Secular Assemblages

Bloomsbury Advances in Religious Studies

James Cox, Steven Sutcliffe and Will Sweetman

This ground-breaking series presents innovative research in theory and method in the study of religion, paying special attention to disciplinary formation in Religious Studies. Volumes published under its auspices demonstrate new approaches to the way religious traditions are presented and analyzed. Each study will demonstrate its theoretical insights by applying them to particular empirical case studies in order to foster integration of data and theory in the historical and cultural study of 'religion'.

Secular Assemblages

Affect, Orientalism and Power in the French Enlightenment

Marek Sullivan

BLOOMSBURY ACADEMIC

LONDON • NEW YORK • OXFORD • NEW DELHI • SYDNEY

BLOOMSBURY ACADEMIC
Bloomsbury Publishing Plc
50 Bedford Square, London, WC1B 3DP, UK
1385 Broadway, New York, NY 10018, USA
29 Earlsfort Terrace, Dublin 2, Ireland

BLOOMSBURY, BLOOMSBURY ACADEMIC and the Diana logo
are trademarks of Bloomsbury Publishing Plc

First published in Great Britain 2020
This paperback edition published in 2022

A catalogue record for this book is available from the British Library.

Library of Congress Control Number: 2019949344.

ISBN:	HB:	978-1-3501-2367-0
	PB:	978-1-3502-7236-1
	ePDF:	978-1-3501-2368-7
	eBook:	978-1-3501-2369-4

Series: Bloomsbury Advances in Religious Studies

Typeset by Integra Software Services Pvt. Ltd.

To find out more about our authors and books visit www.bloomsbury.com
and sign up for our newsletters.

What then am I, my God? What is my nature? It is characterized by diversity, by life of many forms, utterly immeasurable. See the broad plains and caves and caverns of my memory. The varieties there cannot be counted, and are beyond any reckoning, full of innumerable things.
Augustine, Confessions *(1992 [397–400]: 194)*

The conscious and intelligent manipulation of the organized habits and opinions of the masses is an important element in democratic society. Those who manipulate this unseen mechanism of society constitute an invisible government which is the true ruling power of our country.
Edward Bernays, Propaganda *(1928: 9)*

Contents

Preface

This book took shape against a background of massive upheavals in politics around the world. The traumatic events associated with Islamic State, followed by rising 'populism' on the left and right, an apparent unleashing of nationalist sentiment, isolationist fiscal and immigration policies focused especially on Brexit (at least in the UK), and the increasing dominance of political 'strongmen' like Donald Trump, Vladimir Putin, Recep Tayyip Erdogan and Xi Jinping all created, and continue to create, the impression of a dramatic departure from received narratives concerning the progress of secular democracy. Prophets of modernity from Auguste Comte to Francis Fukuyama had led us to believe the world would gradually become more rational, more liberal, less religious, less selfish. Things just weren't supposed to go this way.

The tidal turn of the late 2000s and early 2010s was followed by shocking revelations, still ongoing, over the complicity of social media platforms in stoking political sentiments, and the unwillingness of CEOs to regulate data-collecting and sharing at a significant level. Each day sheds new light on the extent and nature of online political campaigns, waged through fine-tuned algorithms and the relentless propagation of individually tailored, emotionally valenced news. Again, these developments pose challenges to standard teleologies of the secular, by putting increasing pressure on rationalistic understandings of political discourse. Not only has there been a gradual dismantling of Rawlsian and Habermasian assumptions about the existence and rationality of the public sphere (accompanied by resignation in the face of religion's staying power), but a growing acceptance that reason may function less effectively than emotion in shaping the political *demos*. This change is not restricted to the 'affective turn', now well established in academic circles (Connolly 1999; Bennett 2001; Massumi 2002; Ahmed 2014), but extends to mainstream, if not popular, thought on the science of political mobilization. Discussing the issue of a democratic Brexit, children's author Philip Pullman has warned that the only way to change people's minds is through emotion since 'reason doesn't work' (2017, unpaginated). Filmed by undercover reporters in 2018, Mark Turnbull, the former managing director of Cambridge Analytica, confided:

The two fundamental human drivers when it comes to taking information on board effectively are hopes and fears, and many of those are unspoken and even unconscious. You didn't know that was a fear until you saw something that evoked that reaction from you. And our job is ... to drop the bucket further down the well than anybody else, to understand what are those really deep-seated underlying fears, concerns. It's no good fighting an election campaign on the facts, because actually it's all about emotion. (Channel 4 News 2018, 7:00–7:48)

The failure of mainstream institutions to anticipate and account for these changes has been accompanied by a predictable backlash from centrist supporters of the secular order, focused especially on the continuing relevance and value of the historical Enlightenment. Most recently, Steven Pinker has called for 'an Enlightenment newly recharged for the twenty-first century' (2018: jacket cover), against Brexit, Trump, political religion, nationalism, socialism and the parochial forces of a regressive 'Counter-Enlightenment'. Appeals to the Enlightenment have also come from more right-leaning though no less 'secular' circles. The 2000s saw the rise of 'patriotic atheism' (Bullivant 2010) epitomized by the so-called New Atheists (especially Sam Harris and Christopher Hitchens), who have repeatedly demanded a 'new Enlightenment' against the ideological encroachment of Islam across Europe and America. Dutch nationalists Geert Wilders and Pim Fortuyn have warned that excessive Muslim immigration constitutes an attack on the 'fortress of Enlightenment' (Buruma 2006: 28–9).

Whether or not an abstract ideal of reason can resolve our current crisis, this book seeks to move away from simplistic dichotomies of rational/irrational – non-emotional/emotional, channelled through a historical opposition between the Enlightenment and Counter-Enlightenment. Indeed, a principal intention here is to show that appeals to 'Enlightenment reason' as cannon fodder against political religion and rising nationalist sentiment are, in a profound sense, misplaced. They are misplaced for two reasons. First, because the historical Enlightenment, at least in its French variant, was anything but averse to emotional manipulation, especially when it came to nationalism. It is not the case that the Enlightenment sought to do away with emotion or 'overcome' our 'irrational passions' (Pinker 2018: 9). The tendency, as this book argues, was rather to channel the latter into the appropriate avenues for a viable nation-state. And second, because the Enlightenment was already a deeply xenophobic phenomenon – a fact which itself reflects its realpolitik approach to emotion. The Enlightenment deployed racist, Orientalist tropes, not (or not only) because the Enlightenment was racist and Orientalist in itself, but because it was expedient for it to do so: Enlightenment xenophobia was a practical outcome of its demurral to affect, since it was clear to Enlightenment thinkers from Montesquieu to Holbach that racist affects provided a more potent means of bringing about social and political change (e.g. disestablishing the Catholic Church) than good reasons.

Right-wing politicians like Wilders, who seek to co-opt the prestige of Enlightenment reason in a defence of Western values, thereby squaring the circle of a rationalistic nationalism, might think twice about appealing to a historical phenomenon that was already aware of its power to manipulate people through a process of affective othering. In doing so, they become unwitting puppets of intellectual history, rehashing Enlightenment soundbites without any of the latter's self-awareness and scepticism. Indeed, it is no small irony that affect's shift to the mainstream and a concomitant explosion of Islamophobic sentiment in Europe and America in some ways marks the fulfilment of Enlightenment thought on the mechanics of public discourse, and a return to the rhetorical theory and method of the eighteenth century. Conversely, modern advocates of reason like Pinker, who seek succour in European intellectual history in the fight against modern, national passions, may find themselves short-changed on this front, since the Enlightenment was already a nationalistic and emotive phenomenon, based on a postrationalistic understanding of the political subject. It was not Cambridge Analytica but Claude Adrien Helvétius who, in 1758, called for a treatise on 'the art of inspiring [the passions]' (1759 [1758]: 217) that would bestow sovereignty on whoever mastered its secrets. Today we are closer than ever to this dream.

Acknowledgements

A first book affords many opportunities, perhaps especially the opportunity to thank friends and colleagues for their support, whether recent or in the past. As the *philosophes* well knew, we are made by what surrounds us, or, to paraphrase Baron d'Holbach, 'the very particles we breathe'.

Donovan Schaefer has been a consistently warm presence, a brilliant supervisor, an insightful mentor and a true friend. I do not think it is an exaggeration to say that his teaching and personality set a gold standard for universities everywhere. Sondra Hausner's experience, wit and humanity have likewise been an invaluable education, from early days in Oxford to the present. Graham Ward, Martyn Percy and Monique Scheer provided incisive feedback on various aspects of my doctoral work. It is a privilege to have been read and criticized by such a stellar cast.

I owe a great debt to Benedict Mackay, who provided more support through the last eight years than it would be possible to summarize here.

The research behind this book was sustained by a combined grant from the Clarendon Fund and Balliol College, and by the generosity of the De La Salle Brothers in North Oxford. I am infinitely grateful for the doors these have opened. I am also grateful to the Ian Ramsey Centre for funding the symposium 'Senses of the Secular' in 2018; to Roxana Willis, for the opportunity to present aspects of my research at the Centre for Criminology, Oxford; to Lois Lee, Chris Cotter and David Robertson for their tireless work at *Secularism and Nonreligion* and *Implicit Religion*; to Lucy Carroll at Bloomsbury for the warm guidance; and to Sharday Mosurinjohn and the anonymous reviewer, who gave very generous feedback and thoughtful suggestions for improvement. I have tried to incorporate as many of these as possible. All remaining weaknesses are mine.

Other people whose ideas and passions have grown into my life include but are not limited to: Max 'MC Wally' Harris, Justine Ellis, Francesca Po, Joseph Currie, Achas Burin, Ruby Magic, Ed Allistone, Tom Francis, Sian Bo Beynon, Nicholas Mackay and my brother, Arie. Francesca Kay and Mark Currie's openness and generosity provided an island of peace in the last stages of research.

Lastly, thank you to my mother for the love and strength, and for teaching me to question everything. And thank you to Arabella, for the swifts.

Note on translations

I have used existing translations where available and reliable. In certain cases, I have used my own translations to convey the significance of key terms and to sidestep an Anglophone tendency for rationalization. In other instances, I have used an adapted version of an existing translation (e.g. Henry Carey's translation of Jean-François Senault's *De l'Usage des Passions*, 1641) for convenience. All translations have been checked against the original texts.

Introduction

The 'deeply boring' case of Saint-Genis-Pouilly

On 8 December 2005, just seventy days after *Jyllands Posten* published a series of cartoons mocking Muhammed, and in direct response to the ensuing controversy, theatre director Hervé Loichemol staged Voltaire's 1741 play *Le Fanatisme* in the Genevese town of Saint-Genis-Pouilly. Loichemol had already attempted this once in 1993, on the occasion of Voltaire's 300th anniversary. But his plans had been thwarted by a chorus of complaints driven by scholar of Islam, Tariq Ramadan, and a battalion of leftist government officials charged with cultural affairs. In an open letter in October 1993, Ramadan described the play as 'one more stone in this edifice of hatred and rejection in which Muslims feel entrapped' and – to the outrage of many libertarian critics – appealed to 'tactfulness' against absolute principles of free speech and censorship (Ramadan 1993; Fourest 2007: 80). Geneva authorities eventually dropped the play, citing 'financial reasons' (Higgins 2006: unpaginated).

In 2005, the Enlightenment won out. *Le Fanatisme* was booked for two dates in the municipal theatre of Saint-Genis-Pouilly and Geneva's Théâtre Carouge. A small riot broke out on the first night: a car was burned and rubbish bins set on fire by local youths. Yet the play went ahead, protected by police reinforcements brought in by mayor Hubert Bertrand for the occasion. Although Bertrand expressed concerns about Muslim feelings, he also insisted on the sanctity of freedom of expression, the 'foundation stone of modern Europe'. He later belittled the riots as 'the most excitement we've ever had down here' (Higgins 2006).

One striking element of this drama is the way emotionality became mapped exclusively onto aggrieved Muslims. According to Andrew Higgins, writing for the *Wall Street Journal*, 'The production quickly stirred up passions that echoed the cartoon uproar'. Predictably, it was Muslims who 'raised a furore', not Loichemol (2006). For many critics of the Muslim reaction, not only was this 'stirring of the passions' an illegitimate response, given its untranslatability into the language of secular reason, but it stemmed from a failure to grasp the metaphorical nature of the play. A correct approach began from the assumption that the play should be decoded into an alternative set of identities relevant to Voltaire's immediate context. As Ross Mullin wrote at the time, 'Voltaire wasn't actually attacking Mohammed. His main targets, thinly disguised, were religious fanaticism in general, and Christian fanatics in particular. When his play reached Paris on 9 August 1742, the right-wing Catholic Jansenists well knew at whom the barbs flew' (1994: unpaginated). According to François Rochaix, director of the Théâtre Carouge, *Le Fanatisme* 'is a metaphor and is not blasphemous' (Armanios 2005: unpaginated). Loichemol reminded 'the censors' that 'no one is forced to attend a theatre', and that those who cross the threshold accept entry into a 'game of identities' where 'interpretation is practiced' and truth emerges from 'an ironic exchange of significations' (2006: unpaginated). The same reasoning underpinned Rochaix's spurious claim that 'theatre has no taboos' (Armanios 2005). For Loichemol and Rochaix, speech regulations could have no bearing on the stage, since theatre-goers could always choose not to be harmed by properly interpreting the play, refusing to attend or making the appropriate aesthetic leap. (In the recent words of *Guardian* columnist Rachel Cooke, 'plays … don't groom people … Read a book or watch a play and see how you/we have changed'; 2017: unpaginated.)

By reaching into the past to disambiguate the metaphorical underside of *Le Fanatisme*, supporters of the play not only ignored its extraordinary flexibility as it journeyed across religious and political landscapes over nearly three centuries, but obfuscated the specific context of its performance in France in December 2005.[1] There was very little question over what it was intended to do or provoke at Saint-Genis-Pouilly. *Le Fanatisme* was performed explicitly as a response to the *Jyllands Posten* cartoons, in a context of heightened tensions between French Muslims and non-Muslims. The play was therefore more likely to challenge Muslims than Christian fanatics or religious fanaticism in general – a fact which, ironically, went against the grain of the Enlightenment. Jean Goldzink described the face off between Muslims and Loichemol as 'the same situation as in the eighteenth century': 'Then it was Catholic priests who were angry. Now it is parts of the Muslim community' (Higgins 2006: unpaginated). But it could only be the same if France had a twenty-first-century Muslim monarch, and non-Muslims had recently suffered a revocation of their right to practice, equivalent to Louis XIV's 1685 Revocation of the Edict of Nantes. Voltaire's France was dominated by Catholicism and his work so powerful and vulnerable to censorship because it spoke to, not for, power. Outside of this highly specific context and just two months after *Jyllands Posten*, the irony of the play easily collapsed into the veneer of representation. It would take a feat of self-reflexive detachment and contrivance to see Mahomet as anything other than Mahomet. No wonder Bertrand Hubert found the play 'deeply boring' (Higgins 2006: unpaginated).

The events at Saint-Genis-Pouilly became an important flashpoint of twenty-first-century debates about the place of Islam in Europe, free speech and the politics of representation. They demonstrated the ongoing relevance of the Enlightenment to recent permutations and refractions of religion, and the knotty relation between hermeneutics and power on the twenty-first-century stage. They also demonstrated a striking tendency to project the modern distinction between aesthetics and politics onto the past. For the idea that one could, or should, distance oneself from the enchantment of a play, aestheticize one's hurt and experience it as mere spectacle or an 'ironic exchange of significations' would have surprised Voltaire. Not only did Voltaire believe in the appropriateness of 'veiling' certain theatrical ideas and images, but he recognized and deliberately exploited theatre's privileged access to the formation of the emotional self.[2] In a letter to the King of Prussia, prefacing the 1753 edition of *Le Fanatisme*, Voltaire wrote: 'I have always believed that Tragedy must not be a mere Spectacle, which touches the heart without correcting it. What relevance do the passions and ill-fortunes of an Ancient Hero have for the Human Species if they do not serve to instruct us?' (1753b [1741]: unpaginated). The value of tragedy, for Voltaire, lay precisely in its power to 'touch the heart' and 'correct' it. The passions of classical heroes, properly rendered upon the stage, could not but shape our dispositions, uproot certain sentiments and 'instruct' us. Given that a strict distinction between the aesthetic and the private was not only undesirable but impossible, Voltaire took hold of this opportunity with enthusiasm and direction. His aim was precisely to provide a 'disloyal concurrence', an 'exercise in capturing spirits' (Loichemol 2006: unpaginated) that would, in Cooke's words, 'groom people'.

Can secularism be other-wise?

This is the question Saba Mahmood (2010) poses to Charles Taylor in an effort to fill a relative silence over representations of the other in his monumental work *A Secular Age* (2007). *Secular Assemblages* responds to this demand.

I take Mahmood's question as a call to problematize not only the lack of engagement with other places, other religions, other secularities (a problem addressed elsewhere, e.g. by Pellegrini and Jakobsen 2008), but also the presumptions mapped onto others as a means of securing the legitimacy of the secular. This is about the dependence of the secular on these presumptions – presumptions which might entail a disavowal and projection of values and ideas associated with religion, such as immaturity, ignorance, emotionality or irrationality, onto the civilizational other, and the concomitant erasure of secularity's own religious or affective history. An 'other-wise' secularism will need to take stock of this history and proceed self-reflexively if it is to avoid reproducing a binary logic complicit in the legitimization of a Western imperialistic order.

Through a careful re-reading of canonical Enlightenment authors including Descartes, Montesquieu, Voltaire, Diderot, Holbach and Helvétius, *Secular Assemblages* examines, first, the centrality of emotion, the 'passions' and the 'habits' to the foundations of eighteenth-century enlightened reform, and hence to the genealogy of the secular; and second, the historical entanglement of the secular with negative, affect-laden representations of Oriental religions, especially Islam. Against a tenacious assumption that the Enlightenment was fundamentally 'rationalistic' and blind or antithetical to the body, I show that, on the contrary, French thinkers of the eighteenth century were highly sensitive to issues of embodiment and emotion, and generally optimistic about the potential of the latter to support anti-religious, nationalist change. Like early propaganda theorist Edward Bernays, they were also keenly aware of the power of media and representation to mould people's 'habits and opinions' in favour of a post-religious, republican order in the early stages of mass print dissemination.[3] Highly affective representations of the Orient were therefore not mere aberrations – emotional challenges to Enlightenment 'rationalism' to be drawn out through a careful re-evaluation of Enlightenment literatures and material culture 'between the lines' – but a natural outgrowth of enlightened discourse on the power of emotional imagery to generate civic virtue and a sense of national belonging.

In what follows, I will outline what I take to be some common assumptions in the emerging field of secular studies, and outline the potential implications of a more body-centred and other-wise re-evaluation of secular history.

The secular body

In the opening lines of *Formations of the Secular*, Talal Asad asks whether 'the secular' and 'secularism' can be objects of anthropological enquiry, and what this enquiry would look like (2003: 1). The question is knowingly controversial because the secular and secularism, whether taken as 'background understandings' of modern social life or 'foreground principles' (2) of political deliberation, typically evoke our natural condition once freed from the distortive effects of institutional religion. The taken-for-granted 'universal validity' (1) of secularism suggests a degree of cross-cultural translatability not granted to other politico-ethical frameworks under conditions of cultural and ethical plurality, making it *a priori* incompatible with the culturally relativizing project of social anthropology. To raise the question of its embeddedness in specific cultures – that is to say, its embodiment in historically contingent practices and disciplines of body and mind, specific to certain times and places (the modern West), and responsive to specific socio-political dilemmas (e.g. the wars of religion, the Catholic Church-state nexus) – is to undermine secularism's universalist thrust and the many violences this universalism legitimates across the world (Asad 2003; Cavanaugh 2009). A social anthropology of 'the secular' or 'secularism' is a *de facto* critique of the ideological basis of late-modern imperialism since it parochializes, historicizes or 'culturalizes' what is theoretically true and applicable for all times and places, and hence spreadable by force or consent.

By tying secularity to history and body, Asad instigates a new approach to the secular that directly reflects late-twentieth and early-twenty-first-century historicizations and genealogies of its dialectical partner: 'religion' (e.g. W. C. Smith 1964; J. Z Smith 1982, 1998; Asad 1993). Since secularity and modern understandings of religion emerge simultaneously (Asad 2003; Cavanaugh 2009), it was only a matter of time before the first was subjected to the same treatment as the second. As Asad notes, 'religion and the secular are closely linked, both in our thought and the way they have emerged historically. Any discipline that seeks to understand "religion" must also try to understand its other' (2003: 22).[4]

Despite Asad's opening gambit, however, it remains unclear how 'the secular' or 'secularism' can – practically speaking – be read through a social-anthropological vocabulary of cultural sensibility, affect, practice and bodily discipline. As anthropologist Charles Hirschkind has noted, for books that seek to treat the secular or secularism as culturally embedded or embodied 'modes of appraisal', both *Formations* and William Connolly's equally body-centric *Why I Am Not a Secularist* (1999) largely sidestep descriptions of secular 'self-cultivation or practices of self-discipline' (2011: 636). While Asad's *Genealogies of Religion* (1993) provided a densely woven survey of medieval Christian sensitivities, practices, disciplines and forms of devotion, *Formations* and *Why I Am Not* skirt around sustained engagement with their secular equivalents. Indeed, 'we find very little in these books in regard, not only to how the sensibilities and visceral modes of judgment of secular subjects are cultivated but also how they give shape to and find expression in a secular life' (Hirschkind 2011: 635). Asad and Connolly's relative silence on this point leads Hirschkind to a narrower set of questions, focused more precisely on the body: 'Is there a secular body?' or more specifically, 'is there a particular configuration of the human sensorium – of sensibilities, affects, embodied dispositions – specific to secular subjects, and thus constitutive of what we mean by "secular society"?' (633).

Hirschkind himself defaults on a substantive answer, explaining Asad and Connolly's silence in terms of at least two restrictions on the project itself: the methodologically impenetrable character of its subject material (secularism, according to Asad, can only be approached 'through its shadows', since it is the 'water we swim in') and the inherent aversion of secularism to visceral or embodied registers of subjectivity. On this account, the secular body eludes enquiry because 'a secular person is someone whose affective-gestural repertoires express a negative relation to forms of embodiment historically associated with (but not limited to) theistic religion' (638). In other words, the question of a secular body is either moot or theoretically limited, since 'the most visceral element' of the discourses identified by Connolly and re-presented by Hirschkind as 'secular' is their 'rejection of the visceral dimension itself' (636).

In his support, Hirschkind cites the sixteenth- to eighteenth-century 'desensualization' of knowledge analysed by Walter Ong (2005 [1958]), the 'stilling of passionate expression within courtly society' examined by Norbert Elias (1994 [1939]) and Kant's 'dinner party scene', originally featured in Connolly (1999), which he reads as 'a pedagogical device geared to disciplining the emotions and attitudes of a secular subject' (637). This scene, which prescribes a set of social manners appropriate to the Kantian host (such as avoiding contentious topics, 'deadly silence', etc.), is apparently suggestive of a move towards the suppression of excessive emotionality, itself tied to the experiential domain of religion. The party scene functions by analogy as a regulatory blueprint for the control and suppression of religious affects 'in accord with the doctrine of political secularism' (638). Kantian and neo-Kantian political philosophies (e.g. Rawls, Habermas) are seen to carry forward this political project by facilitating the regulation of religion in public life through a continuous devaluation of the sensual register, and transfer of 'vast realms of experience from the surface of public life' to 'the invisible depths of the lonely individual' (638). Since this transfer jettisons valuable resources for a rich and healthy sphere of political debate, and is in fact impossible anyway (religious affects always seep into political discourse whether we like it or not), scholars like Connolly have sought to rehabilitate religious discourse as a valuable asset for ethical and political deliberation.

Important as this rehabilitation may be, neither Connolly nor Hirschkind radically question the implied link between religion, embodiment and emotion, and secularization, disembodiment and non-emotion backgrounding these debates. Why has religion been made the carrier of emotions and secularity the domain of a pure and disembodied rationality? On whose terms? Why has Kant come to stand for the history of the secular?[5] These questions are important because there is a sense in which Connolly and Hirschkind's analyses, while casting a critical eye over secular thought and practice to challenge negative accounts of political emotionality, may in fact contribute to a reproduction of secular categories and their attendant anti-religious bias by tying religion to the emotional body and leaving secularism's own affective history untouched.[6] For both, the secular is simply what religion runs up against: the unemotional counterpart to religion's more depth-sensitive catalogue of affects. But can we plot a history of affects distinctive to secular space, that is, one not defined solely in terms of its rejection of religious emotion?

Critical secular studies

The supposed tendency for secularization to bring about a suppression of emotional or sensual life, and thus to elide – conceptually and practically – more embodied forms of religious commitment and devotion, also backgrounds a wider set of questions about contemporary secularism and its troubled confrontation with 'resurgent' forms of religion the world over, arguably resurgent less because religion really is growing, than because it has become more visible in a presumed secular context. For many, this increased visibility stems from the difficulty of shoehorning non-Christian-Protestant religion into a legal and political structure shaped by a predominantly Protestant or Kantian history. A range of scholars have recently focused their attention on the failure of secular frameworks to recognize and cope with forms of religion not built on Western templates. Saba Mahmood (2008a, 2008b, 2009, 2010) has written extensively on the secular state's convenient blindness to, and antipathy for, the embodied, virtue-centred nature of Muslim devotional practice. Since secular rule, embedded in a predominantly Protestant history, tends only to validate forms of religion that suppress public action and sentiment in favour of an inoffensive (because private) 'cognitive assent to sets of propositions', Muslim offence (e.g. to the *Jyllands Posten* cartoons) remains usefully incomprehensible to Western sensibilities and stands out as a marker of cultural and ethnic difference.

In fact, as Mahmood, William T. Cavanaugh (2009) and Mayanthi Fernando (2014) have argued, the secular state *requires* that 'virtue-centred' or embodied modes of religiosity remain both highly visible and indecipherable to discourses of religious freedom, since this visible opacity allows the construction of a crypto-Protestant democratic standard from which non-Protestant (e.g. Muslim) communities and practices will always seem to be deviating.[7] If Muslims are incapable of drawing the line between text and truth, signifier and signified, and thus tempering their (always 'emotional', 'fanatic') reactions to 'mere' images, perhaps they should relocate elsewhere – a gesture of exclusion that generates and strengthens the boundaries assumed to have been transgressed and weakened by the presence of the other.[8] According to Fernando (2014), the persistent failure of immigrant religions to integrate in French culture, far from a corrosive anti-national force, supports the national bond by opening a space for the endless reiteration of 'national values' against the perceived threat of religious and ethnic alterity. While portraying itself as protective of universal religious rights and freedoms, this discourse tacitly legitimizes discrimination against particular religious groups, reinforcing the unassimilable nature of 'Muslim-French' identity and, by implication, the integrity of France and Frenchness as distinct culturo-ethnic categories.[9]

The operative assumption here is that secularism or the secular – articulated through a Lockean or neo-Kantian language of belief as internal, private or distillable to 'sets of propositions' to which one assents – offers up a hermeneutic lens inherently incapable of dealing (if not unwilling to deal) with embodied forms of religious life, especially those originating in other cultures. And indeed, there is now a rich secondary literature on the tensions and contradictions crossing through secularism and its attendant ethos of religious freedom, much of it highly sensitive to issues of embodiment, colonial representation and power. Twenty-first-century scholars of the secular have done much to unmask secularism as an inherently unstable political doctrine and/or legal principle, wrenched apart by incompatibilities between its constitutive pillars, e.g. disestablishment and freedom to practice, and ridden with Eurocentric biases bleeding through the fault lines (e.g. Mahmood 2009; Fernando 2014; Pellegrini 2015; Sullivan et al. 2015).

Nevertheless, Lockean and Kantian curations of secular intellectual history –
even in critical work like Mahmood, Fernando, Hirschkind and Connolly's –
arguably risk shoring up a secular-rational/religious-emotional double binary
useful to secular power, since it is this binary that enables secular (Western)
violence to be presented as 'rational' and religious (subaltern) violence not. To
the extent this binary is left unchallenged, European discrimination against
non-Western forms of 'embodied' religion (e.g. Islam) can be framed as a logical
necessity inherent in the doctrine of secularism rather than a political decision
based on the arbitrary, but historically highly determined, circumscription of
non-native, 'emotion-driven' cultures.[10] It is precisely this possibility that allows
European secular-nationalists like Geert Wilders and Pim Fortuyn to proclaim
the universal values of the Enlightenment, yet insist on the Christian (i.e.
Western, European) heritage of those very same values.[11] In this context, simply
pointing out that the secular has a Protestant (= Lockean, Kantian) history no
longer has any bite, since it merely confirms what secular-nationalists wish to
believe: that the Enlightenment is both 'theirs' and distillable to a universalist,
anti-corporeal rationalism denying more embodied dimensions of religious
subjectivity, such as the religious offence or 'pain' (Mahmood 2009) caused by
pictographic representations of Muhammed. Again, the political stakes of an
anthropology of the secular or secularism that does not hedge on the possibility
of a history of secular affects should be clear.

Thus, to reframe Asad's questions in historical terms, can we reconstruct a
history of the secular body that does not rule out secular affectivity in principle?
And what would this history look like?

A secular age

Like Asad, Hirschkind takes the secular to be 'conceptually prior to the political
doctrine of secularism' and hence 'part of the background presupposed by our
routine ways of distinguishing secular from religious in law, politics, ethics, and
aesthetics' (2011: 633; Asad 2003: 16). In this view, the secular is still a concept,
but one that precedes any kind of political-theoretical prescriptive content, e.g.
concerning the proper relation of church and state. His understanding of the
secular is more encompassing. For Hirschkind, the secular is 'a concept that
articulates a constellation of institutions, ideas, and affective orientations that
constitute an important dimension of what we call modernity and its defining
forms of knowledge and practice – both religious and nonreligious' (634). As

previously mentioned, it is also 'the water we swim in' and therefore difficult to analyse objectively; it cannot be tackled head-on, but rather 'through its shadows'.

Given this theoretical background, it is perhaps surprising that Hirschkind does not mention Charles Taylor's discipline-defining *A Secular Age* (2007; henceforth *ASA*), despite the fact his work appeared four years before Hirschkind's essay and provides one of the richest analyses of secular experience and embodiment to date. For Taylor, as for Asad and Hirschkind, the secular is irreducible to a political concept: it is the background frame – conceptual, phenomenological, affective – for the 'lifeworld' and 'social imaginary' of the modern West. Taylor patiently (over almost 800 pages) reconstructs the many lifeworlds generated and inhabited by Western subjects in the genesis of secular modernity, drawing on popular literatures, theological, philosophical and political-theoretical thought, and a wealth of social-scientific historical data. His understanding of secularity is thus deliberately vaguer yet richer and more generously encompassing than modern political-theoretical conceptions of the secular that seek to disambiguate or 'decontest' (Freeden 2007) what it means to 'be secular' (e.g. Berlinerblau 2012, 2014). For Taylor, such conceptions, while useful in a limited sphere of application (e.g. dedicated projects of socio-political reform), are merely one facet of an expansive and ultimately irreducible socio-historical phenomenon.

At the core of Taylor's analysis are three types or modes of secularity: 1, 2 and 3. Secularity 1 refers to a normative distinction between church and state; secularity 2 to a general scepticism towards religious truth claims and institutions; and secularity 3 to the most generalizable feature of the modern secular and central focus of *ASA*: the awareness that belief is, for most people in most of the West, no longer a compulsory dimension of social life, but rather 'one human possibility among others' (3). Tied up with this pluralization and relativization of belief/non-belief is an increased phenomenological isolation, whereby bodies formerly located in a complex ecology of visible and invisible beings are cut off and revealed as self-standing, autonomous agents locked in the confines of an unprecedentedly materialistic 'immanent frame'. This isolated, 'disenchanted' secular subject is what Taylor calls the 'buffered self' (27): a self whose self-awareness (or, less cognitively, 'sense of self') as a being hermetically insulated from other beings, and naturally endowed with certain rights (to personal property, freedom of conscience, etc.), is much stronger than at any other point in history. As he sums it up elsewhere, 'One of the big differences between us and them is that we live with a much firmer sense of the boundary between self and other' (2011: 302–3).

In a certain sense, Taylor's 'buffered self' *is* Hirschkind's 'secular body'. Where Hirschkind connects the secular body to a rejection of the visceral dimension articulated through Kant, Taylor connects bufferedness with the rise to hegemony of 'disengaged reason' (especially via Descartes), Hume and Gibbon's 'ironic distance' and Kant's eschewal of 'our embodied feeling, our "gut reactions" in determining what is right' (137, 241, 286, 301, 288; 2011: 34, 35). He also – like Hirschkind – cites Norbert Elias's *The Civilizing Process* (1994 [1939]) as demonstrative of a historical shift away from the body and emotions, and adds Jürgen Habermas's (1989 [1962]) neo-Kantian concept of the public sphere as a means of theorizing the rationalization of political authority in the transition from monarchic to democratic government. Taylor thereby advances almost exactly the theory of rational disengagement advocated by Hirschkind as constitutive of the secular, going so far as to suggest that secularization has brought us to a contemporary situation in which we tend, more than our ancestors, to 'live in our heads' (2007: 555).

The richness of Taylor's analysis, its theoretical focus on the experiential and affective (not simply political or legal) dimensions of secular life and its importance for the emerging field of secular studies, make it an exceptionally relevant source for thinking through the nature and genealogy of secular embodiment. As I will show, it is also a paradigmatic example of the way historiographies of the secular – even those that take a neutral or antipathetic stance towards classical secular ideology – still tend to operate within a set of coordinates driven by secular self-understandings. Though critical of secularist attempts to drive a wedge between religion and the secular, Taylor, like Hirschkind, still links secularity or secularization to a loss of contact with the body in favour of an abstracted ideal of pure reason, thereby reproducing a typically secularist association between religion and embodied or 'engaged' emotionality.

I do not think this association stands up to scrutiny. The secular is, by almost any measure, as embodied or emotionally entangled as 'religion' (Mahmood 2009; Calhoun 2010). Nevertheless, Taylor's complex socio-intellectual analysis provides a strong starting point for constructing a revised genealogy of the secular, one sensitive to ongoing forms of porosity and embodiment in our secular age, and one that does not defer to Kantian rationalism as the paradigm shaper of secular history. Insofar as a secular body exists, and insofar as we can plot its genetic make-up through an analysis of Western intellectual history, *ASA* provides the most comprehensive attempt so far to flesh out (or, as it happens, unflesh) the secular body through time. It therefore stands out as a particularly relevant foil for a comprehensive history of secular affectivity. But what grounds are there for questioning Taylor's narrative?

Reembodying the secular

Consider the following two quotations:

> [M]y physical delight, which has to be checked from enervating the mind, often deceives me when the perception of the senses is unaccompanied by reason, and is not patiently content to be in a subordinate place. It tries to be first and to be in the leading role, though it deserves to be allowed only as secondary to reason.

> [T]he objects of the passions produce movements in the blood which follow so rapidly from the mere impressions formed in the brain and the disposition of the organs, without any help at all from the soul, that no amount of human wisdom is capable of counteracting these movements when we are not adequately prepared to do so. Thus many people cannot keep from laughing when they are tickled, even though they get no pleasure from it. For the impression of joy and surprise, which previously made them laugh for the same reason, is awakened in their imagination and causes their lungs to be swollen suddenly and involuntarily by blood sent to them from the heart.

As mentioned above, Taylor situates a key moment for the genealogy of the secular, and especially the buffered self of secular modernity, in the figure of Descartes. According to Taylor, Descartes's 'neo-Stoicism' yoked the body and passions to the hegemony of the rational will, or 'disengaged reason', thereby downgrading the role of the body, sensations and emotions in the constitution of knowledge, behaviour, 'the good' and the fully realised, immanently self-transparent individual. It is a classic anti-corporeal or at least body-insensitive interpretation of Descartes, usually illustrated by his epistemological deference to the authority of the *cogito*.

The first passage would seem to confirm this interpretation, if it had been written by Descartes. It was in fact written by Augustine of Hippo (1992 [397–400]: 207–8) around 1200 years earlier.[12] The second passage, describing bodily stimulations that 'no amount of human wisdom is capable of counteracting' when we are not prepared, was written by Descartes in his final work *Les Passions de l'Âme* (1985a [1649]: 403). Separated by more than a millennium, Augustine's and Descartes's understandings of reason were different. Yet the essential structure opposing abstract reason and the physical body (or 'the perception of the senses') is precisely mirrored in both authors' works, and – at least here – in the opposite order to Taylor's rationalistic narrative of the secular.

In making this observation, I do not mean to suggest that Augustine was a rationalist and Descartes an anti-rationalist. My point is not to reverse but to complicate Taylor's narrative, by highlighting alternative ways of constructing

Western intellectual history embedded in the very same, contradictory set of materials. At stake here is a wider issue about the way intellectual histories take shape, and the meta-historiographical framework by which certain narratives predominate over others. How do these passages fit into a historical schema plotting the development of our secular age as a gradual process of emancipation from the body and its enmeshment in the world? What presumptions allow Taylor to construe secularization (and especially the European Enlightenment) as the ideological focal point for the rise to hegemony of disembodied reason, given the predominance of anti-corporeal, rationalistic strands within ancient Christianity, and the stubborn presence of the body in later secularizing discourse?

As we shall see, the idea that the body and its affects can or should be isolated from secular aims would have seemed strange to many eighteenth- and nineteenth-century theorists of the self, especially those concerned with forging new, stable models of political organization in a post-revolutionary, post-religious state. The re-creation of a universal basis for good behaviour and the moral obligations of citizenship was, for Enlightenment philosophers from Montesquieu to Holbach, as much a matter of feeling as ideas and reason. Indeed, secular discourse of the time is crossed through with the language of emotionality and passions, a trend that continued into the nineteenth century when, according to Martha Nussbaum, philosophers became 'obsessed' with 'civic emotion' (2013: 55). The primary target of Enlightenment anti-religion was not religious passionality – from a secular perspective this was negligible or non-existent, except in the case of extreme fanaticism – but a split allegiance to the state and supra-national institution of the Catholic Church, as evidenced by authors as wide-ranging as Locke, Montesquieu, Rousseau, Holbach and Helvétius.[13] The aim was not so much to kill off religious sentiment, as redirect it away from the Catholic Church, both inwards towards private virtue and outwards towards the nation-state, so that the cultivation of one became the cultivation of the other. The early modern citizen was thus shaped by a kind of mutually reinforcing *habitus* in which true moral progress would be achieved by harmonizing personal and national motivations. Citizens were held in a secular project of justification by civility alone through which 'the new religion of national identity' (Rothschild 2001: 248) could flourish unimpeded.

This new religion was not – could not be – based on a suppression or erasure of religious affect. On the contrary, powerful emotions were often encouraged and cultivated, so long as they harmonized with the nation-building project.[14] In this respect, it is useful to distinguish three terms that Taylor tends to conflate in his effort to plot an anti-corporeal or anti-emotional history of the secular: 'fanaticism', 'passion' (or 'the passions') and 'enthusiasm'.[15] Throughout *ASA*, Taylor cites criticisms of 'enthusiasm' and 'fanaticism' as examples of an Enlightenment antipathy towards emotion and the body (chief among these, Edward Gibbon's 'ironic distance'). But enthusiasm had a very particular meaning in eighteenth-century Europe, not necessarily attached to excessive emotion. Indeed, it could mean the opposite: an excessive attachment to religious ascetic practice or piety, both of which bred emotional stultification not release. This point is underlined by the fact that both the passions and fanaticism could be and often were praised as *positive* facets of human experience, provided they were directed at the right kinds of end, e.g. support for the nation-state. The *Encyclopédie* entry for *fanatisme*, for example, ends with praise for '*Le Fanatisme du patriote*', since this fanaticism could act as a useful counter to religious fanaticism (2016 [1751–1782]: VI. 401).[16]

As Asad writes, on the subject of secular violence: 'A secular state does not guarantee toleration; it puts into place different structures of ambition and fear. The law never seeks to eliminate violence since its object is always to *regulate* violence' (2003: 8, emphasis original). Similarly, Jakobsen notes that modernity is characterized by a 'market-based sense of freedom' that, she notes, 'is not the repression of activity, but it is the regulated enactment of activity along particular lines' (2005: 285). Clearly, there is something amiss in a rationalistic narrative of the secular that reduces secularization to an eliminatory or repressive model of public consent. It is not simply that emotions were not suppressed by the Enlightenment, through a reluctant accommodation to the visceral or embodied, but that emotions, even strong emotions like fanaticism, were positively encouraged, provided they fell in line with the nation-building project. Indeed, the very discourse (or 'Republic of Letters'; Warner 1990) taken to represent a pivotal moment for the rationalization of society (since it was power-free, rational and self-legitimizing; Habermas 1989 [1962]; Taylor 2007; Hirschkind 2011) was laced with appeals to the body, both theoretically, through articulated strategies for the manipulation of public consent (e.g. education), and formally, through the deployment of highly affective nationalist propaganda – propaganda rooted especially, as we shall see, in negative representations of non-Western religions. We might therefore say the Enlightenment's appeal to the body was twofold: theoretically, it established a basis for shaping or 'forming' bodies in the national interest; and formally, it put this basis into practice through a xenophobic mode of discourse reliant upon affectively charged representations of the Oriental other.

Narratives of recovery

Of course, Taylor is not so blind to the impossibility of corporeal repression or denial that he rules out substantial modes of secular embodiment altogether. *ASA* is full of references to Counter-Enlightenment or 'romantic' figures who upturned the Enlightenment's naïve faith in the autonomy of reason and established the grounds for a thoroughly embodied yet eminently modern nationalism. These are as much part of the history of the secular as the French Enlightenment. The point, however, is that Taylor still operates within the constraints of a narrative timeline that positions a Counter-Enlightenment recovery of affect as the dialectical counterpoint to the originally 'rationalistic' thrust of the Enlightenment, thereby supporting a modern secular-nationalist appeal to 'pure reason' as the historical foundation of the Republic, and hence of the Western nation-state. It is precisely this reasoning that allows hard-line secularists like Christopher Hitchens to simultaneously demand a 'new Enlightenment', join the ranks of American patriotism and reject anti-rationalists like Nietzsche for obscuring the true power of Enlightenment (2007: 277–83). Insofar as the Enlightenment is construed as an uncontaminated domain of pure reason, it will continue to acquire density as the historical focal point or Golden Age of the rational West, and continue to be deployed as the sacred cow of Western secular nationalism.

In challenging Taylor's narrative of disenchantment, however, I am not seeking merely to 'uncover' the ongoing enchantment of the world in the gaps, crevices or cultural 'unspoken' of Western intellectual history. In *The Enchantments of Modernity* (2000), Jane Bennett sets out to critique 'the image of modernity as disenchanted, that is to say, as a place of dearth and alienation (when compared to a golden age of community and cosmological coherency) or a place of reason, freedom, and control (when compared to a dark and confused premodernity)' (3). She summarizes the narrative of disenchantment framing this image as follows:

> There was once a time when Nature was purposive, God was active in the details of human affairs, human and other creatures were defined by a preexisting web of relations, social life was characterized by face-to-face relations, and political order took the form of organic community. Then, this premodern world gave way to forces of scientific and instrumental rationality, secularism, individualism, and the bureaucratic state – all of which, combined, disenchant the world. (7)

Against such narratives, Bennett argues for the ongoing presence of the magical, the awe-inspiring, the enchanting in the very midst of 'modern life', bringing into vision 'a contemporary world sprinkled with natural and cultural sites that have the power to "enchant"' (3).[17]

Despite allowing enchantment to blur the boundary between pre-modernity and modernity, however, Bennett still arguably subscribes to an essential dualism between centre and periphery that reinscribes the conceit of a rational mainstream to be critiqued from the edges. While she admits 'there are plenty of aspects of contemporary life that fit the disenchantment story,' she also claims 'there is enough evidence of everyday enchantment to warrant the telling of an alter-tale' (4).[18] Why conceive of everyday enchantments in terms of an 'alter-tale'? Why seek out the ongoing spell of wonder *behind the back* of the secular enlightenment' or 'in the catacombs of the aesthetic', as Philip Fisher has sought to do (1998: 1–2, emphasis mine)? What models of intellectual storytelling have facilitated a counter-cultural reclamation of the unspoken, enchanted vernacular in the midst of disenchanted, secular modernity?

William Mazzarella has recently taken Bennett and fellow theorist Brian Massumi to task for succumbing to what he calls a 'romantic fetishization' of affect based on an over-enthusiastic (in Mazzarella's words, 'melodramatic') overcoming of 'the death-dealing certitudes of formal determination' in favour of 'the productive, the multiple, and the mobile' (2009: 294). According to Mazzarella, Bennett and Massumi's work, though sensitive to the dangers of invoking 'some prereflexive, romantically raw domain of primitive experiential richness' still risks mirroring and perpetuating a classic anthropological yearning for the untainted human or 'noble savage' of pre-modernity: 'The ideological discourse of modernity not only represses and demonizes the affective but also romantically fetishizes it – particularly insofar as it can be located at the receding horizon of a savage disappearing world, an anthropological other in the classic sense' (Mazzarella 2009: 295). The double effect of this othering gesture, associated especially with Jürgen Habermas's theory of political legitimation in *Structural Transformation of the Public Sphere* (1989), is striking: the 'savage slot' (Trouillot 2003: 7–28) has served not only to preserve the romanticized, fetishized, emotional other as an object of pre- and postrationalist yearning, but to facilitate 'the disavowal through which the discourse of modernity absolved itself from grappling with its own affective politics' (Mazzarella 2009: 295–6). The relative 'savaging' of the past permits the rationalization of the present, as well as the possibility for a recovery of affect in the afterglow of a calcified (and calcifying) discourse of pure reason – a recovery undertaken by scholars like Bennett and Massumi.

Clearly, Mazzarella's point is not so much to question the politics of affect recovered by the latter, as the presumptions enabling them to construe this politics as a recovery in the first place. The excitement of the new has, according to Mazzarella, led to a retroactive construction (or at least exaggeration) of an affect-evacuated past, which, though fantastical, is a necessary support for the unleashing of affect in the present. Following this narrative,

> [t]he stage ... is set for a kind of return of the repressed, whether in the form of a grand revolutionary reversal or a more inconclusive, but no less subversive 'haunting' of the deathly abstractions of modern knowledge by the vitally embodied energies they both require and deny. From the psychoanalytic liberation theology of a Herbert Marcuse or a Wilhelm Reich to the teleological certitude of scientific socialism, affect will out. (295)

For Mazzarella, such staging of the repressed is historically untenable, because 'contrary to the ideological discourse of rationalized modernity, the labile terrain of affect is not in fact external to bureaucratic process'; indeed, 'Affect is not ... so much a radical site of otherness to be policed or preserved but rather a necessary moment of any institutional practice with aspirations to public efficacy' (298). If this is true, then theorists who champion the recovery of affect in public life against the desiccated, alienating rationalism and technicism of late-nineteenth- and twentieth-century ideology, political theory and ideology critique, may be fighting a battle that has already been won – indeed, never got started – since social change has never occurred on a purely rational basis, and was only ever intended to occur on such a basis in rare, unsuccessful instances (e.g. Auguste Comte's Positivism). As Mazzarella puts it, 'modernity is and has always been structurally affective'. This is not simply a claim about a 'vernacular' or 'vital outside' to 'the rationalizing, disenchanting institutions of modernity', but the very possibility of a democratic institution not dependent on the mobilization of affect.[19] According to Mazzarella, all such institutions derive from a social consensus grounded in the contagious spread and amplification of affective intensities – hence his central claim that 'any social project that is not imposed through force alone must be affective in order to be effective' (298-9).

Following Mazzarella, I do not believe the history of our secular age can be equated to the history of the disengagement of the self, whether from its surrounding lifeworld or its body and emotions. Such claims stem from a retroactive rationalization of the secular that downplays the many complexities and contradictions of Western intellectual history, and sustains the illusion of a secular politics evacuated of affect yet endowed with a social efficacy that, interestingly, even Massumi and Taylor deny in principle. As Jonathan Sheehan comments on the 'pathetic' effect of an approach to the Enlightenment that concentrates all social efficacy in the anti-rationalistic dialectic of Counter-Enlightenment:

> [T]he Counter-Enlightenment allows its authors both to tell a story of an eighteenth-century religion untarnished by the patina of decay and also to salvage the traditionally rationalist idea of Enlightenment from the challenge of religion. But its effects are profoundly 'pathetic', for the Enlightenment that results is a *failure*. Even if the modernity of the Enlightenment is preserved, the efficacy of the Enlightenment in actually creating this modernity is denied. Tragedy persists, in other words, in an Enlightenment whose rationalist aspirations fell short of their mark, and fell victim to religion, irrationalism, and enthusiasm. (2003: 1068, emphasis original)

The idea that Enlightenment rationalism 'succumbed' to the corporeal impingements of religion, irrationalism and enthusiasm in the closing years of the Revolution, or later (e.g. through the Catholic Restoration), clearly obfuscates the presence of these same forces within the Enlightenment itself. More specifically, it obfuscates attempts to redirect, not erase, religious emotions in the eighteenth-century transition to the modern nation-state, which can then be portrayed as the result of an entirely rational process of public-sphere creation and constitutional legitimization. Despite revising many secular or secularist assumptions about the genealogy of modernity, e.g. the idea that a neat divide can be drawn between the secular and religion in the first place, Taylor – like Hirschkind and Connolly – still writes out of a historical consciousness framed by rationalist presumptions, resulting in a relative silencing of the body in our secular age and a theoretical blind spot over the possibility of a secular yet emotion-driven nationalism. As noted above, this approach can have the unintentional effect of shoring up a secular-rational/religious-emotional double binary that plays directly into secular narratives of Western exceptionalism.

Secular Assemblages therefore offers a critical re-evaluation of rationalistic narratives of secular modernity. But it does so in two ways: first, by reengaging with the philosophy and political thought of seminal architects of secularity – especially those imbricated in the great crucible of the European secular, the French Enlightenment; and second, by engaging with the same thinkers' visceral representations of 'other' religions and peoples. I have already suggested ways in which the first point might be demonstrated, e.g. through a body-centred re-reading of Descartes's *Les Passions de l'Âme*; this book is the main focus of Chapter 1. The second point, however, requires elaboration. Why might representations of other religions and peoples be relevant to an exploration of the 'secular body'? And what do these have to do with *ASA*?

A (European) secular age

Perhaps the most serious weakness of *A Secular Age* is its Eurocentrism. As several commentators (van der Veer 2001: 160; Brown 2007; Casanova 2010: 278; Mahmood 2010) have noted, Taylor's autochthonous reading of secular history – first in *Sources of the Self* (1989) and later in *ASA* – as a natural twist in the warp and weft of Latin Christendom's 'social imaginary' omits a crucial dimension in the genealogy of secular modernity: Latin Christendom's encounters with non-Christian outsiders and the formative role of such encounters for constructions of the secular self.[20]

This is not simply a matter of scope or nuance. Taylor has responded to criticisms of Eurocentrism by admitting that 'the book could have been – in a sense, should have been – longer … There should have been lots more chapters, describing regions and times that I have left relatively neglected' (2010: 301). But appending further examples gleaned from other times and places would not resolve the issue. As Mahmood has argued, the point is not 'to make Taylor's narrative more inclusive, more copious but to question if indeed Taylor misidentifies the very object of which he speaks' (2010: 289). For Mahmood, Taylor risks misidentifying his object because a proper understanding of modern secularity is impossible without 'taking into account Christianity's encounters with its "others"' (285). For example, the rhetorical power of Hugo Grotius's Christian polemic *De Veritate Religionis Christianae* (1627) is inherently contingent on negative representations of 'pagan religions', Judaism and Islam – representations which feed into a normative, Eurocentric progressivism in which the Christian (then secular) European subject is positioned as the singular bearer of modernity and civilization (285–7). The genealogy of the secular is simply incomprehensible without taking such representations into account.

And neither is the problem simply about the universality or non-universality of secular values and the mistake of confusing one for the other. Asad has criticized Taylor's early (pre-*ASA*) work for assuming that 'although secularism emerged in response to the political problems of Western Christian society in early modernity … it is applicable to non-Christian societies everywhere that have become modern' (2003: 2). In other words, Asad thinks Taylor is wrong to take as universally applicable a set of concepts and values that is in fact highly specific to Western intellectual history and the emergence of modern nation-states. This problem is articulated particularly clearly in John and J. Judd Owen's survey of Enlightenment thought *Religion, the Enlightenment, and the New*

Global Order (2010), where the authors ask: 'Is the Enlightenment based on a set of universally valid principles that merely happen to have emerged first and most robustly in the West? ... Or is the Enlightenment instead a movement inherently particular to a time (roughly the seventeenth through nineteenth centuries) and place (western Europe and North and perhaps Latin America)?' (20). In response to the first question, they suggest that 'If the Enlightenment is indeed somehow universal, then calling for its spread to (or emergence within) non-Western areas of the world is not per se imperialistic, for it entails no domination, but rather liberation from both "East" and "West"' (20).

This reasoning is flawed on two counts. First, the West's exceptionality depends on a double reading of its own position as both universal *and* particular: universal in the sense that its values are understood (from within the West) to be universally applicable, and particular in the sense that only the West holds the keys to modernity.[21] The effect is to split civilizations along a temporal line in which the West comes to represent the present and future endpoint of a steady process of modernization/secularization, against an East condemned to trail in a permanent past. The temporalization of secular values, and the mapping of geographical areas onto a chronological, historical scale, was a distinguishing feature of the Enlightenment. Just as geographically bounded communities delineated by seas and borders conceptually dissolved through a recognition of universal rights and the irreducible dignity of all human beings, these same boundaries were reinscribed by mapping geography onto history; the distinguishing feature of nations would no longer be their location in space, but their distance in time from the arrowhead of Western modernity (Rousseau and Porter 1990: 9; Dube 2009). According to the new dispensation, non-Westerners were not inherently inferior but morally, economically and/or educationally backward, creating new opportunities for what Taylor calls 'human excellences' (e.g. 'the defence of the weak', 2007: 630) even as humanity flattened into a single, global community.[22]

Second, and more significantly, it ignores the extent to which 'East' and 'West' were themselves bound up with the Enlightenment project as conceptual resting points for the construction of the modern, secular subject and its universalisms, including 'religion' and 'the secular'. From this point of view, the problem is not just that 'Western' values (of liberty, democracy, etc.) can be exported elsewhere only on condition that others accept their universality, and through it, the intellectual hegemony of the West (since the West 'got there first'), but that the values and concepts themselves are already built out of, or 'assembled' through, past histories of interaction. Van der Veer puts the point succinctly:

Modernity has a global history. This does not imply a single origin of concepts and blueprints that are developed in the Enlightenment (both American and French) and exported and resisted, and adopted, elsewhere. Nor does it imply the dialectic between an already finished idiom of modernity that confronts an already existing idiom of tradition, out of which a synthesis emerges. Rather, it manifests a history of interactions out of which modernity, with its new historical problematic, arose, offering creative tensions, not solutions. (2001: 160)

According to van der Veer, core facets of the secular, e.g. concepts of modernity, liberty and equality, can only be understood as products of 'a shared colonial experience … created and re-created in the interaction between colony and metropole' (7). Tomoko Masuzawa (2005) and Timothy Fitzgerald (2000) have similarly argued that 'religion', and through it, 'the secular', emerged through the history of Christianity's engagement with non-Western religions.[23]

The problem, then, is not simply that Taylor wishes to export his concept of the secular to cultures that have no share in its intellectual history (as Asad suggests), but that secularity's basic building blocks were themselves generated at the edge of intercivilizational encounters – encounters ideologically and materially biased towards the West. By passing over this oppositional and asymmetrical history, Taylor unwittingly projects elsewhere a socio-political concept already built out of, or affectively secured through, negative representations of that elsewhere. The consequences are severe:

To secure secularism as a uniquely Christian (or, for that matter, Western) achievement is not simply a documentary exercise. Rather, it is to engage in a practice through which the 'North Atlantic' has historically secured its exceptionality – the simultaneous uniqueness *and* universality of its religious forms and the superiority of its civilization. To inhabit this founding gesture uncritically (as Taylor does), by which the West consolidates its epistemic and historical privilege, is not simply to describe a discursive structure but to write from within its concepts and ambitions – one might say even to further its aims and strengthen its presuppositions. (Mahmood 2010: 289–90, emphasis original)[24]

Mahmood's comments suggest that an escape from the reproduction of imperialist ideology will be effected neither by looking elsewhere, into the 'deep space' of foreign histories and cultures, nor by tracing an autochthonous history of the secular rooted in Christianity, but by paying close attention to the ways in which secular concepts and affectivities are constructed and grounded against these foreign histories and cultures. A critical history of the secular must address this opposition.

The buffered self

Unsurprisingly, Mahmood criticizes Taylor for ignoring the formative role of civilizational encounters in the construction of the buffered self. According to her, 'the condition of emergence of the "buffered self" ... was not only an epistemological shift but also civilizational, in that the self-reflection induced by encounters with others was taken as a sign of the superiority and uniqueness of Western European Christianity'. But rather than jettisoning the concept, Mahmood asks, 'Is it possible to think *with* Taylor's conception of the buffered self, which no doubt captures something quite important about modern secular sensibility, while remaining attentive to the relations of power that provided the structural conditions for the emergence of this peculiar self-conception?' (2010: 291, fn. 14, emphasis original).

Returning to Hirschkind's two questions – 'Is there a secular body?' and 'Is there a particular configuration of the human sensorium – of sensibilities, affects, embodied dispositions – specific to secular subjects, and thus constitutive of what we mean by "secular society"?' – what Mahmood seems to be suggesting is that Taylor and Hirschkind's accounts of the buffered self and secular body will necessarily remain incomplete until close attention is paid to the way these selves and bodies are constructed out of the dynamic interplay of oppositional categories, fundamentally the distinction between the West and the rest. This last point must be emphasized, because although critical and body-sensitive scholars of the secular like Asad accept that the secular 'works through a series of particular oppositions' (2003: 25), they are surprisingly silent on the formative role of colonial encounters for the genealogy of secularity, focusing instead on the exclusively *Western* predicament of managing religious strife in the transition to modern nation-states. Similarly, Hirschkind lists secularity's generative binaries as 'religion-secular, belief-knowledge, sacred-profane' (2011: 641), without indexing these to their obvious civilizational correlate: East–West or Orient–Occident. This is a significant omission because insofar as the secular can be analysed as a compound assemblage of concepts, sensibilities and affects (as Asad and Hirschkind seek to do), it seems clear that negative representations of other civilizations – which permeated eighteenth-century 'secular' literature – will play a crucial role in the affective grounding of the secular, and the simultaneous establishment of the West as the standard bearer of modernity.[25] If we want to understand the origins, history and nature of a 'secular body', secular representations of the Orient and Oriental religions may be a good place to look.

Statement of purpose

This book does not provide a comprehensive answer to Asad's call for an anthropology of the secular. Nor does it deny that secularism or the secular constitute the ubiquitous (and for that reason invisible) backdrop to the experience of modernity. It does, however, contest two interrelated ideas, both centred on Charles Taylor's *A Secular Age*: that secularism necessarily entails a negative stance towards emotion, the body, or what Connolly calls 'the visceral register of intersubjectivity' (1999); and that the genealogy of secularity is complete without reference to secular representations of non-Western religions and cultures. I argue that, despite efforts to nuance our understanding of secularity by softening the boundary between religious and secular, the emerging field of secular studies, and especially Charles Taylor's *ASA*, still operates with (a) an overly reductive and rationalistic conception of Enlightenment that casts secularization as a gradual (if rocky) process of disengagement from the body (via e.g. Grotius, Descartes, Voltaire, Gibbon, Kant), and thereby elides ongoing forms of 'porous', 'embedded' and 'embodied' subjectivity in the national age; and (b) an excessively West- or Eurocentric understanding of secularization that ignores the historical dependence of secular discourse on visceral representations of 'other' religions and 'other' peoples.

Through close engagement with a selection of French Enlightenment figures of the seventeenth and eighteenth century, I show that insofar as the buffered self or secular body exist, their history cannot be reduced to a rationalistic rejection of the visceral dimension (Hirschkind; Taylor), nor traced simply to the emergence of a democratic politics based on the free exchange of rational speech acts in the 'public sphere' (Taylor; Habermas), but is instead closely bound up with a conscious manipulation of affects at a founding moment of the nation-state. This manipulation was aided by atheistic, polemical descriptions of Oriental religions, especially Islam, which functioned as a practical, representational extension of the *philosophes'* already 'postrationalist' theories of agency. There is thus an intimate link between the genealogy of our secular age and European representations of the Oriental (Islamic) other.

Secular Assemblages develops in two stages. In the first (Chapters 1 to 3), I suggest that a careful re-examination of key texts of the seventeenth- and eighteenth-century French Enlightenment points to a much more nuanced and embodied intellectual history of Latin Christendom (Taylor) than neo-Kantian histories of the secular like Taylor's and Habermas's suggest. Chapter 1 challenges Taylor's 'rationalistic' reading of Descartes's late work *Les Passions de l'Âme* (1649), arguing that Taylor glosses over important ways in which Descartes involves the body in processes of knowledge acquisition and ethical cultivation, particularly through his conception of 'habit'. Chapter 2 examines the role of 'passions' and 'imagination' in mid- to late-eighteenth-century French philosophy, through authors including Montesquieu, Diderot, Rousseau, Helvétius, Holbach and Condorcet, with a special focus on Holbach's seminal work of Enlightenment materialism *Système de la Nature* (1770). Chapter 3 considers ways in which eighteenth-century epistemologies and *habitus*-based theories of agency explicitly fed into French projects of statecraft and national identity-formation, e.g. through documents of educational reform like Talleyrand's *Rapport sur l'Instruction Publique* (1791) and Condorcet's *Cinq Mémoires sur l'Instruction Publique* (1791).

As I show, the mid- to late-eighteenth-century French Enlightenment did not simply push for a repression of emotionality (religious or otherwise), nor did it consistently endorse a 'neo-Stoic' (Taylor) theory of morality and agency that situated reason as the hegemonic director of the passions within the autonomous realm of the buffered self. Instead, many of the *philosophes* sought to guide – not coerce – private and public emotions towards the imagined community and values of the nation-state through emotional and sensual means, by thinking through the power of experience, representation, the body and bodily habits for creating and sustaining national, post-religious subjects. The theoretical groundwork for this approach can be traced to Descartes, reaches full articulation in Holbach's *Système* and, I suggest, is later erased in a retroactive, post-revolutionary disavowal of emotion and the body, indebted centrally to Kant.

The second stage tackles racialized representations of religion in secular discourse, which, I argue, were a natural outgrowth of Enlightenment postrational epistemology and empiricist virtue ethics. Chapter 4 demonstrates the ubiquity of negative, affectively charged representations of Islam during the Enlightenment, with a special focus on the eighteenth-century anti-Catholic polemics *Lettres Persanes* (1721) and *De l'Esprit des Lois* (1748) by Montesquieu. Drawing on Victor Turner's 'law of dissociation by varying concomitants' (1964: 105), I suggest the 'Oriental despot' – a key figure of Montesquieu's work and of the Enlightenment generally – performed a role analogous to the 'monstrous mask' of pre-modern initiation rites, serving to reduce complex politico-theological problems to the exaggerated, embodied and easily digestible features of the Oriental other, and thereby 'rewire' the structure of affects surrounding religion and the nation-state. Chapter 5 focuses particularly on Voltaire's manipulation of racialized bodies and imagery in his stage-play *Le Fanatisme* (1741) to execute a critique of religion that worked primarily at the affective level, so shoring up two desirables of the emerging secular state: civic virtue and a strong sense of national belonging.

Chapters 4 and 5 indicate that, insofar as our secular age is in any sense anti-corporeal (according to Taylor, 'we relate to the world as more disembodied beings than our ancestors', 2007: 141), this anti-corporeality has a very specific lineage, both in the genealogy of the secular and, by implication, the genealogy of 'religion'. Enlightenment attacks on religious emotion or fanaticism were formulated almost exclusively in terms of non-Christian religions, usually Islam, allowing Christianity to transubstantiate into the category of the secular and escape scot-free (Anidjar 2006). What we today read as an autochthonous development of the West ('Western "disengaged reason" emancipating itself from Western pre-modern porosity and superstition') was bound up at its origins with representations of other religions in other places. I suggest this has important implications for the way we approach contemporary secular-nationalist appeals to a 'new Enlightenment', since these appeals are in a certain sense tautological: the Enlightenment was already an emotive, nationalistic and often xenophobic phenomenon, rooted in a postrationalistic (and to that extent 'postsecular') understanding of the body. For many of the *philosophes*, the commonplace opposition between 'religious culture' and 'Enlightenment principles' would have made no sense; Enlightenment *was* culture.

Secular Assemblages therefore has at least two consequences beyond simply critiquing *A Secular Age*. In the first place, it considerably nuances secular-studies approaches to the history of secularization, which frequently operate with an outdated conception of Enlightenment as focused exclusively on 'reason and science', a point then used to critically re-examine the Enlightenment or modernity between the lines, e.g. through material culture and Enlightenment aesthetics, or eighteenth- to nineteenth-century secular pop-culture (e.g. Modern 2011; Curtis 2016). Second, it challenges a secular-nationalist double-binary linking religion to emotion, and secularity to rationality, that allows contemporary secular nationalists (Geert Wilders, Marine Le Pen, Christopher Hitchens, Sam Harris, Ayaan Hirsi Ali, etc.) to co-opt the 'rational' Enlightenment against the irrational passions of (especially Islamic) religion, while ironically playing up highly emotive fears of the invading other. As this book suggests, the Enlightenment is a deceitful partner in this game. For though it – like modern advocates of a new Enlightenment – exploited negative representations of the other, it did so consistent with a postrationalist epistemology that had already come to terms with the inadequacy of an anti-emotional or anti-corporeal politics, and to that extent deconstructed itself.[26]

Secular assemblages

Although this book suggests that Enlightenment philosophers from Descartes to Holbach in some ways sought to reinstate emotion and the body against the rationalistic tendencies of the past, my aim is not to reverse an existing paradigm concerning the genealogy of the secular body. Emotionalism did not replace rationalism as the dominant epistemological and ethical framework of the Enlightenment. Neither the French Enlightenment nor its precedents are simple enough to be encompassed by a singular narrative, whether rationalist or anti-rationalist. Instead, I highlight points of disagreement, tension and outright contradiction between and within the *philosophes'* works, as postrationalist strands emerged and ran parallel with rationalist appeals to the hegemony of reason. These tensions occurred along several axes: chronological (e.g. the end of the eighteenth century was arguably less rationalistic than the beginning), denominational (e.g. Protestant vs Catholic contexts), national (e.g. Anglophone vs Gallic contexts) and philosophical (e.g. empiricism vs innatism). But they were also, to some extent, embedded in the nature of the material itself, insofar as rationalistic premises (e.g. the senses yield reason) could lead to non-rationalistic conclusions (sensual manipulation, not reason, governs the people). Moreover, many of the works examined here, from Montesquieu's *Lettres Persanes* (1721) to Diderot and d'Alembert's *Encyclopédie* (1751–1772), contain highly heterogeneous images and ideas, collating anti-Catholic polemics with pseudoscientific and pseudohistorical representations of the Orient and Oriental religions. This confluence demands an explanation. Why were some of the most anti-religious documents to emerge from the French Enlightenment also deeply Orientalist? Is it a coincidence that Helvétius, one of the most radical atheists of the eighteenth century, coined the term 'Oriental despotism' in his seminal tract *De l'Esprit* (1758)? What drew atheism and Orientalism together so that, over time, their juxtaposition seemed given, logical, natural?

At a general level, I would suggest that the Enlightenment works examined here are best approached not as unitary systems, but what Deleuze and Guattari call 'assemblages' of knowledges, logical machineries, affects or 'lines of articulation or segmentarity, strata and territories' (1987 [1980]: 4). From this perspective, there is no single conclusion, meaning or 'ideology' to be derived from a literary production, since it is inevitably *bricolé* out of heterogeneous and sometimes contradictory elements. A book is a 'multiplicity' (4), incomprehensible in isolation from the cultural machinery surrounding its production.[27] The meaning of a work is not intrinsic to it, but arises through connections to 'other assemblages', 'other bodies without organs' and other usages. The core question then is not so much what Enlightenment books meant, but how they functioned, contingently, within a given field of knowledge and power; not to detect a hidden unity in the intellectual content of works, but to understand how a fractured document might still achieve its intended effect in the machinery of a discursive 'meta-assemblage' or 'assemblage of assemblages':

> As an assemblage, a book has only itself, in connection with other assemblages and in relation to other bodies without organs. We will never ask what a book means, as signified or signifier; we will not look for anything to understand in it. We will ask what it functions with, in connection with what other things it does or does not transmit intensities, in which other multiplicities its own are inserted and metamorphosed, and with what bodies without organs it makes its own converge. … A book itself is a little machine … when one writes, the only question is which other machine the literary machine can be plugged into, must be plugged into in order to work. (4)[28]

As assemblages, the unity these books stemmed from their social efficacy within a general field of knowledge and their enmeshment in a broad tide of anti-religious propaganda sweeping through France during the eighteenth century. Though full of inconsistencies, and mixing logical argument, empirical data, speculation and highly affective rhetoric, French anti-religious texts nevertheless functioned to secure determinable socio-political goals, e.g. the abolition of clerical privilege and establishment of a limited monarchy or republic.[29] Their primary function was not necessarily to correct or fine-tune an existing system of thought, but to play up visceral reactions to a corrupt church, through the language of freedom, equality and, as I will show, radical ethnic and cultural alterity. Despite their seeming incongruity, the domains of anti-religion and Orientalism could be 'glued' into an expedient assemblage by a common agenda motivating French anti-clerical and anti-monarchic populism, and thereby put to work in the political machinery of eighteenth-century France.

There is, however, another sense in which the concept of assemblage applies particularly well to secular discourse of the eighteenth century. When Deleuze and Guattari developed the concept of assemblage in *A Thousand Plateaus* (1980), they were responding to Freud's theory of consciousness, both advancing and critiquing his dis-integrated conception of the subject. (While Freud dissolved the singular 'Cartesian' ego, he still insisted on a linear, hierarchical model of separation, from the id to the superego.) The 'rhizome' is a conceptual device aimed specifically at arboreal models of knowledge and subjectivity, since it radically decentres the knowing subject of Western intellectual history and fragments all 'root, trunk and branch'-based theories of knowledge into a multiplicity of contingently articulated, divergent vectors or 'lines of flight'. To the extent that we can speak of a subject at all, this subject is, for Deleuze and Guattari, a composite entity assembled by surrounding conditions – social, geographical, historical, etc. – none of which necessarily take precedence over the other, and none of which necessarily bears any relation to the other.

The assemblage is thus a clear attack on Enlightenment conceptions of a fully self-transparent, integrated subject. Deconstructed by Nietzsche and Freud at the turn of the nineteenth century, further fragmented by Deleuze and Guattari, and later reprised and critiqued by Derrida in his seminal paper 'Structure, Sign, and Play in the Discourse of the Human Sciences' (2001 [1967]: 351–370), this self has become a (if not *the*) symbolic *bête noire* of Enlightenment philosophy. It is precisely this self that Theodor Adorno and Max Horkheimer critique in *Dialectic of Enlightenment* (1944):

> According to enlightened thinking, the multiplicity of mythical figures can be reduced to a single common denominator, the subject. ... For the Enlightenment, only what can be encompassed by unity has the status of an existent or an event; its ideal is the system from which everything and anything follows. ... For the Enlightenment, anything which cannot be resolved into numbers, and ultimately into one, is illusion. (2002 [1944]: 4)

More recently, Asad has linked the unitary self to Locke especially:

> After all, human beings do, think, and feel all sorts of disparate things – what is it that brings all of them together? At least as far back as John Locke, 'person' was theorized as a forensic term that called for the integration of a single subject with a continuous consciousness in a single body. (2003: 74)

As the first chapter shows, the singular, self-transparent subject is also intrinsic to Taylor's critique of Descartes, setting the stage for a monumental 'discovery' of the unconscious in the nineteenth century.

In fact, many Enlightenment works are extremely difficult to square with such an integrated understanding of the subject. A careful re-reading of Descartes's *Les Passions de l'Âme* reveals a thoroughly embodied self, formed by histories of habituation not immediately available to reason's introspective gaze; Ivan

Pavlov would later cite Descartes as a formative influence. A century before the *Passions*, Montaigne described humans as unstable, liquid 'wind', and advocated surrendering one's fate to chance or the play of dice since human reason was 'a double-edged and dangerous sword' (1940: 43, 58). Later, Diderot suggested the unity of the subject spoke more of moral delusion than truth to nature. In a fictional conversation between himself (as narrator) and the enlightened figure of 'Dorval' in *Entretiens sur le Fils Naturel* (1757), the narrator asks, 'But isn't unity of character, rigorously interpreted, an illusion [*chimère*]?' Dorval answers: 'No doubt ... It seems to me that it is better to render men as they are [than as they should be]. What they should be is a thing too systematic and too vague to serve as a useful basis for the art of imitation. There is nothing so rare as a totally evil person' (1821 [1757]: 273–4). Against common perceptions, such multilayered, heterogeneous, unstable and dynamic conceptions of the person underwrote virtually all eighteenth-century French philosophy, as was recognized by early historiographers of Enlightenment. Reflecting on the achievements of the preceding few centuries, the anonymous editor of Joseph Fouché's collected writings *Matériaux pour Servir à la Vie Publique et Privée de Joseph Fouché* (1821) wrote that:

> Certain Greek philosophers believed themselves to have made an incredible discovery by proposing that man is *double*: we have gone much further, and the precise analysis of his faculties today demonstrates that he is *multiple*. Should we therefore be surprised that in the forced conjoining of these qualities, there should be some that are diverse, opposed, contradictory? It would, on the contrary, be more surprising that they be homogenous and reconcilable. (34, emphasis original)

Subjective multiplicity and contradiction are here presented not as the antithesis of Enlightenment, but its culmination. That this passage could be written in 1821 – more than a hundred years before Freud's major works of psychoanalysis – highlights the inadequacy of conceiving Western intellectual history in terms of a straightforward dialectic movement between a rationalistic Enlightenment and a Freudian recovery of the unconscious at the end of the nineteenth century. The Enlightenment was already sensitive to the problematic nature of a unitary, integrated conception of the self; this conception was already, in a sense, 'assembled'.

Cartesian secularity: 'Disengaged reason', the passions and the public sphere beyond Charles Taylor's *A Secular Age* (2007)

Though love is but a passion of our soul, it has this advantage in common with divinity: that it is as secret as it is public, and that there is nothing in nature more evident yet more hidden ... our hopes divulge it and all our passions discover it, yet it is retreated in the bottom of our hearts, and all the traces that reveal its presence are as so many clouds, concealing it from our understandings.

Jean-François Senault, *De l'Usage des Passions* (1641: 214–15)

Introduction

Talal Asad has criticized Charles Taylor's *A Secular Age* (2007) for privileging belief as the pivot between pre-secularity and secularity. Against Taylor's primary interest in the emergence of ubiquitously optional belief (what he calls 'secularity 3'), Asad argues for 'the importance of studying the senses in order to identify ways they can build sensibilities and attitudes that are distinct from beliefs' (2011: 37). This alternative approach sidesteps a Christo- or ratiocentric tendency to take faith, doctrine, propositional truth or even 'enchantment' as the essence of religion, and it clears the way for an analysis of the modern subject that crosses the secular/religious divide. If 'belief' and its accompanying term 'religion' are today better understood as performative elements in a language game that facilitates rule by liberal democratic government, 'studying the senses' promises an avenue into both religious and secular subjectivity that is not already *interpreted*.[1] Asad's counter-Taylorian emphasis on the pre-interpreted, sensual and disciplinary dimensions of secularism extends his earlier project, first outlined in *Formations of the Secular*, to develop an 'anthropology of secularism' (2003: 1).

This chapter agrees with Asad but goes further in questioning the 'disenchantment' narrative at the heart of *A Secular Age*. Indeed, it suggests that Taylor's focus on belief not only presents a methodological problem vis-à-vis the genealogy secularity, but leads to a distorted *factual* understanding of this genealogy, by overemphasizing the importance of a historical break between belief and practice, reason and emotion, and mind and body in the intellectual history of Europe – a tendency that is particularly clear in Taylor's treatment of the historical 'Enlightenment'. While explicitly challenging over-simplistic dichotomies between secular reason and religious affect, I argue Taylor overstates the division of reason and emotion in the thought of certain secularizing thinkers, especially Descartes, and thus unjustifiably associates secularization or Enlightenment with an epistemological and ethical disengagement from the body. To take this position is to grant the Enlightenment both too much and too little. It grants the Enlightenment too much, because it allows it to step outside of politics and power and assume the voice of an idealized pure reason. It grants the Enlightenment too little, because it does not recognize the sophistication of its engagement with the question of human subjectivity and the importance of its legacy for modern psychology, especially theories of mass manipulation by manufactured consent. Against such idealistic conceptions, I show that Enlightenment thought – beginning with Descartes – is indissociable from the body, politics and power.

Why Descartes? According to Taylor, Descartes marks a key moment in the simultaneous transition from theism to 'exclusive humanism', and from the 'porous' to the 'punctual' (1989) or 'buffered self' (2007) of secular modernity. The sixteenth- to seventeenth-century shift from medieval practices of piety and devotion rooted in the body, to the mind-based, 'rational-critical' world of the eighteenth-century Enlightenment situates Descartes in a pivotal position for the erasure of bodily experience, and eventual hegemony of autonomous, 'disengaged reason' (1989, 2007, 2012). This in turn feeds into a disembodied conception of a 'public sphere' founded on the dialogical unfolding of pure reason exempt from social conflict and the distortive influence of power (2007: 185–96). Within this broad historical context, Taylor reads Descartes with a clear anti-corporeal or anti-emotional inflection: he opened the way for the 'cold rationalism' of the Enlightenment and its distrust of religious sentiments or 'enthusiasm' later epitomized by Gibbon and Hume; and he helped lay the ground for an effective 'immanentization' of ethics, by drawing previously external sources of moral authority (e.g. God or Nature's order) under the judgement of autonomous reason, an internalizing movement partially revoked by the subsequent rise to dominance of communicative rationality in the public sphere.

The assumption that Descartes sought to downgrade or dominate the passions by force of reason is so engrained that even researchers more sensitive to the presence of the body in the Enlightenment still associate Descartes with an antithetical stance towards the body and emotions. According to Jessica Riskin, whose work on the Enlightenment body is central to the following chapter, Descartes 'treated the passions as innate tendencies of the human constitution, the antithesis of the rational faculty, and inherently destructive' (2002: 49). This is false, even by Taylor's account. Descartes's last major work *Les Passions de l'Âme* (1649) – according to Philip Fisher, 'the most significant modern work on the passions' (1998: 16) – testifies to an acute awareness of the limits of internal, autonomous reason, emphasizing the entanglement of reason in the workings of the body; the importance of external, environmental factors for the shaping of human experience and response; and the centrality of 'habit' or 'habits' to the cultivation of virtue. In this respect, Descartes's theories share more in common with Aristotelian virtue ethics than a reason-based framework of moral decisions, or a neo-Stoic 'honour ethic' founded on coercive acts of sovereign will meted out to subjugated and immediately accessible passions or acts. Although Taylor accepts that Descartes adopted an instrumentalist approach to the passions that allowed for a positive reassessment of the latter, he still reads Descartes in terms of a rationalistic, 'disengaged stance' towards the body that, among other things, elides his theory of the habit entirely. This chapter redresses the record.

Given the depth and complexity of Taylor's analysis, I begin with a detailed summary of the intellectual history leading up to Descartes, as outlined in *A Secular Age*, then summarize Taylor's reading of Descartes, both in *A Secular Age* and *Sources of the Self*. I briefly compare the chief arguments of the *Passions*, as read by Taylor, to the arguments of an earlier, lesser-known treatise, *De l'Usage des Passions* (1641), by the Augustinian philosopher Jean-François Senault, in order to draw out the distinctiveness of Descartes's contribution. My own close reading of the *Passions* suggests that, if Descartes played a pivotal role in the genealogy of the secular, it is not because he rationalized the ideal thinking, feeling, acting subject (a feature of *De l'Usage*) but, on the contrary, because he provided a striking anticipation of postrationalist scepticism, articulated through his theory of the associational habit. Excavating Descartes's sceptic side will later serve as a basis for deconstructing two key premises of *A Secular Age*: that the 'Counter-

Enlightenment' marked a recovery of affect or the unconscious, following the failures of the rational Enlightenment; and that modern secularity is conditioned by a moment of pure rationality at the foundation of the nation-state.

In the broader scheme of secular history, a careful re-evaluation of Descartes problematizes Taylor's narrative arc casting the eighteenth-century Enlightenment as the culmination of a gradual suppression of sentiment, and rise to hegemony of affectless, disengaged reason. As I will argue later, this culmination narrative is both inaccurate, since it relies on an illegitimate reification of pure or disengaged reason that in fact never existed, and masks important ways in which the 'radical Enlightenment' (Taylor 2007: 149) of the eighteenth century combined 'rational-critical' (Habermas 1989 [1962]) elaboration with nationalistic propaganda. This propaganda played heavily on sentiments and passions to manipulate an emergent public opinion and build up a secular-nationalist structure of affect with revolutionary and long-lasting consequences.

From porous to buffered selves: Questions and categories

Taylor begins Part I of *A Secular Age* with a thematic question tying the whole of the book's almost 800 pages together: 'why was it virtually impossible not to believe in God in, say 1500 in our Western society, while in 2000 many of us find this not only easy, but even inescapable?' (25). This simple question, laying out two poles on a temporal continuum stretching over 500 years, establishes a binary narrative structure based on the historical progression from one state of affairs to another. State 1 is characterized by three principal features:

(1) People's 'natural world', including both the world of daily experience and the imagined cosmos in which this world was situated 'testified to divine purpose and action'.
(2) God was implicated in 'the very existence of society'.
(3) People lived in an 'enchanted world', that is, a world inhabited by visible and invisible spirits that interacted with fleshly humans in ways we now find difficult to imagine (e.g. 'possession' by a spirit could take the form of a physical substance, e.g. black bile). (25)

State 2 (our 'secular age') is characterized by the overwhelming absence of these features. Taylor devotes the bulk of *A Secular Age* to fleshing out the gap between states 1 and 2.

To this end, Taylor develops several conceptual categories based upon challenges to the above features. (1), (2) and (3) all suggest a pre-modern openness to transcendence that is gradually 'fragilized' by encounters with alternative (e.g. materialist) construals of the natural order, society or the good, leading to the eventual establishment of 'the immanent frame': a metaphysical outlook that tends to elide (indeed, make impossible) all appeals to transcendence. The subject position most closely linked to this closure of transcendence is what he calls the 'buffered self' in contradistinction to the 'porous self' of the enchanted Middle Ages. Whereas the porous self lived in a universe crossed through with invisible forces and beings, and was constantly threatened by forms of divine and/ or malign agency that may enter, possess or destroy human bodies and ecologies, the buffered self is characterized by its confidence in the invulnerability of the self to forces beyond the immanent (or empirically accessible) realm.

Crucially, whereas the porous self typically derived its conception of the good from transcendental sources of moral authority (e.g. Platonic forms, divine commandments and fear of retribution), the buffered self has, through a number of intermediary stages, brought moral judgement into the exclusive realm of an immanent Natural Law or secular ethics (e.g. utilitarianism) determinable (if not determined) by human powers. In this sense, the modern self is not only buffered against forces we would now consider imaginary (e.g. divine or satanic possession) but against the arbitrary judgement of a divine legislator or *a priori* world of pure forms not answerable to, yet determinative of, rational principles. Immanent ethics emerge through an individual process of rational deliberation or inward reflection accessible to anyone endowed with the capacity to think; the outcome may or may not reflect God's will. The tendency was in fact to move from the first to the second possibility: from rationally inferred Natural Law as the disclosure of God's blueprint for creation (e.g. Hugo Grotius), to rationally inferred ethics established in independence from the legitimating force of divine sanction (e.g. Holbach). Bufferedness is thus as much an ethical as an ontological or physical condition – indeed, Taylor's thesis can be seen as an attempt to shift weight from the latter onto the former, since pre-*A Secular Age* genealogies of the secular tended to overemphasize the power of empiricism to debunk theological imaginings on physical grounds alone.

The buffered self therefore involves at least two interrelated shifts, both of which reflect a broader shift from an enchanted to a disenchanted universe: (1) the gradual disappearance of supernatural forces and spirits inaccessible to empirical verification; and (2) the internalization of sources of moral authority, as guidance no longer issues from a tension between our falling short of an objective standard set by Platonic forms existing 'out there', or divine commandments disclosed via the intermediary of an external arbitrator, e.g. the Church or Prince, but from the internal domain of the reasoning self. The 'aura' surrounding traditional, external sources of moral authority has disappeared.

According to Taylor, however, bufferedness also entails a third, less explicit shift in subjectivity: it calls for a negative, objectifying or instrumental stance towards the body and affective registers of experience, morality and agency – a stance Taylor associates especially with Descartes's 'disengaged reason' (1989, 2007, 2012), and later with the eighteenth-century Enlightenment. This aspect of his analysis demands careful attention. For in his effort to track a coherent thread running through Western intellectual history, Taylor tends to underplay Descartes's more positive assessments of the body and its entanglement with the mind. Since Taylor links Descartes strongly to the 'neo-Stoic' tradition of sixteenth-century reformism, I will begin by outlining the neo-Stoic background to Descartes's thinking, as presented in *A Secular Age*.

The neo-Stoic backdrop

A Secular Age situates a key moment for the genealogy of the buffered self in the sixteenth-century neo-Stoic reformer Justus Lipsius. Like the Stoics, Lipsius broke from existing ethical frameworks based on divine command, empathy or virtue by formulating an ethical theory rooted exclusively in the reasoning mind. Where Christian ethics might emphasize the power and necessity of *agape*, love for our neighbour, or *miseratio* and *misericordia* (the 'compassion of feeling' embodied in the figure of Christ), Lipsius rejected all these in favour of the Stoic goal of *apatheia*, 'a condition beyond passion' (2007: 115). His 'Christianized Stoicism' had no place for the body or emotions but rather sought moral perfection 'on the basis of a full inner detachment' (115). This did not mean detachment from God, however; Lipsius was not what Taylor calls an 'exclusive humanist'. Rather, the use of reason was itself a crucial element of God's plan, since 'God is the source of the ratio on which we base our lives' (115), an idea later systematized in Grotius's formulation of Natural Law – one both rationally inferable and 'God given' (129). For Lipsius and Grotius, to be rational was to exercise one's faith, and vice versa. Reason was a route into the mystery of divine order. Indeed, it was its fundamental principle, for unlike 'opinion, which comes from the earth and the body', or 'external calamities', 'Reason tells us to hang on to what is unchanging' (115–16). The focus on eternal truth naturally tended to downgrade Christological emphases on the temporality and embodied suffering of Christ, and from there to downgrade the body in general. As Lipsius's predecessor Erasmus put it: 'Transfer your love to something permanent, something celestial, something incorruptible, and you will love more coolly this transitory and fleeting form of the body' (Taylor 2007: 116).

Along with the rationalization and internalization of morality came a new-found confidence in man's ability to manipulate both himself and his environment. Lipsius 'set the tone' for the reformers of the following century, that is high civil servants, administrators and generals who sought to 'reconstruct various dimensions of society' (118). A new optimism took over during this period, grounded in self-discipline and the training of the subordinate masses, so that eventually the belief emerged that 'nothing in principle stood in the way of ... social engineering' (121). Whereas the Middle Ages were still 'steeped in the view ... that there are severe limits to the degree in which sin and disorder can be done away with in this world' (119), the new 'protestant work ethic' and 'inner worldly asceticism' propagated by Calvinism and Pietism tended to remove limits on human improvement and bring other-worldly utopianism into the present. The thrust of this new optimism was an unprecedented faith in the powers of human reason. The eventual hegemony of reason, still understood as the ultimate expression divine order, would allow humans to reach maximal control (and hence happiness) in this life, not just the next. In other words, the body was not just relegated to a subordinate position in the hierarchy of human flourishing; it was *to be subordinated* by force of will and reason.

Cartesian reason

It is in this context that Taylor presents Descartes, as a transitional figure for the closure of self at the onset of early modernity. According to Taylor, Descartes 'clearly [stood] in the neo-Stoic stream of thought' (130), yet departed from traditional neo-Stoicism in important ways. He retained and intensified the neo-Stoic emphasis on disengagement from the body and, like Lipsius and Grotius, elaborated an understanding of virtue as 'dominance of the will over passion' (130). Virtue increased to the extent that unruly passions were brought under the hegemonic reach of autonomous reason. Unlike the Stoics and neo-Stoics, however, Descartes (1) jettisoned any sense that rationally derived principles of virtue reflected something about the order of things existing 'out there' – his moral framework was 'all in the mind', marking a further inward shift towards the self-sufficiency of the buffered self; and (2) did not seek to annihilate the passions, but rather, to channel them towards a rationally inferred or *a priori* deducible good. While for the Stoics, the passions were 'false opinions' that would disappear in the light of wisdom, for Descartes, they were 'responses we are endowed with by the Creator to help us respond with appropriate vigour in certain, appropriate circumstances'. The goal was therefore 'not to do away with them, but to bring them under the instrumental control of reason' (131). As Descartes puts it, in a key passage cited by Taylor:

> The customary mode of action of all the passions is simply this, that they dispose the soul to desire those things which nature tells us are of use, and to persist in this desire, and also bring about that same agitation of spirits which customarily causes them to dispose the body to the movement which serves for the carrying into effect of those things. (*Les Passions de l'Âme,* Article 52, in Taylor 1989: 150)

Instead of eradicating or suppressing the passions, Descartes yoked them to the principle of reason through a dual process of objectification and instrumentalization that reduced the body to a mere crutch: '[The soul] has to support itself on [the body] to climb free of it' (1989: 146). Taylor speaks of 'the Cartesian picture of total self-possession' (2007: 349), of 'self-mastery' which 'consists in our lives being shaped by the orders that our reasoning capacity constructs according to the appropriate standards' (standards themselves derived from rational introspection; 1989: 147), of Cartesian 'disengaged reason' and 'dispassionate impersonality ... taken as sufficient for universal benevolence' (2007: 250).[2] The Cartesian understanding is characterized by a 'sharp division between mind and non-mental reality' that supports 'a conception of thought and will as something self-contained, in principle quite clear and present to themselves, and capable of establishing their independence from the world of matter' (348).

Taylor also links Descartes to a Lockean rejection of external culture and practice, e.g. 'bodily habitus and mimicry' and 'symbolic expression in art, poetry, music, dance' characteristic of 'aboriginal culture' (615). Cartesian attitudes to embodied practice and the cultivation of 'habits' run parallel to the modern ethic of disengagement, since ritual 'form' and bodily 'emotion' are rendered equally irrelevant against the absoluteness of eternal, unextended principles. As he puts it:

> In both cases the key is to grasp correct prepositional truth – about God and his Christ in one case, about correct action in the other. In the first case, right worship follows, but the forms that it takes are secondary, and can be varied at

will. In the second case, a successful imposition of reason brings about right action, but what this amounts to is to be known purely by reason – either the calculation of utility consequences, or the universalizability of the maxim. In no case, is a paradigm bodily emotion seen as *criterial* for right action – as in the case of New Testament agape. (615, emphasis original)

The assumption is not that Descartes ignored or sought to do away with the body and its emotions completely – this was the neo-Stoics' position – but that he did not recognize or deal adequately with the mind's dependence on the body. For Descartes, power only travelled one way: the properly trained body submitted completely to the mind, for knowledge of both itself and world, and for directing its actions. Thus, '[right action] is not defined as what comes from properly ordered desire, but rather as what disengaged reason demands of desire, to which desire has to be trained to be docile' (614). The 'clarity and distinctness' necessary for the control of desire required that we 'distance ourselves from our embodied understanding of things' (614) or do 'violence to our ordinary, embodied way of experiencing' since embodiment inevitably embroiled us in an 'irremediably confused and obscure way of grasping things' (1989: 146). Against this, Descartes recommends 'objectify[ing] the world, including our own bodies … in the same way that an uninvolved external observer would' (145).[3]

Descartes's legacy I: The unconscious 'reversal'

As noted above, Taylor takes Descartes's understanding of 'total self-possession' to represent a historical transition between 'two great cosmic outlooks' – between an enchanted universe in which meaning resided in the structure of existence itself and 'a mechanistic universe, providentially ordered for the sake of souls whose destiny was elsewhere' (2007: 349). The naive sense that 'what I really am' was discoverable through 'purely immanent self-clarity, clear and distinct self-consciousness', and that human reflexes and behaviour could be controlled through the sheer power of reason, (a) became definitive of the age of Enlightenment and (b) would later be replaced by more sceptic theories of human consciousness and agency based on a new awareness of the power of the 'cerebral unconscious'. This new awareness, outlined in Marcel Gauchet's *L'Inconscient Cérébral* (1992), was more sensitive to the body's imbrication in processes of deliberation, action and will formation. Further, it marked an epochal shift in the entire experiential framework or social imaginary in which we live:

Gauchet shows how in the nineteenth century ... the sense [develops] that our thinking and willing emerges out of cerebral/nervous function, through the concept of the reflex arc and sensorimotor scheme. The second half of the century comes to be dominated by a psycho-physiological outlook, which tries to place consciousness, thinking and will within its bodily realization. ... [T]his is more than just a change of theory. It is a shift in the whole framework in which theories are propounded ... the reality of thought to its material substrate, from being an issue of external relations for Descartes, has now become the key question about its very nature. On the new understanding, conscious willing grows out of the reflex arc, and is of the same nature as it. This ... has helped to produce our sense of the deep subject, opaque to herself, the locus of unconscious and partly impersonal processes. (2007: 349)

In other words, Descartes's transparent and rational subject laid the grounds for a monumental return of the repressed in nineteenth- and early-twentieth-century thought, the most important exponent of which was of course Freud, but which later received expression in the behavioural conditioning theories of Pavlov and others. The very idea that consciousness might be shaped by or subservient to unconscious orders of experience and reflection secured in independence from the self-reflective, reasoning mind was anathema to Descartes's faith in the transparency of the subject and the power of virtuous persons to force through actions on the basis of sheer will.

This assumption had important political implications, since it removed any limit on human reason and its potential for challenging external sources of authority. Since everything true began from the thinking mind, a process of rational inward reflection could not but corrode the causal relation between individual action and the externally imposed demands of social convention or hierarchical structures of authority headed by the sovereign will of Prince and King. Such corrosion was in fact a double-edged sword: it eventually buttressed the emancipatory ideology of the Revolution, but it also generated a 'weak' understanding of human nature and a naive faith in the autonomy of reason, so that Revolutionary utopias were quickly run aground and replaced with traditional Catholic structures and strictures during the nineteenth-century Restoration. For Taylor, this in turn provides a historical illustration of the weakness of rationality and conscious will vs the power of the unconscious. French revolutionaries could temporarily exterminate religious practices and institutions, but the background texture of affects, largely unconscious, and generated by richly sedimented histories of liturgy, ritual and social convention eventually won out.

Descartes's legacy II: The public sphere

Nevertheless, at least one aspect of Descartes's thought survived and became definitive of early modernity: his 'procedural rationality', i.e. a rationality based not on substantive ends but the method used to reach those ends. As is well known, Descartes's starting point for accessing the true nature of things rested fundamentally on correct procedure. The search for truth began with a process of subtraction and partitioning (especially of the soul/mind from the body) to facilitate the bottom-up reconstruction of knowledge by reason alone. The *way* in which Descartes's epistemological building blocks were manoeuvred into place following the initial act of deconstruction itself guaranteed the truth of his conclusions.

For Taylor, this procedural rationalism mirrors a crucial development in the social consciousness of early modernity, one inherently bound up with the genealogy of *A Secular Age*. Drawing on Habermas (1984 [1981], 1989 [1962]), Taylor explicitly links Descartes to the eighteenth-century emergence of the modern public sphere, seeing in his model of 'clear and distinct thought' a paradigmatic precursor for the later emergence of communicative rationality, since both Descartes's ethics and the legislative products of the public sphere rest on a rejection of substantive ends. Whereas substantive ethical frameworks assume that practical wisdom rests on 'seeing an order which in some sense is in nature', i.e. external or existing independently of the thinking self, Descartes's method and the dialogically constituted public sphere require a radical 'proceduralization' of the good (1989: 86). For both Descartes and the public sphere, moral justification becomes a matter not of discovering external goods embedded in the fabric of nature, or obeying the dictates of a transcendental God, but of correct procedure within the confines of the thinking mind (in the case of Descartes) or the circumscribed domain of public reason (in the case of the public sphere).

Though Descartes's pure reason and the public sphere may not seem, at first sight, to share much in common (Descartes's reason is internal; the public sphere is, well, public), in fact both see justification as procedural since 'It can't be defined by the particular outcome, but by the way in which the outcome is arrived at' (86). In neither case can there be *a priori* ascertainable ends, or 'once-for-all' moral judgements dispensed by a sovereign deity to subordinated humans (2007: 188). Even Descartes's certainties (such as the *cogito*) only attain absoluteness in light of a retroactive ratification linking ends to means. His conclusions, like the public sphere's, are not true because God has willed it, but because they derive from the correct method of attaining them. This is why the public sphere is fundamentally 'secular': it closes off transcendence by legitimizing itself on the discursive unfolding of immanent rationality, carried forward by reciprocal speech acts in the 'meta-topical' space – real and imagined – of free debate (a space constituted by a rich interconnecting network of communication media, including letters, pamphlets, books, face-to-face meetings, salon gatherings, etc.).[4] This debate is purely immanent. It happens within time and space, and hence within secularity, defined against the eternal, unextended plane of the divine.

Descartes's reasoning parallels and anticipates the eighteenth-century public sphere at another level, too. According to Taylor, the public sphere designates a universe of strictly self-contained 'rational-critical' debate outside social conflict and structures of power yet nevertheless able to influence those same structures. Indeed, its uniqueness stemmed from the fact it was 'extra-political', 'emanating from reason … not from power or traditional authority', yet still applied normative pressure on existing authorities; it was 'a discourse of reason *on* and *to* power' that stood outside of power (2007: 190, emphasis original).[5] Habermas is central to this part of *A Secular Age*. According to the latter, the eighteenth century saw Prince and Church become answerable, for the first time in history, to a self-legitimizing system of norms, constructed by the people (or more accurately 'the bourgeois reading public'; Habermas 1989 [1962]) and their public use of private reason. This extra-political system was deeply threatening and for that reason subject to censorship: 'Reason, which through public use of the rational faculty was to be realized in the rational communication of a public consisting of cultivated human beings, itself needed to be protected from becoming public because it was a threat to any and all relations of domination' (1989 [1962]: 35). According to Habermas, the Enlightenment – which generated the fundamental architecture of the public sphere, e.g. its 'Republic of Letters', salons, coffeehouses and other open spaces of discussion – only became political after the publication of the *Encyclopédie* (68), and then only to *rationalize* politics: 'The critical process that private people engaged in rational-critical public debate brought to bear on absolutist rule, interpreted itself as unpolitical: public opinion aimed at rationalizing politics in the name of morality' (102). In general, 'The salons were removed from practical politics' (34) and engaged in politics only to the extent that they could '*transform* voluntas *into a* ratio *that in the public competition of private arguments came into being as the consensus about what was practically necessary in the interest of all*' (83, emphasis original). Despite its eventual imbrication in politics, the enlightened discourse of the public sphere was itself untainted by power; it only assumed the appearance of a dominating force by reason of the system it fought against:

> The bourgeois idea of the law-based state, namely, the binding of all state activity to a system of norms legitimated by public opinion ... already aimed at abolishing the state as an instrument of domination altogether. Acts of sovereignty were considered apocryphal per se. Since the critical public debate of private people convincingly claimed to be in the nature of a noncoercive inquiry into what was at the same time correct and right, a legislation that had recourse to public opinion thus could not be explicitly considered as domination. ... Although construed as 'power', legislation was supposed to be the result not of a political will, but of rational agreement. (82)

For Habermas, this process of shaping public opinion and formulating legislation through 'rational agreement' alone was characteristic only of a limited period during the eighteenth century. It was eventually overturned by the rise of mass communications, the commodification of information and the politicization of news publishing and broadcasting corporations. Under the pressure of forces not subject to judgement by public reason, rational debate and public will-formation were replaced by manufactured consent.

As should be obvious, the free-floating-yet-hegemonic nature of rational-critical discourse directly parallels Descartes's distancing of reason from the body. Both Descartes and the public sphere take autonomous reason and its hegemony over the passions (or their worldly equivalent, the people or politics) as their basis. For both, 'power was to be tamed by reason' (Taylor 2007: 190). The Cartesian rationalistic procedure and its emphasis on freedom of will therefore parallels, and indeed *motivates*, the rise to hegemony of the public sphere – a kind of external, inter-subjective mind – and its self-generated system of justification on the basis of 'the better argument' alone. The 'modern idea of freedom' encapsulated in Cartesian and Kantian conceptions of the hegemony of reason and will is, according to Taylor, 'the strongest motive for the massive shift from substantive to procedural justifications in the modern world' (Taylor 1989: 86).

Summary

To summarize, Taylor reads Descartes as (1) standing in the neo-Stoic stream of thought, insofar as he advocates disengagement from the body and its unruly passions; (2) departing from the Stoics, in that he does not seek to suppress or annihilate the passions, but to objectify and instrumentalize them for the greater good; (3) understanding the passions as extensions of the will, or an intensifying bridge between reason, the will and the body; (4) emphasizing the absolute hegemony of reason and will among the virtuous, as well as (5) the transparency of self to the scrutinizing gaze of rational introspection, and (6) a sharp distinction between thinking mind and brute matter; and finally, (7) recommending a 'third-person', objectifying perspective on the self. Taken together, these points anticipate and motivate a shift from substantive to procedural justifications in the rational-critical discourse of the eighteenth-century public sphere, thus laying a foundation stone for the immanentization of sources of the good, a golden age of discursive rationalism and the ultimate secularization of Latin Christendom.

Each one of the above points can be challenged following a close reading of *Les Passions de l'Âme*.

Existing critiques of 'Cartesian dualism'

A number of existing works have challenged the Taylorian consensus of a rationalistic and/or dualistic Descartes. In 'Descartes' Embodied Psychology' (2001), Geir Kirkebøen argues against Antonio Damasio's seminal work *Descartes' Error* (1994) that 'Descartes never considered what we today call thinking or cognition without taking the body into account' (173). Whereas Damasio criticizes Descartes for imagining the thinking process as 'an activity quite separate from the body' (1994: 248, cited in Kirkebøen 2001: 173) and uses him as a historical foil for the elaboration of his own embodied psychology, Kirkebøen considers this critique flawed at the outset since '[Descartes's] explanations of psychological phenomena are all embodied' (174). Similarly, John Cottingham has written on the impossibility of separating reason from the passions in Descartes's thought, arguing that, post-*Méditations*,

> Descartes became increasingly preoccupied with the need for a genuine 'anthropology' – one which would do justice to the inescapable fact that we are not merely incorporeal ends inhabiting an alien mechanism, but creatures whose welfare is, in a special and intimate way, bound up with the operations of the body, and with the feelings, sensations, and passions that arise from our embodied state. (2008: 238)

Conversely, Victoria Kahn reads the innovations of the *Passions* in terms of an attempt to grapple with politics, arguing that, although Descartes initially favoured 'the more traditional language of Stoic virtue and Stoic detachment', he began to change his views following his correspondence with Princess Elisabeth of Bohemia (which Kahn views as a kind of trial run for the *Passions*). At this point, 'Descartes began to see the relevance of baroque politics and theatrical manipulation for a scientific treatment of the passions' (2006: 95). When Elisabeth requested his opinion of Machiavelli's *Prince* in September 1646, Descartes could no longer hide behind the abstractions of the *Méditations* and instead responded by 'touch[ing] on major themes of baroque political thought: the legitimacy of reason of state, the management of the people's passions, the relationship between force and ideology, as well as between *virtù* and virtue' (2006: 97). According to Kahn, the 'old-fashioned aristocratic ideal of self-mastery' was replaced by Descartes with 'the modern individual, whose body has become a foreign territory, one that requires new indirect techniques of government'. Such 'indirect techniques' represented a departure from Descartes's 'original ambition to establish ethics on a secure scientific basis' and led to 'a conception of government and self-government based on units of energy, mechanical operations, relations of forces' that transcended 'Hobbes's and Grotius's "modern" juridical language of rights, obligations, and consent'. Thus, the *Passions* 'deserves to be seen as one of the inaugurating texts of a new regime of politics, one inscribed in the body itself' (110).

While these works provide necessary rejoinders to the standard reception of Descartes represented by Taylor, Riskin and others, they do not touch upon some of the most central aspects of the *Passions*, notably its technical and ethical similarity to previous works like Jean-François Senault's *De l'Usage des Passions* (1641), its presentation of the soul–body relation and some of the deeper intricacies of the relation between the will, the passions and the habits – the last of which may be the most important contribution of the *Passions*. There is also a tendency (e.g. in Cottingham's work) to gloss over some of the basic contradictions in Descartes's work, reading divergent viewpoints in terms of a 'reconciliation' narrative that culminates in a strained harmonization of the Cartesian body-mind.

In order to draw out the complexity and heterogeneity of the *Passions*, the following sections delve extensively into the background and content of Descartes's work, referencing Kirkebøen, Cottingham and Kahn where appropriate, and reframing their analysis, along with my reinterpretation of Descartes, in terms of a response to *A Secular Age.*

De l'Usage des Passions (1641)

Perhaps the first question arising in response to *A Secular Age* concerns the weight placed upon Descartes as a major pivot upon which a putative rationalization of the European subject turned: to what extent were the Cartesian developments outlined by Taylor really 'Cartesian'? I suggest at least one author anticipated the majority of ideas taken by Taylor to define Descartes, and hence a crucial node in the genealogy of our secular age: Jean-François or 'Father' Senault (1599–1672), an Augustinian philosopher and priest whose work *De l'Usage des Passions* (1641) is among the most extensive and systematic treatments of the passions pre-Descartes, and sometimes listed as an important influence on the latter (Koch 2008: 303, fn. 67). A brief examination of this work will leave us better placed to pinpoint the exact contribution made by Descartes, eight years later.

To some extent, *De l'Usage* can be situated within the rationalistic theological lineage of Lipsius and Grotius. Like these, Senault saw no antagonism between reason and faith, for reason itself 'flowed' from the Godhead, and was therefore 'the true good of man' (1641: 6).[6] Senault did not think that approaching godliness and using one's reason meant rejecting the body or passions, however. Like the *Passions, De l'Usage* is a manual for the correct use of the passions, not their destruction. He explicitly aligned himself with Aristotle on this point: 'I had rather follow Aristotle's opinion than Seneca's, and rather govern passions than destroy them' (142). According to him, invectives against the passions merely exacerbated the problem, for he 'who seeks to oppose this torrent by making a dam will only increase its fury' (118). Whereas the Stoics failed to consider that man is 'endowed with a body' wherefrom 'the soul is not disengaged' and 'sought to stifle the passions' by 'elevating him to the condition of angels' (2–3), the wise man, 'knowing very well that he is composed of a soul and body ... endeavours to employ both parts in the exercise of virtue' (142).

Senault was especially incensed by a contemporaneous tendency to conflate Christianity with Stoicism, precisely because the Stoic, exemplified by Seneca, 'pleads always for the soul against the body' (292). Whereas Epicureans 'submitted the soul to the body and reduced men to the life of beasts', Stoics 'filled the

Soul with arrogance' by pretending that salvation is accessible through reason and 'words' ('paroles') alone (unpaginated). The skilled Christian, by contrast, understood the centrality of the body to the cultivation of virtue and hence to God's work. 'Though [God] may deal with the soul without the interposition of the senses', wrote Senault, 'he rules himself according to man's condition, and knowing that they are composed of a soul and body, he undertakes nothing upon the former but by the means of the latter' (191). The passions were the 'seeds' ('semences') of all virtues and could, through careful cultivation, yield 'pleasant fruits' (137). Indeed, no passion was not 'useful to virtue, when ... governed by reason' (9). Conversely, ignoring the passions would 'leave unused one of the most beautiful parts of our soul', for 'virtue herself would become idle, had she no passions, either to subdue or regulate' (7).

As this cursory outline makes clear, the 'Cartesian' ideal of a rational regulation of the passions predates *Les Passions de l'Âme* by at least eight years, raising questions over Descartes's distinct contribution. In fact, I argue the *Passions* is important not for parsing the mind from the body and subjecting the latter to the former, as Senault had advocated, but for introducing a complex theory of the habits and their power to structure the passions. Descartes's innovation, if anything, indicates a shift towards not away from the body and ironically reinstates the transcendental foundation of the good epitomized by Senault and his appeal to divine grace. In order to unpack this claim, I now return to the *Passions*, while continuing to highlight similarities and contrasts with *De l'Usage* where relevant.[7]

Les Passions de l'Âme (1649)

The *Passions* is not a systematic document. It combines speculation about the nature and 'seat' of the soul, scientific theories about the bodily mechanisms linking thoughts and passions to actions; an extended enumeration of the passions, with explanations of their distinct qualities; and an early theory of behavioural conditioning. It is unintegrated and sometimes contradictory. It even contains jokes.[8]

Rather than summarize the entire work, I will focus on a number of points responding directly to Taylor's 'disengaged' reading. These are: Descartes's location of the soul not just in the 'kernel' or pineal gland, but the whole body; his complex soul–body structure and the formative role of the habits within this structure; his understanding of rational/passional annexation by habit and experience; his nuanced understanding of the hegemony of reason or the will; his thoughts on the moral authority of 'nature'; his non-transparent subject; his understanding of the human reflex arc; his understanding of the true function of the passions as resting in their memory-reinforcing properties; and finally, his faith in the inherent (not merely instrumental) goodness of certain passions. I will argue that while Taylor's reading of Descartes is accurate from a certain perspective, it ultimately fails to engage with the full diversity of ideas contained in the *Passions*. Descartes's late work in fact testifies to a basic double tension within his thought between the power of reason and the power of the passions, and the autonomy of mind and dependence of mind on the body. This tension is never fully resolved, instead echoing throughout the Enlightenment and its explorations into the bases of human agency.

The location of the soul

Against conventional assumptions, Descartes's soul-mind does not simply reside in the brain or even the *glande*, that uniquely undivided part of the brain joining each lobe now understood to be the pineal gland.[9] Although Descartes on occasion insists that 'Apart from this gland, there cannot be any other place in the whole body where the soul directly exercises its functions' (1985a: 340),[10] he also, perhaps contradictorily, understands it as an emergent epiphenomenon dependent on the entire body, at least for its worldly existence. As he explains in Article 30, 'The Soul is United to All the Parts of the Body Conjointly':

> We need to recognize that the soul is really joined to the whole body, and that we cannot properly say that it exists in any one part of the body to the exclusion of the others. For the body is a unity which is in a sense indivisible because of the arrangement of its organs, these being so related to one another that the removal of any one of them renders the whole body defective. (339)[11]

That the soul can coexist with the body, indeed, be fundamentally dependent on it, yet still be indivisible and eternal, is because the soul (a) has no extension and (b) relates to the body as an assemblage of interrelated parts. As he puts it: 'the soul [does not] become any smaller if we cut off some part of the body, but it becomes completely separate from the body when we break up the assemblage of the body's organs' (340).[12] The relation between the body and the pineal gland is not entirely clear but may be understood in terms of a quantitative distinction. If the gland still plays a special role in housing the soul, it is arguably one of degree not kind: 'there is a certain part of the body where [the soul] exercises its functions more particularly than in all the others' (340). The gland is merely the 'principal seat' (341) of the soul, not its unique dwelling.

This more embodied conception of the soul subtly nuances Taylor's interpretation of Descartes as arguing for a 'disengaged perspective' wherein our usual embodied perspective, which conceives of surrounding objects as 'really qualified by colour or sweetness or heat, [or] tend to think of the pain or tickle as in [our] tooth or foot' (1989: 145), is replaced by the singularly rational perspective of the thinking mind. If the soul-mind is in fact co-extensive with the body (insofar as it makes sense to speak of an extended, non-extended entity), then it becomes difficult to speak of sensation – whether experienced by the body or soul-mind – as *not* being in the tooth or foot. For Descartes, the pain resides in both, e.g. tooth and soul, since the soul is (at least partly) in the tooth in any case.[13] As we shall see, this understanding corresponds well with the broader framework of the *Passions*. Although Descartes on occasion seems to emphasize the 'ontological cleft' between body and soul, e.g. by insisting on the non-extendedness of the soul or by claiming that 'it is to the body alone that we should attribute everything that can be observed in us to oppose our reason' (1985a: 346), a careful breakdown of his soul–body structure yields interesting bridges between the two.

The soul–body structure

After distinguishing the body from the soul by explaining their different functions, Descartes equates the soul with 'our thoughts' and divides these thoughts into two kinds: 'actions of the soul' and 'passions of the soul'. The actions of the soul are equivalent to 'our volitions', and the passions of the soul to 'the various perceptions or modes of knowledge present in us' (335). Volitions are further broken down into two sorts: actions of the soul which terminate in the soul itself and actions which 'terminate in our body, as when our merely willing to walk has the consequence that our legs move and we walk' (335). Our perceptions are also of two sorts: those caused by the soul and those caused by the body (335). These points may be diagrammed as follows:

1.	a. Body	b. Soul

$$\downarrow$$

2.   = Our thoughts

$$\swarrow \qquad \searrow$$

3.   a. Actions of the soul   b. Passions of the soul

$$\downarrow \qquad\qquad\qquad \downarrow$$

4.   a. = Our volitions   b. = Our perceptions

$$\swarrow \;\; \downarrow \qquad\qquad \downarrow \;\; \searrow$$

5.   a. End in   b. End in   c. Caused by   d. Caused by

          the body   the soul   the body   the soul

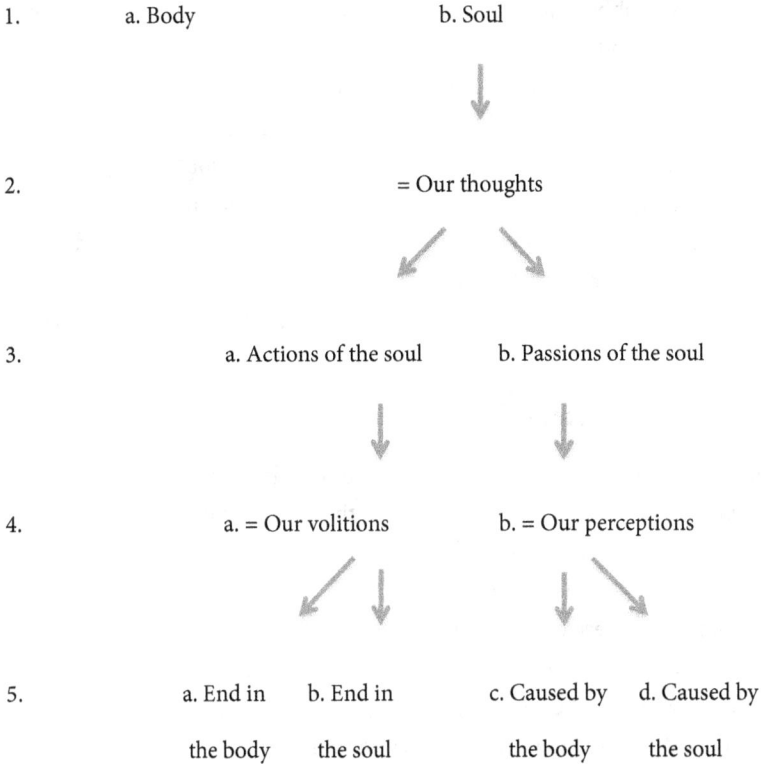

As this schema shows, the initial clear-cut distinction between body and soul is mitigated considerably by stage 5. It is not just that the soul generates actions or wills which end in bodily action (e.g. walking) – the one-way process that Taylor takes as indicative of reason's hegemony in the properly disciplined subject – but that the passions of the soul (and hence one half of 'our thoughts' or 'soul') are at least partially caused by and hence dependent upon the body (stage 5c). Descartes elaborates on this point considerably. From Articles 21 and 22, on 'Imaginings Which Are Caused Solely by the Body' and 'How These Other Perceptions Differ from One Another': 'Among the perceptions caused by the body, most of them depend on the nerves. … [W]e refer some to external objects which strike our senses, others to our body or to certain of its parts, and still others to our soul' (336–7). The perceptions which stem from 'things outside us' are caused by objects which 'produce certain movements in the organs of the external senses and, by means of the nerves, produce other movements in the brain'. Although perceptions attributed only to the soul (including 'the feelings of joy, anger and the like') are distinguished by the fact their effects are felt 'in the soul itself', as well as, presumably, originating there, they may also (somewhat mysteriously) originate in the body, too, since '[they] are aroused in us sometimes by the objects which stimulate our nerves' (337). In other words, although Descartes opens the *Passions* by proposing to focus only on the third element of his triadic structure of apprehensive causes (those passions attributable to the soul itself, hence the title of the book) this third element is in fact very similar to the first. Perceptions of 'things outside us' and perceptions 'from the soul' are both stimulated by 'objects which stimulate our nerves'. Perceptions which in principle derive only from the soul are in the end as traceable to the body as those deriving from without.

Mind–body dualism, habits

To understand how our thoughts or 'perceptions' link up with the body and can be shaped by it, it is necessary to engage with a crucial concept at the heart of the *Passions* and completely absent from Taylor's analysis in both *Sources of the Self* and *A Secular Age* – the concept of 'habit'.[14]

According to Descartes, 'our soul and body are so linked that once we have joined some bodily action with a certain thought, the one does not occur afterwards without the other occurring too' (365). Indeed, he feels strongly enough about this to later repeat the same point:

> For the rest, so as to put in a few words all the points which might be added regarding the different effects or different causes of the passions, I shall content myself with repeating the principle which underlies everything I have written about them – namely, that our soul and body are so linked that once we have joined some bodily action with a certain thought, the one does not occur thereafter without the other occurring too; but we do not always join the same actions to the same thoughts. (375)

These passages confirm Descartes's emphasis on the mutual engagement of soul and body. But they also show that (a) this engagement stems from a pre-rational linkage of specific thoughts to specific actions, since these thoughts and actions are not 'willed' but 'present themselves' to us involuntarily; and (b) although corporeal actions and thoughts arise outside of our immediate control, it is still *us* who 'join' or 'annex' specific actions to specific thoughts in the first place. Taken together, points (a) and (b) present a fascinatingly complex picture of agency that suggests neither the sovereignty of reason or will over the body and passions, nor the absolute submission of reason to bodily experience or 'providence', but the dependence of agency on a process of behavioural self-conditioning through the manipulation of habits, themselves shaped and modified by external conditioning factors. This point needs unpacking.

The annexation of passions through habit, the hegemony of reason/will

To grasp what Descartes is getting at, we first need to understand how 'volitions' become joined to thoughts and passions, and (what amounts to the same) thoughts to actions and experiences. I will quote extensively from the *Passions* in order to demonstrate the centrality of the concept for Descartes's ethics.

According to Descartes, 'each volition is naturally joined to some movement of the gland, but through effort or habit we may join it to others' (344). This applies to every possible movement, even those that seem most naturally joined to their respective wills: although 'nature seems to have joined every movement of the gland to certain of our thoughts from the beginning of our life, yet we may join them to others through habit' (348). Descartes illustrates this by reference to the work of language:

> Words represent to the soul only the sounds of their syllables when they are spoken or the shape of their letters when they are written, yet, because we have acquired the habit of thinking of this meaning when we hear them spoken or see them written, do they tend to make us conceive their signification rather than the shape of their letters or the sound of their syllables. (348)[15]

In other words, the repeated juxtaposition of specific wills and motions gradually generates a firm bond between them – a bond so strong that it bypasses the conscious level of sense perception. We do not primarily perceive the shape or sound of letters and syllables but their signification. Despite the general necessity of reiteration, however, the process of annexation can also be immediate if the experience is disturbing enough:

> A habit can be acquired by a single action, and does not require long practice. Thus, when we unexpectedly come upon something very foul in a dish we are eating with relish, our surprise may so change the disposition of our brain that we cannot afterwards look upon any such food without repulsion, whereas previously we ate it with pleasure. (1985a: 348)

Or again,

> Those who have taken some medicine with great aversion when they are ill … afterwards cannot eat or drink anything approaching it in taste without immediately feeling the same aversion; and similarly they cannot think of the aversion they have for medicines without the same taste returning in their thought. (1985a: 365)[16]

Anticipating modern theories of child development that trace latent affects and phobias to childhood experiences (e.g. Damasio 1994: 131, 134), Descartes suggests early life is a particularly sensitive time for the annexation of experience to affects. This explains why some people may have irrational or otherwise inexplicable distastes, e.g. for roses or cats:

> The strange aversions of certain people that make them unable to bear the smell of roses, the presence of a cat, or the like, can readily be recognized as resulting simply from their having been greatly upset by some such object in the early years of their life. Or it may even result from their having been affected by the feelings their mother had when she was upset by such an object while pregnant; for there certainly is a connection between all the movements of a mother and those of a child in her womb, so that anything adverse to the one is harmful to the other. And the smell of roses may have caused severe headache in a child when he was still in the cradle, or a cat may have terrified him without anyone noticing and without any memory of it remaining afterwards; and yet the idea of the aversion he then felt for roses or for the cat will remain imprinted on his brain till the end of his life. (1985a: 376)[17]

For Descartes, then, the arising of thoughts is conditional on past histories of association that wire the soul and body in certain ways, through unintentional or intentional reiteration. This wiring is evidence of the inseparability of body and soul, and it is 'pre-rational' insofar as it involves soul–body annexations not immediately governed by reason or the will. It may also be altered through an alteration of habits, or by undergoing a traumatic experience that shocks the soul–body nexus into a new configuration.

These points place considerable limits on the power or 'hegemony' of reason, which Taylor takes as a defining feature of Descartes's virtuous subject. If anything, Descartes is here demonstrating the opposite: the secondariness of reason to predetermined bodily psychic pathways, established by contingent histories of habit and experience. We do not 'choose' our reactions in given situations, except insofar as we are able to condition ourselves *before the event* to respond in certain ways. This conditioning may be aimed at a rationally derived telos beyond the immediate content of the passions (though not necessarily – see below), but the declension from thought to action is not itself a rational process dictated by the sovereign will or reason. There is no question here of the soul or will coercing the passions or body to respond in rationally sanctioned ways. Though it is true Descartes frequently emphasizes the virtue of a soul that has achieved 'absolute mastery' ('un empire très-absolu'; 1649: 78; 1985a: 348) over the passions, this is simply impossible from the perspective of his total psychology. As he himself puts it, 'the soul cannot suddenly [*promptement*] change or stop [*arrester*] its passions' (1985a: 345).[18] It cannot because the habits connecting motions of the body to motions of the gland override everything else, as he explains with the example of tickling cited in the Introduction.

Even more fundamentally, thoughts – the basis of reason's power – are themselves, to some extent, conditioned by habits. As he explains in Article 161, on 'How Generosity May Be Acquired': 'It should be noted that what we commonly call "virtues" are habits in the soul which dispose it to have certain thoughts: though different from the thoughts, these habits can produce them and in turn can be produced by them' (1985a: 387). The idea that virtues are based on habits which can both produce and be produced by thoughts, seriously compromises any putative Cartesian *point d'origine* founded on the sovereignty of will or reason. All that exists is a cycle from habits to thoughts and back to habits, continually inflected by our external environment. The will's control over the passions is far from absolute: it can only be exerted indirectly, e.g. through a shaping of our interaction with this external environment.

> Our passions ... cannot be directly aroused or removed [*ostées*] by the action of our will: but only indirectly through the representation of things which are usually joined with the passions we wish to have and opposed to the passions we wish to reject. For example, in order to arouse boldness and suppress fear in ourselves, it is not sufficient to have the volition to do so. We must apply ourselves to consider the reasons, objects or precedents which persuade us that the danger is not great. (1985a: 345)[19]

For Descartes, it is futile to imagine that one can alter one's behaviour and achieve a 'struggled-for-domination' (Taylor 2007: 133) over the passions through an antagonistic imposition of the will. Virtue is less a matter of neo-Stoic 'struggle' than of gradual, Aristotelian self-fashioning (Kahn 2006: 100; Cottingham 2008).[20]

According to Kirkebøen, Descartes's radical insight did not concern the distinctiveness of soul and body, or the hegemony of the soul over the body and passions, but precisely the opposite: 'the *limitations* [of] the human soul and its functions' (2001: 173–4, emphasis original). Kahn even goes so far as to suggest that, for Descartes, 'the body might be a better sovereign than the soul' (2006: 109). Such a radical externalization of the factors shaping knowledge and behaviour undermines not only Taylor's instance on the hegemony of reason, but his association of Descartes with a Lockean rejection of external practices, e.g. liturgy and ritual. For Descartes, everything we think, feel and do is contingent on bodily practices and environmental factors that fix certain thoughts to passions, and certain passions to actions and experiences, throwing the very distinction between 'internal' and 'external' into doubt.

Article 52 and the moral authority of nature

As noted above, Taylor hinges much of his argument on Article 52 of the *Passions*, in which Descartes seems to explain the sole utility of the passions as residing in their power to 'dispose the soul to desire those things which nature tells us are of use, and to persist in this desire' (Taylor 1989: 150). Following this reading, the passions function as a causal link between the soul and the body, as a kind of extended arm or ontological bridge allowing the soul to manipulate the body in the immediate present.[21]

Two points must be made here. First, the book contains several statements about the true function of the passions, some of which expand on Article 52 considerably. As Descartes writes elsewhere, under Article 74, 'How the Passions are Useful, and How They Are Harmful':

> The utility of all the passions consists [only] in the fact that they strengthen and prolong thoughts in the soul which it is good for the soul to preserve and which otherwise might easily be erased from it.[22] Likewise the harm they may cause consists entirely in their strengthening and preserving these thoughts beyond what is required, or in their strengthening and preserving others on which it is not good to dwell. (1985a: 354)[23]

Or again, on the particular passion of wonder (*admiration*):

> Of wonder ... we may say that it is useful in that it makes us learn and retain in our memory things of which we were previously ignorant. ... [W]hen something previously unknown to us comes before our intellect or our senses for the first time, this does not make us retain it in our memory unless our idea of it is strengthened in our brain by some passion, or perhaps also by some application of our intellect as fixed by our will in a special state of attention and reflection. (1985a: 355)[24]

These alternative passages suggest that, insofar as the passions can extend or even alter the soul's disposition, it is not because they further the soul's power directly by acting as a causal link between the soul and the body, but because they precondition the soul to interact in certain ways with the body, by inscribing memories at a deep level – an idea that ties in seamlessly with Descartes's theory of habituation.

Second, even if we accept that Article 52 contains Descartes's definitive statement on the function of the passions, Taylor's translation of this passage is clearly inflected by his effort to reinforce Descartes's putative hegemony of will and shoehorn him into the neo-Stoic mould. The problem stems from his translation of two key words: *vouloir* and *volonté*. Taylor translates these as 'desire' (verb and noun), thus bringing home the power of the passions to extend the power of the will, which may manipulate desire to its own end. The 'sovereign will' remains untouched.

But as is well known, *volonté* typically refers to the Cartesian will itself, not desire. Thus, Robert Stoothoff renders the passage in straightforwardly volitional terms: 'The function of all the passions consists solely in this, that they dispose our soul to want the things which nature deems useful for us, and to persist in this volition' (1985a: 349). The earliest (anonymous) translation of 1650 follows a similar model: 'The use of all the Passions consists only in this, that they dispose the Soul to will the things which Nature dictates are profitable to us, and to persist in this will' (1671 [1649]: 46). Both translations arguably reflect the semantic universe of the *Passions* more naturally than Taylor's. For example, if desire is the passion in question, it is likely Descartes would have written *désirer* and *désir* instead of *vouloir* and *volonté*, to match his specific treatment of the passion of desire in Article 57, 'Le Désir'.

'Will' or 'want' are not only more accurate than 'desire'; they make more sense. Desires are by definition unwilled (desire happens; the will makes things happen) and thus not subject to the Stoic or neo-Stoic virtue of persistence: e.g. it makes no sense to 'persist in desiring pistachio ice-cream'.[25] But the problem with Taylor's translation emerges particularly acutely when we try to understand how the passions could ever 'dispose' the soul to desire something, since, according to Descartes, desire is itself a passion. This would suggest desire can dictate desire – an idea that could make sense in terms of Descartes's wider theory of habituation, but undermines any conception of the absolute hegemony of will, since desire could unfold and intensify through its own closed system.[26]

What Descartes seeks to demonstrate, I would argue, is not simply the idea that desires can be manipulated to affect other desires under the coercive direction of the sovereign will, but that they – like habits – can influence the will itself. The passions 'dispose our soul to want the things which nature deems useful for us'. This idea is problematic for Taylor on two accounts. First, because it unseats the will as the sovereign dictator of the passions but ties in very well with the broader context of the *Passions*. And second because it relocates the sources of moral authority away from the sovereignty of the thinking self and towards 'nature', thus challenging Taylor's assertion that for Descartes true virtue is an entirely internal matter. This may be seen through a breakdown of Article 52's key points: (1) the passions are instrumentalized by the will; this is a condition of their being 'useful'. (2) They in turn reflect back on the will, since they 'dispose the soul' to will certain things. (3) Nature dictates that these things are 'profitable to us', i.e. the passions (and hence nature itself) work in our interests. This breakdown evinces a direct link between the will's surrender of authority and Descartes's faith in the inherent goodness of nature, which replaces introspective certainty as the ground of morality. This ground has existed for time out of mind and it is *external*, i.e. not dependent on human powers of reasoning. For Descartes, we can no more control our physiology than 'other events in the physical universe': 'The natural (or divinely ordained) correlations between physiological events and psychological states are not within our power to set up from scratch; they were laid down, as part of our human nature, long before we came on the scene' (Cottingham 2008: 244). As Cottingham points out, these psychophysical correlations are 'crucial for our survival', a point that would today be accounted for in evolutionary terms. Descartes, however, like Senault, invoked the standard source of morality at the time – the benevolence of God – as the ultimate origin and dispenser of 'information about what is harmful for the [human] mind-body composite' (250). Point three above reinstates an external, i.e. transcendental or non-rationally derived, source of morality grounding what is effectively a feedback loop between the passions and the will. The perpetual mutual influence of one on the other undoes any sense that true morality issues from a single internal source (e.g. reason or the will); there is instead an ongoing process of mutual reinforcement, guided towards the good by the dictates of external reality, God or nature.[27]

Descartes's reflex arc

According to Taylor, Descartes envisioned spontaneous bodily reflexes as one side of a double response involving both reflex and rational deliberation. Whereas animals always respond impulsively and mechanistically, humans have a unique capacity to subjugate the initial 'animalistic' response to the dictates of autonomous reason, which may then *use* passion to bolster the appropriate physical response:[28]

> The sight of a dangerous animal ... will typically have three kinds of consequences. It may trigger off a reflex of flight. This is the only consequence which occurs in

animals, which must be understood as complex machines. With man it will also bring about the rational recognition that he ought to make himself scarce. The man is rationally motivated to do what his animal reactions have perhaps already started. But then passion will strengthen the response, because the animal spirits connected with the perception of the animal and the flight reflex also incite fear in the soul. (Taylor 1989: 150)

For Taylor, Descartes's rationalistic reflex arc underscores the utility of the passions as extenders of the will over the body. The passions have no value in themselves, but are useful insofar as they strengthen the causal relation between will and action, or 'beef up the *already existing* rational movement towards flight' (150, emphasis mine).

This reading of Descartes is puzzling, since the *Passions* makes quite clear that reflex actions are distinctive precisely because they do not involve a rational process. Summarizing the work ahead of its publication in 1649, Descartes wrote that 'even in us [humans] all the motions of our limbs which accompany our passions are caused not by the soul but simply by the machinery of the body' (1991a: 374). In the *Passions* itself, Descartes discusses uncontrollable, knee-jerk reactions to external stimuli, e.g. a hand that threatens to strike, to illustrate the *absence* of reason in the reflex arc.

> If someone suddenly thrusts his hand in front of our eyes as if to strike us, then even if we know that he is our friend, that he is doing this only jest and that he will take care not to harm us, we still find it difficult to prevent ourselves from closing our eyes. This shows that it is not through the mediation of our soul that they close, since this action is contrary to our volition. (1985a: 333)[29]

At least for the Descartes of the *Passions*, it is not the case that the passions strengthen an 'already existing rational movement towards flight'. Insofar as the passions are involved in the reflex arc at all, they bypass the rational process. The soul does not intervene in reflexive action, let alone precede it.

The transparency of the subject

It should be clear from the above that any idea of a completely 'transparent subject' accessible to and guided by 'immanent clarity' or the unrestricted gaze of pure reason is out of the question in the context of the *Passions*. Without explicitly naming the unconscious as such, Descartes clearly carves out a space for it in his theory of the reflex or non-rational action generally. As Kirkebøen writes, 'Descartes's understanding of his own emotional reaction to people with squints [see fn. 20] indicates the degree of importance, often neglected, that the rationalist Descartes attaches to unconscious motives (e.g. acquired emotional mechanisms) as determinants of behaviour and decision-making' (2001: 185). Similarly, Cottingham has argued at length that Descartes's 'affective modes', such as joy, excitement and stress, are not under 'direct conscious control' since 'the causal genesis of those states ... is largely opaque to the conscious subject' (2008: 243). A good example of this opacity and the *benefits* that come from recognizing and accepting it is provided by his understanding of the subservience of the will to habits in terms of the non-cognitive forces animating bodies in day-to-day activities, e.g. conversation:

> When we speak, we think only of the meaning of what we want to say, and this makes us move our tongue and lips much more readily and effectively than if we thought of moving them in all the ways required for uttering the same words. For the habits acquired in learning to speak have made us join the action of the soul (which by means of the gland, can move the tongue and lips) with the meaning of the words which follow upon these movements, rather than with the movements themselves. (1985a: 344–5)

In other words, our bodies may work *better* when the mind surrenders its power over individual movements of the mouth to the naturally formed bond between signification and muscle-memory – a bond again established first by habit and only later ratified, if at all, by reason.

Disengaged, disembodied reason and the inherent goodness of passions

As explained above, a cornerstone of Taylor's interpretation of Cartesian ethics rests on a distinction between internally and externally derived goods. For Taylor, Descartes marks a profound shift in ethical consciousness, whereby goods previously located 'outside' in a Platonic order of things or partially constructed through a neo-Stoic Natural Law are fully internalized, dissected and reconstructed from the bottom up by the power of autonomous reason. Since everything 'opposed to reason' originates in the body, the properly trained, neo-Stoic subject stands 'above' the body and orchestrates the passions accordingly, guiding body and soul to the correct, rationally derived telos. He only reengages with the passions and body to the extent that they can further the soul's aims: e.g. by coercing the body into desiring virtue. This is why Descartes does not seek to eradicate the passions, but to co-opt them in pursuit of the good; the soul uses the body to 'climb free of it' (1989: 146).

A key question here concerns Descartes's ends. Are these really so detached from the body as Taylor makes out? Here again, a careful reading of the *Passions* nuances the picture. On the centrality of the body for our conception and experience of the good, Descartes is clear: 'if we had no body, I venture to say we could not go too far in abandoning ourselves to love and joy, or in avoiding hatred and sadness' (1985a: 378). Note that the passions of love and joy are here valued as goods in themselves; their value does not derive from their utility in bringing the soul closer to full flourishing; they *are* full flourishing. (Contrast with Taylor's claim in *Sources of the Self*, that it is only during the late-eighteenth and nineteenth centuries that 'Experiencing certain feelings [including "married love"] comes to be an important part of the good life', 1989: 294.) Again, from the final article of the *Passions*, on the notion that 'It Is on the Passions Alone that All the Good and Evil of this Life Depends': 'For the rest, the soul can have pleasures of its own. But the pleasures common to it and the body depend entirely on the passions, so that persons whom the passions can move most deeply are capable of enjoying the sweetest pleasures of this life' (1985a: 404).

Cottingham has challenged classical, 'dualistic' misconceptions of Cartesian ethics that drive a wedge between passions and the good. According to him, the *Passions* is aimed at redressing precisely this misconception: 'the major task of Descartes's closing years [was] the task of coming to terms with – and trying to mitigate the harsher effects of – that alienation of man from nature which his own dualistic metaphysics and mechanistic science had threatened to generate' (2008: 238). While the Greeks tended to take on a 'ratiocentric bias' and the Cartesian model 'at first seems to be even more ratiocentric', the *Passions* presents a somewhat different picture. Here,

> Although the deliverances of reason reveal a rigidly dualistic world of extended matter plus incorporeal consciousness, our own daily experience as human beings provides a very different kind of awareness – one coloured by intimate and urgent feeling and emotion, one that projects us into the very centre of a 'substantial union' of mind and body, where, so far from operating as cognitive pilots of an alien bodily machine, each of us finds the operations of the body that is in a special and intimate sense his *own* giving rise to a rich and vivid sensory and emotional life. (239, emphasis original)

If there is any restriction on the ethical worth of the passions, it is based not on a categorical distinction between means and ends, but the degree of intensity of these same means, since 'the bodily movements accompanying these passions may all be injurious to health when they are very violent; on the other hand, they may be beneficial to it when they are only moderate' (Descartes

1985a: 378). Of course, even here Descartes ultimately equivocates, since he also removes any restriction on the intensity of passion (e.g. desire) provided this passion is geared towards the right end.[30] What is clear, however, is that Descartes at no point reduces his concept of the good to a disembodied set of virtues attained through a coercive imposition of the will on instrumentalized passions. The soul does not simply use the body to 'climb free of it', as Taylor claims. Descartes was clear on this point, writing in his *Sixth Meditation*: 'I am not merely present in my body as a sailor is present in a ship, but ... am very closely joined and, as it were, intermingled with it, so that I and the body form a unit' (1984 [1641]: 56). He further speculated in his *Letter to Regius* of January 1642, that 'If an angel were in a human body, it would not have sensations as we do, but would simply perceive the motions which are caused by external objects, and in this way would differ from a real human being' (1991a [1619–1615]: 206). This is a direct continuation of Senault, who one year earlier had attacked 'profane philosophy' for representing 'the soul in the body as an intelligence in the heavens ... as a pilot who guides his vessel, sometimes as a sovereign who governs his state' (1641: 11). According to Senault, by seeking to cut the soul loose from the body, the Stoics had 'elevated man to the condition of angels' (3).

Unresolved tension

Despite Descartes's insistence on 'our daily experience as creatures of flesh and blood' (Cottingham 2008: 240), it is difficult to ignore other, more ratiocentric aspects of the Cartesian self. At points Descartes clearly advocates the independence, distance and dominance of reason from and over the passions. For example, he writes in his *Letter to Princess Elisabeth* of August 1645:

> The right use of reason ... makes virtue easy to practice; and by making us recognize the condition of our nature, it sets bounds to our desires. So we must conclude that the greatest felicity of man depends on the right use of reason; and consequently the study which leads to its acquisition is the most useful occupation one can take up. Certainly it is the most agreeable and delightful. (1991 [1619–1650]a: 258)

In another letter to Elisabeth, cited by Taylor, Descartes describes 'the greatest souls' as those 'whose reasoning powers are so strong and powerful that although they also have passions, and often even more violent than is common, nonetheless their reason remains sovereign' (May 1645, in Taylor 2007: 131).

Many more quotations could be provided along these lines (see e.g. Cottingham 2012: 116, fn. 30).

It should be clear from the foregoing, however, that the idea of an *absolute* sovereignty of the will or reason is both impossible from the perspective of Descartes's total psychology and explicitly denied by Descartes himself, since we cannot stop or alter the course of the passions 'at will'. Descartes's work is contradictory and often seems to involve two quite different conceptions of agency.[31] While Cottingham reads Descartes's alternative, embodied mode of thought as suggestive of 'reconciliation and integration' (2008: 252), I suggest Descartes *failed* to think away a basic tension between the sovereignty of will or reason, the undeniable power of the passions, and their inscription through external conditioning factors. In the case of Descartes, this tension is easily dissimulated by the obscurity of his descriptions. As Kirkebøen explains:

> In general statements, Descartes often declares that the soul or will is free. However, in his analysis of concrete volitions he often gives the opposite impression. His discussions of this topic are complex, partly because they presuppose his highly complex concept of causation and partly because he is often vague and cryptical when he discusses the power of the will over the body. For example, 'Those I call [the soul's] actions are all our volitions, for *we experience them* as proceeding directly from our soul and *as seeming* to depend on it alone.' (2001: 187, emphasis original)

Beneath the contradictions and careful qualifications lies a double tension underpinning all Descartes's explorations into human subjectivity between the power of reason and the power of the passions, and the autonomy of mind and the dependence of mind on the body. It is never fully resolved. Descartes swings between affirming a necessary independence and hegemony of reason, and the impossibility of ever reaching that goal. The *Passions* is an assemblage, not a system.

The unconscious reversal

As I hope to have shown, almost every one of Taylor's arguments regarding Descartes can be challenged in light of a close reading of the *Passions*. In the first instance, Descartes's putative disengagement of the soul from the body can be problematized in at least three ways: (1) the soul is inherently dependent on the total body for its earthly existence and not simply restricted to the gland or kernel. Insofar as the latter plays a distinct role for the soul, it is only as its 'principal' seat; the gland is a concentrating, not delimiting, area of the body. (2) Descartes's soul–body structure, while fundamentally dualistic, entails important points of contact and mutual influence between soul and body, so that a very strict distinction is unsustainable in view of his total picture of the subject. (3) Descartes's understanding of the role of bodily habits for tracing and reinforcing pathways between wills, thoughts, passions and actions radically undoes any possibility of a strict mind–body dualism, since what is 'thought' at any time is contingent on the body and past histories of bodily/intellectual iteration and reiteration.

Second, Descartes does not understand the passions as mere extensions of the will. They are inscribing forces, carving memories and thoughts deeper into the subject. Without passions to 'thicken' the connection between thoughts and actions, ethical cultivation would be impossible.

This in turn feeds into the third problematic aspect of Taylor's analysis: Descartes's reason and will are not as hegemonic as he suggests. It is not just that the will cannot stop or change the passions at will, since they are often too powerful to resist, but that the habits, and through them the passions, may themselves snap back to influence the will and thoughts of the soul.

Fourth, it is clear from the above, and from Descartes's comments on reflexes and the act of speaking, that the Cartesian 'fully transparent' self, possessed of 'immanent self-clarity' is incompatible with the self of the *Passions*. This self is deeply divided, even strange to itself. Phobias emerge uncontrollably from unknown depths. Bodies react in independence from the thinking mind. Mouths, tongues and vocal chords move more efficiently by sidestepping the dictates of reason. The Cartesian self is at least partially opaque to itself.

Finally, Descartes does not simply relegate the passions to an instrumental role, as crutches for the 'real' goal of ethical fulfilment based on reason alone. Certain passions, e.g. love and joy, are inherently good. They are constitutive of life's 'sweetness'. Their value does not lie in aiming at anything else.

Despite this clear emphasis on the inextricability of the soul/mind from the body and external world, however, it is impossible to ignore Descartes's more reason-centred assessments of subjectivity, either. I therefore conclude by suggesting Descartes never fully resolves a basic tension at the heart of his work, between the autonomy of reason and its dependence on habits and passions, and between the independence of the soul/mind from the body.

Before considering the wider consequences of these points for Taylor's genealogy of the secular and especially the 'public sphere', I would like to address the specific issue of Descartes's position in the history of psychological science. As noted above, Taylor interprets Descartes's 'disengaged reason' and 'rationalistic' understanding of the reflex arc as weak theories of agency later overturned by nineteenth- and twentieth-century discoveries and excavations of the unconscious. Following this approach, Descartes marked one moment in a dialectic process of secularization (i.e. a process taking us from 'state one' to 'state two', above) linking the Enlightenment, Counter-Enlightenment and the emergence of depth psychology through William James, Freud and Pavlovian theories of behavioural conditioning. Latin Christendom needed Descartes to effect a split between soul and body, or reason and passion, for later 'more sophisticated and adequate [theories] of embodied agency' (2007: 30) to re-establish their connection and 'reembody' the mind.

Clearly, there can be no strict temporal delineation between pre- and post-eighteenth-century psychology in the light of Descartes's total anthropology. Cottingham reads Descartes as 'in some respects at least [representing] a striking anticipation of the Freudian line' (2008: 247), and Kirkebøen has drawn together a host of modern claims to this effect from psychological scientists themselves, who – aside from Freud – saw in Descartes not the antithesis, but the father of modern psychology. As Pavlov put it: 'Our starting-point has been Descartes' idea of the reflex ... [which] was constantly and fruitfully applied in these studies' (1960: 7–8; 4).[32] That Descartes was a 'pioneer' (Cottingham 2008: 244) of the theory of the conditioned response is undeniable: in a 1630 letter to Marin Mersenne, he lays out the Pavlovian method three hundred years before Pavlov:

> Secondly, what makes some people want to dance may make others want to cry. This is because it evokes ideas in our memory: for instance those who have in the past enjoyed dancing to a certain tune feel a fresh wish to dance the moment they hear a similar one; on the other hand, if someone had never heard a galliard without some affliction befalling him, he would certainly grow sad when he heard it again. This is so certain that I reckon that if you whipped a dog five or six times to the sound of a violin, it would begin to howl and run away as soon as it heard that music again. (1991 [1619–1650]a: 20)

Similarly, although Damasio contrasts William James's psychology with Descartes's, arguing that 'James ... produced a truly startling hypothesis on the nature of emotion and feeling' and '[stripped] emotion down to a process that involved the body', it is now recognized that '[James-Lange's] well-known hypothesis was essentially the view proposed by Descartes' (LeDoux 1996, cited in Kirkebøen 2001: 182). As Kirkebøen notes, even Damasio's distinctive anti-Cartesian theory of the 'somatic marker' is 'in accordance with Descartes' general principle of habituation' (185). Finally, Cottingham has emphasized at length the Freudian bent of Descartes's self-opaque subject. According to him, one of Descartes's most fundamental contributions to the history of psychology is not his faith in immanent, self-reflexive clarity, but, on the contrary, the idea that '*the causal genesis and subsequent occurrence of the passions is intimately linked to corporeal events in ways that often make the force of the resultant emotions opaque to reason*' (2008: 246, emphasis original). Whereas traditional 'logocentric' models 'assumed a kind of transparency about the operation of the passions', the viewpoint of the *Passions*

> reveals the full extent to which [the influence of the passions] depends on factors below the threshold of consciousness. We now have a striking paradox: Descartes, the very thinker who is often accused of having a naive theory of the perfect *transparency* of the mind, is actually telling us that our emotional life as embodied creatures, as human beings, is subject to a serious and pervasive *opacity*. (247, emphasis original)

The idea that Descartes laid the groundwork for a total reversal of the psychological field and post-Cartesian 'discovery' of the unconscious in the nineteenth and twentieth centuries is radically misleading. Descartes anticipated key developments in modern psychology and arguably paved the way not for a radical reversal or paradigm shift during the nineteenth century but a steady elaboration of existing ideas.

Conclusion: Cartesian secularity?

What is the relevance of the above for 'secularism', 'secularity' or 'the secular'? Recall that Taylor sees Descartes as standing in a pivotal position for the closure of self at the onset of modernity. The disengagement of reason from the body and its blustery passions is taken as a signal shift for the eventual rise to predominance of a buffered self whose self-understanding drew heavily on an idealized conception of pure, autonomous reason later epitomized by the cold rationalism of the Enlightenment. According to Taylor, reason is inextricably bound up with 'the meanings things have for us' and hence with the bodies and emotional reactions which generate such meanings in the first place. Since the reasoning process itself can only take place through 'our reactions' as embodied beings, and since we grasp truth not by disengaging from experience but '[inhabiting] the meanings things have for us' (2012: 19), it is wrong to imagine that truth can be secured on the basis of a 'post-Enlightenment notion of "reason alone"' (17).

Taylor pins the blame for this development on Descartes, who opened the way for Enlightenment philosophers like David Hume to drive a wedge between reason and affect, reason and experience or reason and aesthetics (18). By implication, Descartes, while not himself atheist or even deist, laid a critical foundation stone for the later disassociation of religion from reason, as religion became increasingly tied to emotionality or 'enthusiasm', while its opposite – what we would now call 'secularity' – became tied to an essentialized understanding of pure, disengaged reason. According to a conventional narrative (W. C. Smith 1964; Asad 1993, 2003; Fitzgerald 2000), this development had crucial implications for the evolution of 'religion' as a conceptualizable category of the secular and for the practice of religion itself. Since eighteenth-century religion was still bound up with bodily practices and emotions, and since reason had nothing to do with the body, everything not rooted in reason could be thrown into the catch-all categories of religion or 'false' religion – 'true' religion in the latter case being a matter of ground-up reconstruction on the basis of reason alone (as seen in later advocates of rational religion from Kant to Swinburne) and usually involving some form of religious internalization (e.g. Locke and some of the *Encyclopédistes*). Descartes's crisp distinction between reason and the passions, and his prescription to dominate the latter through the former, resulted in a crisis of religious subjectivity, as traditions that were historically anchored in practices and disciplines of the body found themselves scrambling for rational justifications. In a discursive atmosphere where 'good reasons' suddenly predominated over traditional forms and expressions of virtue, true religion quickly became rationalized as 'sets of propositions to which one assents' (W. C. Smith 1964; Asad 1993). This led to a levelling of religious and philosophical truth-claims (cf. Milbank, Pickstock and Ward 1999) and the ultimate hegemony of a non-transcendental, rationalistic mode of secular subjectivity, since religious reasons could not hold against the ineluctable force of secular science and ethics.

As noted above, Taylor argues for a direct link between the procedural rationality of the *Méditations* and the eighteenth-century Republic of Letters, since both relied on faith in the process of argument itself and a rejection of substantive ends. With this rejection, claims Taylor, came a sharp step away from transcendental or 'auratic' forms of the good, which morphed into the worldly goods and values of the immanent frame (e.g. the order of mutual beneficence) that, by definition, were visible for public inspection and accessible to human powers. This transformation can be understood in terms of a regulatory strategy for the control and pacification of 'dangerous' religion during the eighteenth-century creation of liberal nation-states. At this time, religion became false and dangerous because it was affective, external and invisible to the logic of public reason; secularity or 'true' religion were good and true because they were rational, internal and constitutive of public reason. Anything that escaped the logic of public reason or the force of 'the better argument' was potentially subversive of national stability and thus to be eradicated or suppressed. As Cavanaugh and others (e.g. Fitzgerald 2000; Asad 2003) have shown, the very concept of religion was crafted out of these concerns, since it enabled secular powers to circumscribe non-public forces and brand them with the label of subversion.

> The religious/secular distinction is a modern invention that directly parallels the invention of the modern state. … As religion was invented in the early modern struggle between ecclesiastical and civil powers in Europe, it was envisioned as occupying an essentially non-rational and non-public sphere to which the concerns of the church should be confined. As the liberal state developed, 'religion' became a category into which to dump ideologies and practices that are judged antithetical to the liberal state's goal of excluding substantive ends from the public sphere. (Cavanaugh 2012: 29)

There is a strong sense in which eighteenth-century approaches to religion mirror Descartes's approach to the passions. In both cases, the pure rationality of the mind/public sphere seeks to dominate the threatening force of the body, theorized as non-private (yet non-discursive and therefore non-regulatable) activity in the case of the public sphere and unwilled physical action in the case of the Cartesian mind. Descartes's 'warning' against the passions thus serves as an early adumbration of polemic attacks on emotional or 'fanatic' religion during the mid- to late eighteenth century.

Taylor clearly writes out of a concern to undo the dichotomies religious/secular, affect/reason, external/internal, public/private, that underpin the genealogy of our secular age, with all the implications this has for the deconstruction of secularism *qua* political ideology of national melioration. But his analysis itself rests on a deeply problematic assumption: that Descartes played a distinct role in underscoring the absolute incompatibility of affect and reason, and generating faith in a politics by reason alone.

In fact, I argue, the protoplasmic form of secularity developed by Descartes was less a matter of procedural rationality than of consent manufactured by controlling people's experiential environment, or, as it came to be expressed in the eighteenth century, 'what passed before people's eyes'. It was less a matter of competing reasons than the affective structure in and through which such reasons were presented. Against common assumptions, Descartes expressed a keen awareness of the transcendental limitations placed upon introspective reason, and insisted on the impossibility of ever knowing exactly *why* people speak or act as they do. In one sense, this was determined by factors in place from time immemorial, i.e. nature or God. In another, it was determined by man-made systems of power that preceded and encompassed the formation of the individual self. This sceptical standpoint effectively theorized the relation between the elite, who controlled the people's sensual environment (through mass media: print, education, stage shows, etc.), and the masses who were controlled by them.

Descartes thus testifies to a sophisticated and *critical* understanding of the political subject, which – as we shall see – later became the bread and butter of eighteenth-century theories of secularization. Contra Cavanaugh and others, the *philosophes* did not just reject affects from the public sphere by throwing them into the bucket of 'religion' but saw in them a deep facet of human nature, as inextricable as life itself. Like Descartes, they sought to preserve intact what makes us 'real human beings' by re-annexing, not destroying, emotions traditionally associated with religion. The Enlightenment and the public sphere were never neutral, apolitical entities guided solely by the workings of discursive rationality but were from the outset generated out of a political desire to shape public opinion through the language of the senses. The eighteenth century did not simply mark the emergence of the public sphere *qua* disengaged sphere of rational-critical speech acts; it also marked the genesis of modern propaganda.

At one point Descartes reflects on his theory of the passions that 'These things are useful to know [*utiles à sçavoir*] … For since we are able, with a little art [*industrie*], to change the movements of the brain in animals devoid of reason, it is evident that we can do so more easily in men'.[33] According to Descartes, 'Even those who have the weakest souls could acquire absolute mastery over all their passions, if sufficient art were employed in training and governing [*conduire*] them' (1985a: 348).[34] For Descartes, art and industry were a matter of manipulating external factors or 'objects of representation'. Such objects might include book adventures or stage plays, which may more readily alter the disposition of the passions than a desiccated process of reasoning: 'when we read of strange adventures in a book, or see them acted out on the stage, this arouses sadness in us, sometimes joy, or love, or hatred, and generally any of the passions, depending on the diversity of the objects, that offer themselves [*s'offrent*] to our imagination' (1985a: 380).[35] From Voltaire's *Le Fanatisme* to Helvétius's phantasmagoria of Islam in *De l'Esprit*, the Enlightenment exploited these tools relentlessly.

Enlightened bodies I: Secular passions, empiricism and civic virtue in the 'radical enlightenment'

[M]any a one
Owes to his Countrey his Religion;
And in another, would as strongly grow,
Had but his Nurse and Mother taught him so.

John Donne, *Poems* (1633: 390)

The passions destroy more prejudices than philosophy.

Denis Diderot, *Entretiens sur le Fils Naturel* (1821 [1757]: 172)

Introduction

How is it that not believing in God today is so easy, but experiencing oneself out of the nation so difficult? For many, nationalism is generated by reiterative processes of interpellation and performative identification that secure one's sense of belonging to a people, a distinct geographical area, a set of values, cultural norms and/or symbolic structures (Connor 1994; Anderson 2006; Smith-Rosenberg 2010). This sense is not primarily cognitive, or a matter of conscious assent to sets of propositions. Nationalism is at heart an affective condition, arising out of the rich texture of practices, rituals, symbols and literatures that constitute modern life; we are born into and die within its boundaries.[1] We can no more 'stand outside' of this texture than we can the secular. Indeed, there are clear parallels between nationalism and Charles Taylor's understanding of secularity. Both are more or less non-negotiable, and both pertain to the 'background understandings' (Asad 2003: 2) that inform decision-making and principle-building in modern life.

But this parallel between secularism and nationalism raises a curious conundrum, based on the historical role of the Enlightenment. On one hand, we know that the Enlightenment 'fragilized' religious imaginaries (Taylor 2007) in Western societies or at least helped render belief a matter of choice (as outlined at length in *A Secular Age*). On the other, we know that the Enlightenment played a decisive role in the creation of the modern nation-state and its accompanying ideology of nationalism (Rothschild 2001: 213; Asad 2003: 181–204; Anderson 2006: 11; Calhoun, Juergensmeyer, and VanAntwerpen 2011: 9, 15).[2] The conundrum lies in the fact that an anti-religious movement ubiquitously construed in terms of a rejection of emotion and the body gave rise or at least contributed to a form of life that is, by common understanding, fundamentally affective. How does an embodied understanding of nationalism square with the historical fact of its incubation in the 'rational' Enlightenment?

The conundrum can be resolved in several ways. For example, it could be argued that the two aspects are only contingently related, that the rise of nationalism merely happened to coincide with an erosion of religious commitments. Or one might weaken the bearing of philosophy on history, suggesting the changes I have described occurred for other reasons – economic, political or otherwise – with Enlightenment literatures retroactively claiming both victories for themselves; or, depending on one's position, that the Enlightenment started off successfully with the downfall of the Catholic Church but ended in failure with the rise of nationalism – in other words, that the 'real' essence or bulk of the Enlightenment had nothing to do with the latter.[3] Yet another solution is to focus not on the essence of Enlightenment per se, but the background conditions under which both developments occurred, with an eye to the fundamental telos of the social body. Taylor, for example, connects the rise of nationalism to the emergence of a socialized concept of virtue in which true flourishing became a matter of aligning self and social interests, as found in Rousseau. This new theory of virtue facilitated the simultaneous closure of religious transcendence and emergence of a collective, national identity, yoking secularism and nationalism together at the level of changing 'hypergoods' (2007). Finally, the rise of nationalism may be explained through the expansion of colonialism and a concomitant need to define and consolidate a sense of national or European superiority against the subaltern. Again, this explanation tends to read nationalism's rise in terms of a failure of the universal Enlightenment principles of liberty, equality and fraternity (e.g. by raising questions about who counts as a rights- or principle-privileged person) rather than a natural extension of the Enlightenment itself.

Regardless of the strengths and weaknesses of these positions, one assumption is held virtually unanimously: that the Enlightenment was at heart (and Rousseau aside) a universalist movement inherently averse to the regressive and parochial forces of authentic nationalism, and fixated on cleansing social space of historically cultivated commitments, habits, practices and emotions. To the extent that the Enlightenment played a role in forming and sustaining the modern nation-state, this role is construed as idealistic, indirect or paradoxical. The Enlightenment may have generated certain conceptions of the individual, of the good and of social progress that intentionally or unintentionally supported the rise of the nation-states, but these conceptions were predominantly universal and rationalistic in their self-understanding. Lacking a language to make sense of the passional forces of true nationalism, Europe had to wait for Rousseau and the Counter-Enlightenment to articulate the undergrowth of affect into the canopy of discourse.

Like *A Secular Age*, this book argues for a close connection between the rise of nationalism and the rise of our secular age. But unlike *A Secular Age*, it does not limit this connection to a shift in the nature of European transcendental ends, 'hypergoods' or conditions of intelligibility. It does not begin from the end and work backwards to the material conditions or phenomenology of everyday life. Instead, it traces the combined genealogy of nationalism and secularism to an explicit, sustained effort on the part of Enlightenment thinkers to generate emotional attachments to the homeland, absolutely consistent with their appraisal of the body, affect and the passions. In other words, it reframes secularity and nationalism as the result of a conscious project of *cultivation* at a founding moment of our secular age.[4] On this reading, secularity and nationalism were not simply deduced from a 'secularized' set of ultimate goods, and neither did they emerge as a 'trickle-down' effect of these same goods.[5] Instead they were – at least in eighteenth-century France – inculcated, taught and disciplined into breathing, feeling bodies. If today religious belief may feel more flexible and optional than one's sense of national identity, this is due, at least in part, to the efforts of Enlightenment thinkers to generate a long-lasting and viscerally engrained secular habitus. We still, arguably, live within this cultivated condition.

It is now a commonplace of Enlightenment studies that the Enlightenment was not so unemotional or coldly rationalistic as traditionally assumed. Whereas in 1979 Isaiah Berlin could still associate Enlightenment with a straightforward 'desiccating spirit of excessive rationalism' (Hausheer 1979: xxxiii), intellectual historians now view the Enlightenment as a period and socio-intellectual movement crossed through with ethical and epistemological contradictions (e.g. between rationalism and empiricism) and accepting of the force and necessity of the passions. A number of works have addressed this problem directly. Albert Hirschman's *The Passions and the Interests* (1977) is a detailed account of the transition in Western enlightened thought from outright rejection or suppression of the passions, to their accommodation and manipulation in modern projects of statecraft, through to their supersession by the priority of 'interest' (self and social) under conditions of free-market capitalism. According to him,

> a considerable change ... took place in the attitude towards the passions from the seventeenth to the eighteenth century: they were first viewed as wholly vicious and destructive ... But gradually, toward the end of the seventeenth and more fully in the course of the eighteenth century, the passions were rehabilitated as the essence of life and as a potentially creative force. (2013 [1977]: 47)

As Emma Rothschild notes in *Economic Sentiments* (2001), the latter half of the eighteenth century in particular marked the emergence of a solid discourse on emotion and its relation to reason, since enthusiasm for a science-based, utopian enlightenment was already a subject of 'extensive derision' by the 1750s (2001: 20). Through a close reading of Enlightenment philosophers, especially Adam Smith and Condorcet, Rothschild shows that during the period 1770s–1820s 'The life of cold and rational calculation was intertwined with the life of sentiment and imagination' (1); for both authors, 'Sentiments influence reasons in economic life, and reasons influence sentiments' (9). The dichotomy between '"cold," rational, and reflective calculation' and '"warm" and instinctive sentiment' is actually 'unrecognizable' in the period 1770s–1780s, only emerging *after* the Revolution and usually through the voice of the Enlightenment's enemies. Although Johann Gottfried Herder reduced the 'spirit of France' to its 'cold language and mentality', 'cold reason', 'cold blood', 'politeness' and 'spirit of prosperity', Rothschild argues the period leading up to the Revolution was neither cold nor hot but marked by a permanent 'conflict of thermometers' (25–6).[6]

Despite such redressive work, assumptions about Enlightenment rationality continue to reproduce in new iterations, from popular works of intellectual history to some of the most sophisticated contributions to secular studies. Steven Pinker's *Enlightenment Now* (2018) is a startling example of how little has been learnt over the last four decades.[7] More pertinently, the 'rationalist Enlightenment' persists in Charles Taylor's *A Secular Age*, ironically perpetuating a dichotomy between secular reason and religious emotion that scholars of the secular, including Taylor, often set out to undermine. For example, while continuously emphasizing the embodied and historical dimensions of secularity, Taylor still maintains that Enlightenment thought entailed a detachment from the body, a 'disengaged stance' of autonomous reason, a suppression of the passions, enthusiasm or fanaticism, which (a) rejoins religion to emotion and secularity to anti-emotion; (b) generates a Habermasian sphere of free-floating, 'rational' discourse removed from power; and (c) legitimizes his own work as a late-modern advocacy for a return to the body and its embeddedness in unique socio-historical and intellectual contexts.

Taylor's turn to the body is in line with a relatively recent turn to material culture, ritual, practice, discipline and affect for a fuller, post-Protestant understanding of religious subjectivity. But what discourses must be silenced for the body to 'win out'? What must be forgotten for affect to be discovered in the seams rather than the substance of Western intellectual history? These questions are highly charged because Taylor's evisceration of the Enlightenment – like Pinker's – allows more corporeally oriented philosophies or ideologies centred especially on nationalism to be gathered up in the exclusive domain of the Counter-Enlightenment. The Enlightenment's cold but rational universalism can thus be represented as the innocent foundation of the modern secular state, setting up an objective, absolute, rational, universal (not subjective, relative, emotional, particular/nationalist) standard from which non-national, non-rational others will be taken to deviate. In other words, the Enlightenment can simultaneously be construed as the essence of rationality *and* deployed in the highly emotive context of Euro-American nationalism, as we increasingly see played out in contemporary Dutch and French right-wing politics.[8]

In order to unpack the constitutive elements of 'Enlightenment' as a historical and cultural object and thereby lay the grounds for a sustained critique of the classical Enlightenment historiography underpinning much of contemporary secular studies, I begin by outlining some popular assumptions about the Enlightenment found in one majorly influential work, Isaiah Berlin's *Against the Current* (1979), considering ways in which Berlin's narrative shapes *A Secular Age*. As I show, Taylor, whose doctoral work at Oxford was supervised by Berlin, operates within a broadly Berlinian framework that associates Enlightenment with three principal antipathies: the Enlightenment's rejection of the body and emotion in favour of 'disengaged reason'; its hermetic rationalism, against the Counter-Enlightenment's radical empiricism; and its rejection of habitus-based disciplines of virtue cultivation (psychological and physical) in favour of an abstract ethical idealism usually reducible to Kantian deontology or Benthamite utilitarianism.

The subsequent sections flesh out an alternative, affective history of the French Enlightenment through key *philosophes*, including Montesquieu, Diderot, Holbach, Helvétius, Rousseau and Condorcet, all of whom evinced a sophisticated understanding of the limits of reason and the emotional and practical complexities involved in steering European society away from religion. I analyse the *philosophes*' explicit statements on the passions and provide a broad outline of three further dimensions central to the French Enlightenment: its adoption and elaboration of Lockean empiricism in the context of debates on mind–body dualism and the freedom of the will, its ambivalent attitude towards the 'imagination' and its almost Nietzschean understanding of historical (anti-) process. By connecting these issues to the specific problem of nationalism in the following chapter, I show that, insofar as 'culture' can be defined in terms of history, tradition, acquired habits and embodied practices, the Enlightenment was construed by its founders as a cultural project with the well-being of the nation-state as its governing telos. The *philosophes* generally did not seek the erasure, suppression or repression of affect, imagination or habits but their Cartesian reorientation towards the imagined community and values of the emerging nation-state.

Crucially, the reorientation model of human passions was not always consistently endorsed, even within the same work. The passions could be, and were, uniformly rejected as often as they were defended. Indeed, a principal motive here is to show the contradictoriness of many Enlightenment works and hence the inadequacy of relying upon ideal-type reconstructions of secular intellectual history (e.g. focused on changing 'higher goods'; Taylor 2007). One work in particular assembled an incredible diversity of mid-eighteenth-century ideas surrounding human subjectivity and agency: Baron d'Holbach's major work of materialist philosophy, *Système de la Nature* (1770). I appeal to the *Système* for three principal reasons. First, because Holbach is so frequently listed as an archetypal representative of the 'cold', 'rational' Enlightenment, and presented as the first 'true' atheist against ambiguous figures like Spinoza or Hume (Buckley 1987: 32; Ruse 2015: 25; LeDrew 2016: 18); he is thus a paradigmatic representative of eighteenth-century French 'secularism'. Second, because the *Système* is relatively unknown and understudied, certainly in the fields of secular and Enlightenment studies, despite the extraordinary popularity of this work at the time of publication. Referring to the book-trading records kept by the Société Typographique de Neuchâtel, Robert Darnton has shown that Holbach was the most popular author of 'religious publications' after Voltaire, with his *Système* generating the most demand (1991: 68).[9] And finally, because the work is both expansive, covering an enormous array of topics central to enlightened discourse from 1750 to 1790, and eminently contradictory, serving as a prime example of the 'assembled' nature of the Enlightenment. Ironically, the *Système* offers anything but a system.

Although a number of authors, such as Jessica Riskin (2002) and Amy Schmitter (2006), have recently gone further than Hirschman and Rothschild in challenging the consensus of a rational, acorporeal Enlightenment, there is a surprising tendency – particularly in Riskin's work – to treat Enlightenment appeals to the body in the abstract, in separation from issues of institutional power and religion. As we have seen, a similar depoliticization of the Enlightenment is discernible in *A Secular Age*, where Enlightenment discourse is construed as 'standing outside of' yet 'speaking *to*' power (Taylor 2007: 190). In contrast, the following chapters reframe the Enlightenment body in thoroughly political terms, showing that Holbach and many other *philosophes* never thought of themselves in isolation from the real work of governing people. On the contrary, they were explicitly concerned with the problem of managing the general will or public opinion: in other words, *statecraft*. Statecraft – then as now – was not a matter of rational demonstration, but of regulating public emotions. These emotions were understood to gravitate around two principal affects: 'love' and 'fear'. This chapter and the next deal principally with 'love', examining Enlightenment thought on the generation of positive sentiments of national solidarity in order to affectively 'imagine' (or in Joan Landes's words, 'visualize', 2001) the nation into being. The fourth and fifth chapters deal with 'fear', focusing on representations of the eighteenth century's principal object of political and moral antipathy, the Oriental despot.

At the broadest level, my analysis testifies to the difficulties of conceiving the genealogy of the secular – as Taylor does – as a gradual (if rocky) process of detachment from the body and its enmeshment in the world. The mid- to late-eighteenth-century French Enlightenment did not replace a 'porous self' with a 'buffered self' but sought to reconfigure the structure of porosity by tying subjectivities to the body of the nation through the manipulation of desire and fear. We cannot therefore unproblematically think of Enlightenment as generating or even slotting into a great narrative of 'disenchantment' or 'disembedding' (Taylor 2007: 155). Enlightened modernity simply brought about new kinds of embeddedness, new modes of inhabitation and openness to the world, linked (especially, I argue) to the rise of the nation-states.

Before beginning, a brief note on methodology and the remit of this chapter is necessary. Since I will be dealing with the historical categories of 'Enlightenment' and 'Counter-Enlightenment', it may be useful to clarify what I mean by these terms and why I think they may benefit from reappraisal here.

Enlightenment/Counter-Enlightenment

The European Enlightenment can be approached in a number of ways. One is to gather authors together on the basis of their geographical and historical location, and project their combined intellectual output as representative of enlightened thought in general. Thus, according to Jonathan Israel, a typical 'French' approach is to focus on the writings of six authors in particular, 'Montesquieu, Voltaire, Diderot, d'Alembert, d'Holbach, and Rousseau', with Descartes and Spinoza performing a background formative role (Israel has emphasized Spinoza's role especially). An 'English' approach might focus instead on Newton and Locke, both of whom were highly influential on European thought (Israel 2001: v–vi). Alternatively, the Enlightenment can be divided along different epistemological or disciplinary strata; for example, Tore Frängsmyr develops a tripartite theory of Enlightenment as (1) a philosophical attitude, (2) a historical period and (3) an intellectual movement (centred in France). Like Franco Venturi, however, he ultimately defaults to the third sense, thereby returning to the 'French' approach (Rothschild 2001: 16). J.G.A. Pocock instead plays down any sense of philosophical, historical or intellectual unity, parsing the monolithic Enlightenment into a series of disjointed, heterogeneous programs to reform the relationship between historically particular religious and political institutions, and thus emphasizing the non-unified and plural nature of Enlightenment, or 'Enlightenments' (2000).

Responding to writers like Pocock, Israel has insisted on the relative homogeneity of the Enlightenment, seeking to convey 'a sense of the European Enlightenment as a single highly integrated intellectual and cultural movement' (2001: v). Similarly, although Owen and Owen recognize disparities between individual Enlightenment thinkers, they also move towards consolidation:

> The Enlightenment grew out of a revolutionary movement in philosophy and science in the West, the roots of which are debated, but can arguably be traced to the sixteenth century. The Enlightenment began to blossom in the seventeenth century with such thinkers as Descartes, Bacon, Hobbes, Bayle, Locke, Newton, and Spinoza. As a movement, it enjoyed its most visible heyday in the eighteenth

century, with such thinkers as Hume, Kant, the *philosophes* in France, as well as Madison, Franklin, and Jefferson in America. ... The term *the Enlightenment* refers to a range of views that is far from unified. The disagreements between Descartes and Locke and Hume and Kant fill volumes. Yet a unifying thread is indicated already in the name: the Enlightenment aimed to benefit humankind through a widespread transformation of public opinion, a transformation in the direction of and effected by reason and science. The Enlightenment was to usher in an unprecedented condition for human kind: the Age of Reason. No longer content to remain a preserve of the few, no longer content to maintain an emphatic orientation to purely speculative thought, reason and science were on the march. (2010: 16–17)

I include this quotation for two reasons. First, to provide a paradigmatic summary of enlightened thought, predictably focused on the compound of 'reason and science' as its 'unifying thread' or dominating epistemological and procedural category. But also to highlight the power of historiography for establishing an unspoken consensus concerning the content and significance of historical periods and their characteristic modes of discourse. This second point requires elaboration.

The question of defining Enlightenment is impossible to close. This is not simply because the scope of the 'historical' Enlightenment is so broad, beginning – as classically understood – anywhere from the sixteenth to the middle of the seventeenth century, beginning to fade towards the beginning of the nineteenth and incorporating an incredible diversity of thinkers across times and places, but because what gets to count *as* enlightened is always based on *a priori* assumptions about the Enlightenment, assumptions themselves derived from a necessarily arbitrary circumscription of relevant thinkers and materials taken to define the essence of enlightened thought. In other words, Enlightenment is an inherently unstable concept not just because it is vague, but because its content is both *defined by* a particular set of literatures and *defining of* the boundaries around this set. For example, Cartesian thought is 'enlightened' because it follows enlightened principles (of rational enquiry, etc.), but these principles are 'enlightened' only because 'rational enquiry' has been taken as definitive of Enlightenment. Enlightenment is thus infinitely expandable in principle and restricted only by social consensus and the historiographical authority this consensus yields. The force of this consensus is strong; it explains how Owen and Owen can take the progress of 'reason and science' as 'indicated already in the name', Enlightenment.

A more critical approach might begin not with 'the Enlightenment' per se, but ways in which Enlightenment discourse has been represented and deployed in intellectual histories of modernity. A particularly interesting and powerful entry point for this genealogical project, I submit, is provided by tellings of the classical Enlightenment/Counter-Enlightenment narrative now ubiquitous in intellectual histories of the West. Since the Enlightenment is, like every movement, most densely and integrally represented through its antagonist, literatures on the Counter-Enlightenment provide some of the richest insights into the constitution of Enlightenment or 'the' Enlightenment as epistemic and historical categories. I am particularly interested in two dimensions of this narrative: the idea that the Enlightenment entailed the suppression or erasure of embodied experience (affect, the senses, habits, etc.) in favour of 'disengaged reason'; and the related idea that the Enlightenment was universalist and therefore inherently incompatible with the particularistic ontology of German nationalism. Both are amply represented in Isaiah Berlin's seminal work of intellectual history *Against the Current* (1979) and, as I will show, substantially replicated in Taylor's *A Secular Age*.

Against the Current (1979)

Although Isaiah Berlin is often credited with coining the term 'Counter-Enlightenment', he neither invented the word, since it already existed in Germany in the late nineteenth century (*Gegen-Aufklärung*) and had been printed in English at least fifteen years before he came to use it, nor the concept, which can be 'traced within the age of Enlightenment itself to debates about its own achievements and failures' (Mali and Wokler 2003: vii, 13). 'Counter-Enlightenment' was already an established idea before his seminal essay 'The Counter-Enlightenment' (1973) and the book that popularized it, *Against the Current* (1979). Nevertheless, as Mali and Wokler, point out, 'More than any other figure since the eighteenth century ... Berlin appropriated the term ... made it the heart of his own political thought, and imbued his interpretations of particular thinkers with its meanings and significance' (2003: vii).[10] The richness of his engagement with a wide array of authors and the importance of *Against the Current* for late-twentieth-century intellectual history make it an ideal starting point for thinking through the construction of Enlightenment as an integrated historical category.

Against the Current contains thirteen essays, each dealing with a thinker or group of thinkers linked to the Enlightenment or Counter-Enlightenment. This division is represented by, on one side, authors like Voltaire, Hume, Gibbon,

Diderot, Helvétius and Holbach; and on the other, Machiavelli, Vico, Hamann, Herder and de Maistre. A handful of authors fall somewhere in between, e.g. Montesquieu and Rousseau. Instead of addressing Berlin's approach to these authors individually, I will base the following outline on four key sets of oppositions: 'cold' reason vs 'warm' emotion; reason and rationalism vs imagination, the senses and 'dispositions'; abstract idealism vs 'concrete' history, habituation and education as 'directors' of the passions; and universalism vs nationalism. These oppositions all make their way into Taylor's *A Secular Age*, and particularly, I will suggest, through two conceptual constructions: the subject category of 'Modern Exclusive Humanism' and 'subtraction story' representations of the secular.

'Cold' reason vs 'warm' emotion

Throughout *Against the Current*, a basic opposition is set up between Enlightenment rationalism and Counter-Enlightenment emotionalism. According to Berlin, the Counter-Enlightenment is characterized by its insistence on the power of emotion over reason – a position that flew in the face of the Enlightenment and its 'proclamation of the autonomy of reason' (1979: 1). The archenemy was of course Descartes, with his doctrine of 'clear and distinct ideas, his contempt for historical and humane studies generally, and his attempts to assimilate all forms of knowledge to ... mathematics' (Hausheer 1979: xxv).[11] Against Descartes and the *philosophes*, the Counter-Enlightenment insisted on the 'hard and timeless core of base human passions and emotions, relationships and needs' (xlvii). Thus Verdi 'speaks directly and unselfconsciously ... in terms of primal human passions and emotions' (xlvi); De Maistre claimed 'Reason is the thinnest of walls against the raging seas of violent emotion' (Berlin 1979: 22); and the *Sturm und Drang* movement of the German Counter-Enlightenment attacked 'the entire tidy ordering of life by the principles of reason and scientific knowledge advocated by the progressive thinkers of France, England and Italy'. Against Herder's ardent call to arms 'I am not here to think, but to be, feel, live!' or 'heart! warmth! blood! humanity! life!', the French rationalists appear 'pale and ghostly'; Goethe described Holbach's *Système* as 'a repulsive, "Cimmerian, corpse-like" treatise' (14). Although Diderot and Rousseau in some ways marked a counter-movement within the Enlightenment, becoming 'major liberator[s] of feeling and natural passion' (Hausheer 1979: xxxiii), they ultimately succumbed to the same elegant but deathly rationalism or 'cold political dehumanization' (Berlin 1979: 9) characterizing the Enlightenment as a whole. Berlin condemns even Rousseau for 'conceding the authority of natural law, a vast, cold, empty abstraction' (9).

As noted in the previous chapter, Taylor's *A Secular Age* is structured around a binary narrative spanning the gap between all-pervasive belief and belief as merely 'one option among many'. A significant part of this narrative involves a shift from pre-secular 'porousness' to secular 'bufferedness': whereas our ancestors inhabited the world as agents 'open' to transcendence, invisible spirits, possession, etc., we now live with a much firmer sense of the boundaries between self and other, or self and world. Taylor outlines key stages in this shift, such as Descartes 'disengagement' of reason from the body, the development of Newtonian science, the socially and politically motivated 'civilizing process' examined by Norbert Elias, and, crucially for this chapter, a generalized suppression of affect and embodiment in eighteenth-century Enlightenment ethics and epistemology.

The conceptual gathering point for each of these shifts is a subject category stemming from Descartes's 'disengaged reason' Taylor calls 'Modern Exclusive Humanism' (henceforth Modern Exclusive Humanism), a condition in which transcendental goals, or goals 'beyond human flourishing', have become obsolete (2007: 19). According to Taylor, Modern Exclusive Humanism, with its roots in 'neo-Stoicism' (2007: 250), 'commands us to obey the demands of rational disengagement' (249), advances 'an ideal of disciplined rational benevolence' (250) and is characterized by an admiration for 'the power of cool, disengaged reason' which alone was 'capable of liberating us from illusion and blind forces of instinct' (9). 'The tyranny of reason over feeling' (314) is associated most closely with Kant, Hume and Gibbon, who recur frequently throughout *A Secular Age* as archetypal representatives of 'cool self-possession', 'unflappability' and 'ironic' distance (241, 286, 301), and thus of a general devaluation, withdrawal from and rejection of the body (e.g. 'the disengaged stance ... leads to the drawing of boundaries, and a withdrawal from certain modes of intimacy, as well as taking a distance from certain bodily functions', 137).[12] Perhaps the most direct expression of this occurs on page 288, where Taylor suggests that, to the extent that 'the stance of disengagement' and 'eclipse of God' transform ethics into a revelation by reason alone, so *'The body tends to fall away'* (288, emphasis mine). This falling away may lead to two possible positions:

> One tells us that we have to factor out our embodied feeling, our 'gut reactions' in determining what is right, even set aside our desires and emotions. This move finds a paradigm statement in the work of Kant. Or else, we turn against the excessive claims of reason, and base morality on emotions, as we find with

Hume. But just for that reason we undercut the aura of the higher that usually surrounds these feelings, giving them a purely naturalistic explanation. (288)

Hume is here rehabilitated as a soft emotionalist against Kant and his desiccated rationalism, with one important qualification: that his naturalistic approach 'undercuts the aura of the higher' surrounding these emotions. This is in line with Taylor's narration of the loss of auratic power in nature descended from Plato explored earlier in *A Secular Age*. Yet two points should be noted: (1) Taylor's unjustified shift from a focus on the emotions in themselves, to the 'aura' surrounding these emotions; (2) the fact that this more qualified claim is inconsistent with Taylor's construction of Modern Exclusive Humanism as a subject position inherently antithetical to the body and emotions *as such*. In other words, Hume's emotionalism is effectively denied any real significance in *A Secular Age*, since the very category of Modern Exclusive Humanism (carried forward by Hume and Gibbon) is constructed against emotions and the body. Significantly, it is Kant who is taken as the paradigm figure for the rationalism and bodily disengagement of Modern Exclusive Humanism – a disengagement then projected onto the 'mainstream Enlightenment' as a whole.

The anti-emotional basis of Modern Exclusive Humanism is further brought out by Taylor's focus on its opposite, Romanticism. This alternative mode of unbelief recognizes the limits of reason and seeks to 'heal the division within us that disengaged reason has created, setting thinking in opposition to feeling or instinct or intuition' (9). According to Taylor, the Romantics are distinguished by their belief that 'the sources of power are not transcendent' but found in 'Nature, or in our own inner depths, or in both' (9). A crucial representative here is D. H. Lawrence who 'rediscovered' emotional depth in the aftermath of the Enlightenment (138). Another is Schiller:

> From the standpoint of [Schiller's] anthropology of fusion and beauty, we can understand one of the central criticisms that the Romantic age levelled at the disengaged, disciplined, buffered self, and the world it had built. ... The accusation against the dominant conceptions of disciplined self and rational order was that they had divided us, confined us in a desiccating reason which had alienated us from our deeper emotions. (314)

Reason vs imagination, the senses and 'dispositions'

A parallel to the Counter-Enlightenment's 'restoration' of the body and emotion is, according to Berlin, its insistence on the value of memory, imagination and dispositions. Thus, for Vico, unlike the Enlightenment,

Memory and imagination, and the potential dispositions (most of which lie unactivated) of one's own mind, provide the basic tools ... upon which all humane studies ultimately rest: we know at first-hand what it is to feel fear, love, hate, to belong to a family or a nation, to understand a facial expression or a human situation or a joke, to appreciate a work of art, to form and live by ideals, and to have an inexhaustible (and developing) variety of other kinds of immediate 'inner' experience besides. (Hausheer 1979: xxxi)

While Enlightenment philosophers like Fontenelle were 'suspicious of all metaphor, but especially of *images fabuleuses*, which spring from a "totally false and ridiculous" conception of things' (Berlin 1979: 97), Vico's historical-hermeneutic method relied on *fantasia*, or 'imagination', through which it is possible to 'enter' minds from different epochs and in different places (98). Similarly, Hamann 'took little interest in theories or speculations about the external world; he cared only for ... art, religious experience, the senses, personal relationships, which the analytic truths of scientific reason seemed to him to reduce to meaningless ciphers' (8–9). Against Descartes and the *philosophes'* mutilation of humanity, Hamann advocated 'the union of spirit and flesh that constitutes the real world'. This union could only take place through a proper understanding of the relation between knowledge and reality, a relation ultimately reducible to history ('History alone yields concrete truth') and poetry ('the language of passion and inspired imagination'). For him, 'The entire treasure of human knowledge and happiness lies in images' (8–9).

The importance of memory, the imagination, images, feelings and first-hand experiences was itself a natural outgrowth of the Counter-Enlightenment's dual emphasis on history and the character-moulding power of man's lived context, accessed through the senses. The Counter-Enlightenment developed on the basis that 'new, richer and deeper forms of collective self-knowledge ... emerge from the historical interaction of men with men – collectively and individually, with their own past, with other nations and cultures, *and with their physical environment*' (Hausheer 1979: xlix, emphasis mine). Again, a paradigmatic representative is Hamann. While the philosophes 'blinded themselves to concrete reality, to *the real experience which only direct acquaintance, especially by the senses, provides*' (Berlin 1979: 7, emphasis mine), Hamann claimed 'True knowledge is given to us immediately by the senses, and by spontaneous imagination, instinct and insight' (Hausheer 1979: xxxiv). The Enlightenment and its 'artificial utilitarian contraptions' had nothing to say on raw, sensual reality: 'No man can love, or see his innermost nature expressed in, the web of lifeless categories spun by the rationalistic Spinoza or the de-spiritualized play of cause and effect of the vast materialist machines constructed by Holbach or Helvétius' (xxxiv, 7).

As we saw in the previous chapter, Taylor explains 'disengaged reason' as entailing a withdrawal from the external world, epitomized by Descartes: 'The crucial *démarche* [of disengagement], as we see it in Descartes, is to isolate the agent from its field, to zero in on it, and to bring out what it has in itself, in abstraction from the surroundings' (2007: 257). Cartesianism directly shapes Modern Exclusive Humanism as a subject category closed off from feeling, experience, environmental context and history. Exclusive humanism also deadens the imagination, a commonplace idea also found in Asad's *Formations of the Secular* (2003), which takes Fontenelle and his claim that 'the imagination and reason have little commerce with each other' as representative of the Enlightenment position (2003: 28, 44). The background assumption is clear: the secular Enlightenment, unlike the Counter-Enlightenment, drew a radical division between reason and imagination, and downgraded the latter in favour of the former. For the *philosophes*, imagination would simply evaporate under the pressure of reason and the certifiable 'facts' of experience – a shift that later became definitive of secularity.

Abstract idealism vs 'concrete' history, habituation and education as 'directors' of the passions

A related node in the Enlightenment/Counter-Enlightenment opposition concerns history and the formation of habits and culture. For Berlin, man's historical condition – the irreducibly unique set of contingencies, rituals, habits, feelings and emotions which structure human life – is central to true self-understanding and cannot be dismissed in the name of an abstract and universal ideal, or 'system of nature' (Hausheer 1979: lii). Montesquieu, portrayed as a kind of rebel figure within the mainstream of the Enlightenment, is a particularly strong representative: unlike the broader French Enlightenment, Montesquieu's 'central conception' was that 'Men are governed by … climate, religion, law, the maxims of government, the examples of past things, customs, manners' (Berlin 1979: 134–5). Whereas Helvétius, Condillac, Holbach, Condorcet, Diderot, Turgot, Voltaire and d'Alembert all believed that '[scientific] knowledge alone could make men happy and virtuous, wise and free', Montesquieu's writings evince 'a sceptical note' emphasizing the non-negotiability of historically embedded, embodied practices and external physical factors (e.g. climate) in the determination of knowledge and behaviour (136).

Of course, this insistence on external conditions went directly against the grain of Cartesian innatism and rationalism, despite the fact Montesquieu considered himself a follower of Descartes: according to Berlin, 'one of [Montesquieu's] greatest merits lies in the very fact that although he claims to be founding a new science in the spirit of Descartes, his practice is better than his professions' (138). Unlike Descartes, Montesquieu sought not to destroy but to *reorient* the passions:

> Montesquieu believed that only reason could solve human problems, but that by itself it could not effect much. He did not, like Hume, think reason to be necessarily the slave of the passions, only feebler than them, and maintained that since reason was weak and the passions strong, and, in any case, indestructible, they should not be fought but harnessed, and conditions created to direct them into desired channels. (148)

Similarly, Fourier is positioned against the Enlightenment for advocating 'the end of repression and the need for the rational canalization of the passions by careful vocational guidance which would enable all human desires, capacities, inclinations, to develop in a free and creative direction' (335).

The idea that the passions could and should be directed into 'desired channels' or 'canalized', not 'repressed', is of course exactly what Descartes argued in the *Passions*. Nevertheless, Berlin contrasts Montesquieu with Descartes, arguing that, whereas Montesquieu aimed to show that 'laws are ... the expression of the changing moral habits, habits, beliefs, general attitudes of a particular society', Descartes and Leibniz placed their faith in 'universal, unvarying, rules discovered by the faculty of reason' (154). In contrast to the latter, Montesquieu and the Counter-Enlightenment sought to redirect the passions by manipulating man's external environment, and especially his educational context. Since external factors determined the shape and scope of human knowledge, people were most effectively modified through 'intensive moral education'. For Montesquieu unlike the rest of the Enlightenment, 'One can modify or regulate ... almost everything' (151).

A significant dimension of Taylor's narrative involves challenging 'subtraction stories', or the notion that secularity and its characteristic features (Modern Exclusive Humanism, universal beneficence, etc.) emerge spontaneously once the distortive effects of 'unfavourable conditions' (e.g. religion) are removed. Whereas the 'subtraction' view construes secularity as a quasi-ontological state of nature corrupted by non-secular accretions, whose erasure will yield a fully formed, ethical self – in its most extreme form, the Modern Exclusive Humanist –

Taylor points to the contingency and historical constructedness of secularity itself, and especially its ethical commitment to Modern Exclusive Humanism. In his words, 'exclusive humanism wasn't just something we fell into, once the old myths dissolved, or the "infamous" *ancien régime* church was crushed ... [Universal beneficence and sympathy require] training, or inculcated insight, and frequently much work on ourselves' (2007: 255). The idea that virtue requires 'work on ourselves' is implicitly positioned against the Enlightenment's naïve faith in innate goodness, or the notion that 'human beings are endowed with a capacity of benevolence or altruism which will emerge if it is not stifled by unfavourable conditions' (247).

This innatist reading of Enlightenment psychology directly reflects Berlin's opposition between the Enlightenment's idealist program of reform and Montesquieu's insistence on education and historically contingent, cultivated habits. According to Berlin and Taylor, the Enlightenment (minus Montesquieu and Rousseau) took for granted that humans would turn out good once freed from the influence of invariably negative institutions; education would not come into it. This is why Taylor reads Rousseau's idiosyncratic 'struggle for virtue' in terms of a departure from the 'mainstream Enlightenment' (203).

The radical Enlightenment

The multilayered binaries underpinning Berlin's Enlightenment/Counter-Enlightenment narrative thus generate a number of assumptions about the Enlightenment: that it elevated reason as the ultimate value in civilized societies, even to the exclusion of empiricism; that it rejected the body and emotions in favour of a 'corpse-like', 'cold' and 'analytical' rationalism; that it was antithetical to the imagination; and that it ignored history and processes of habituation determined by education and man's lived context. As we have seen, many of these assumptions are partially if not identically replicated in Taylor's *A Secular Age*.

Such assumptions are of course not unique to Berlin or Taylor. On the contrary, the point is not that they are unusual, but that Berlin and Taylor present a particularly clear articulation of beliefs and assumptions about the Enlightenment widespread enough to have been absorbed into the generic self-understanding of secular modernity. We have already seen subtle ways in which this understanding informs critical analyses of secularity, like Asad's approach to imagination in *Formations of the Secular*. More recently, Calhoun, Juergensmeyer and VanAntwerpen have written that the Enlightenment's 'new way of thinking' was characterized by 'reason and secular ideals', and that 'Many [Enlightenment figures] preferred a "reasonable" religion … opposing excessive "enthusiasm"' (2011: 7). Finbarr Curtis's recent critique of American religious freedom similarly contrasts the profoundly sentimental 'theological liberalism' of Horace Bushnell with 'enlightenment thought that grounded liberal ideals in an autonomous reasoning individual' (2016: 51).[13]

Interestingly, Taylor accepts the body was not always excised from Enlightenment discourse. Indeed, he briefly notes that the Enlightenment could 'even' involve a return to the body, since 'positive invocations of the body … abound in many forms of atheist materialism'. It is not entirely clear what Taylor means by these 'positive invocations', first because he does not elaborate on what these might be, and second because they are dismissed in principle, since the issue is not 'how many' of these invocations we hear, but 'whether our relation to the highest – God for believers, generally morality for unbelieving *Aufklärer* – is mediated in embodied form, as was plainly the case for parishioners "creeping the Cross" on Good Friday in pre-Reformation England' (554). With these comments, Taylor transitions from a generalized critique of rational disengagement to a more refined variant based on a theory of ends – a variant contrasted with the limit case of medieval Christian praxis, 'creeping the Cross'. Following his earlier argument in *Sources of the Self* (1989), that our sense of identity is bound up with our higher goods, the problem now is not whether the body is valued positively or not, in contrast to his earlier emphasis on a general Enlightenment antipathy towards the body, but 'to what degree our *highest desires, those which allow us to discern the highest,* are embodied' (2007: 554, emphasis mine). According to Taylor, eighteenth-century atheist-materialist restorations of the body implicitly reject any sense that the highest good may be 'mediated through the body' not simply because they devalue the body (Taylor now accepts they do not), but because they reject the illusion of 'highness' to which the body was formerly oriented. Thus, although the aspiration to fuller embodiment surfaces among 'the partisans of maximal instrumental reason as well', this aspiration aims at nothing more than the 'maximization of human desire' detached from transcendental ends:

> What else should this reason aim at than the maximization of human desire? And doesn't this require that we set aside all hankering after illusory 'higher' goals, like spiritual purity, or the dedication to virtue? So argued the proponents of the radical Enlightenment. (609–10)

Who are the 'radical Enlightenment'? Taylor usefully lists these on the following page: 'Helvétius, Holbach, Bentham'. These figures are distinguished, first, from the 'mainstream' Enlightenment of Gibbon, Voltaire and Hume, which flatly rejected the body, but also from Romantic figures like Schiller and Goethe, since the return to the body of radical Enlightenment did not involve 'transforming sensual desire itself', but 'giving ordinary sensual desire its outlet, its space where it could be fulfilled on its own terms'. For the radicals, 'any talk of fusing or transforming desire [as Schiller sought to do, e.g., by fusing desire with form to yield beauty] is just another attempt to sideline the sensual in the name of some specious "higher"' (610).

There are serious problems of accuracy here. First, the transformation of desire and its reorientation towards higher goods, as well as the cultivation of and dedication to virtue, were central to the radical Enlightenment and its double project to destroy religion and build the nation-state on autonomous foundations. As Holbach wrote:

> There must be enthusiasm for transcendent virtues as well as for atrocious crimes. Enthusiasm places the soul, or brain, in a state similar to that of drunkenness; both the one and the other excite in man that rapidity of motion which is approved when good results, but which is called folly, delirium, crime, fury, when it produces nothing but disorder. (1889 [1770]: 64)

Second, the radical Enlightenment did not conceive of the passions as mere means or instruments for the end of the secular project, since, as Holbach put it, 'To interdict passion to man, is to desire of him not to be a human creature' (158). Holbach, like Senault and Descartes before him, understood the passions as both means to and inherent in the final goal; they were at least partly constitutive of the good itself: '[Man's] passions are essential to him … they constitute the happiness of a being who feels, who thinks, who receives ideas' (156). For Helvétius, the passions were to the moral 'what movement [was] to the physical'. Just as movement 'created', 'destroyed', 'conserved' and 'animated everything', the passions likewise '[gave] life to the moral world [*vivifient le monde moral*]' (1759 [1758]: 297). The passions were no more 'instrumental' to morality than movement is instrumental to matter.

Yet even if we assume – wrongly or simplistically – that the radical Enlightenment was as anti-transcendental and anti-corporeal as Taylor makes out, two deeper issues underpin *A Secular Age*: its methodological strategy of distilling secular intellectual history to the 'higher goods' of various thinkers; and its reliance upon a more or less arbitrary distinction between centre/mainstream and periphery/radical Enlightenment. For insofar as these conceptual demarcators are respected, elements of intellectual history that fall on the negative side of either dichotomy (lower goods, peripheral Enlightenment) will remain excisable in principle from the main story of the secular West, and the Enlightenment will retain its status as the rational epicentre of European modernity.

Higher goods and the mainstream

Although Taylor uses *A Secular Age* as an opportunity to focus on the rich texture of ideas and affects that make up our common experience in premodernity, modernity and postmodernity, what underlies this embodied experience ultimately derives from a highly abstracted chain of analytic reasoning. For example, Descartes's self-reflexive, procedural rationality is taken as the motive force for a 'great shift' in perceptions in the seventeenth century towards procedural conceptions of justice and the good, suggesting the tell-tale advance of the age can be encapsulated in what Descartes adds to Augustine and the Stoics. Locke's 'punctual self' similarly stems from an objectifying stance towards the body and senses – a stance then expanded into a defining moment of Western Christendom. Having arrived at each thinker's distinct contribution to the ladder of cunning reason – one might say, each thinker's unique selling point – Taylor treats other aspects of their or others' work as more or less insignificant. What matters is what is added to the ladder vertically, not what extends horizontally and in other directions. Hence his claim that it is irrelevant 'how many' invocations of the body we hear during the Enlightenment.

One problem with this approach is that an exclusive focus on the incremental new and transcendental higher can obfuscate a variety of alternative viewpoints or indeed outright contradictions, between and within the thinkers and movements Taylor examines for his genealogy of the secular. It is now quite uncontroversial to maintain that the contours of an intellectual age, its texture and feel, are not simply set by hierarchies of philosophical reasons deduced through a process of analytic reduction, and that, in order to understand something as general as a 'social imaginary' (Taylor 2007: 171), one has – at the very least – to plunge into the entirety of its discourse, not simply the elements supporting a pre-curated, narrativized genealogy. A more materialist approach would treat every speech act in the so-called public sphere as potentially if not actually significant. It would pay attention to the density of ideas, their reproductivity, their material presence in books, pamphlets, etc., *as well as* their contribution to the genealogy (or genealogies) of ideas. From this perspective, it will always matter how many 'positive invocations of the body' we hear.

A critical genealogy of the secular must therefore expand the scope of engagement beyond the 'ultimate goods' of a given period. But it must also question the categories typically used to delineate the boundaries of historical relevance. Even if the authors of the radical Enlightenment were not as anti-transcendental as Taylor makes out, why accept their status as 'radical' in the first place? For Taylor, the mainstream implicitly or explicitly condenses around figures like Voltaire, Hume and Gibbon – especially the latter, and especially their more negative appraisals of embodied modes of subjectivity (e.g. religious 'enthusiasm' or 'fanaticism'). This is how he can summarize the eighteenth century as 'the time of Gibbon, Voltaire, and Hume' (546), directly mirroring Isaiah Berlin's claim that these three authors 'probably did more than anyone else to determine the entire direction of the Enlightenment' (1979: 92). Why is the eighteenth century the time of Gibbon, Voltaire and Hume? What was 'the entire direction of the Enlightenment' and on what basis did these three authors determine it?

Taylor's construct of a rationalist mainstream arguably depends upon two principles at the heart of *A Secular Age*: first, that what qualifies as mainstream depends on the same *a priori* assumptions used to delimit the field of Enlightenment itself. On this reading, a body of work is more or less central to the degree that it approaches a pre-established Enlightenment norm, i.e. rationalism, universalism, anti-emotionalism or disembodiment, that is never radically questioned.[14] Second, the idea of a rationalistic mainstream is *historically* supported by a crucial assumption concerning the rational nature of secular modernity. Despite his insistence on the plurality of contemporary secular and non-secular positions, Taylor sometimes shifts to a more generalized outlook in which the 'disengaged' (mainstream) position of Modern Exclusive Humanism is taken to characterize secularity as a whole – not just an option of late-modernity or a singular, ideal-type position in intellectual history but a ubiquitous fact of modern life. For example, while stating that 'This disengaged, disciplined stance to self and society has become part of *the essential defining repertory* of the modern identity', he also claims 'It is … a central feature of secularity' (2007: 136, emphasis mine). According to Taylor, Modern Exclusive Humanism 'corresponds to a powerful moral experience in the modern world' (251), since 'In general, [today] we relate to the world as more disembodied beings than our ancestors; that is, the centre of gravity of the person each one of us is, as we interact with others, has moved out of the body. It stands outside, in the agent of disengaged discipline, capable of dispassionate control' (141).

Has it? Do we really 'tend to live in our heads' (555)?[15] And can disembodiment or 'dispassionate control' be taken as *distinctive* to modern secularity? The claim that we are more dispassionately disciplined or 'head-centred' than our ancestors surely relies on a questionable erasure of practices of emotional and bodily control dating from at least the fifth-century BCE, whether Stoic, Buddhist or otherwise, regardless of the higher goods to which such practices pertained.[16] Yet although Taylor's anti-corporeal reading of late modernity might be dismissed as too idealistic, contradictory or vague, I suggest it helps us understand his construction of the 'mainstream' Enlightenment as inherently antithetical to the body; for it is *this* that is taken as the dominant ideology and social force behind the formation of modern secular subjectivity, not 'radical' Enlightenment.

Why? And what happens when we expand the scope of 'mainstream' Enlightenment to the 'radical' Enlightenment? Can we still take Hume and Gibbon's 'cool unflappability' or Descartes's 'disengaged reason' as representative of secular subjectivity in general? As I will show, insofar as we can speak of the eighteenth-century Enlightenment as a bounded historical period or set of discourses including the full range of 'classical' authors from Montesquieu to Diderot and Holbach, this period testifies to a rich and heterogeneous vocabulary of the passions, demonstrating an acute understanding of the limits of reason and the dependence of historical progress on extended projects of secular cultivation through practices of mind and body. These practices were generally aimed at buttressing the nascent nation-state, suggesting unexplored links between Enlightenment thought, secularism and nationalism.

Enlightenment passions: Mainstream and radical

This philosophical spirit ... which wishes to see everything and suppose nothing, has spread even to the Belles-Lettres *... Our century ... seems to want to introduce cold and didactic discussion even in matters of sentiment. It is not that the passions and good taste do not have their own Logic, but this Logic follows principles utterly different to that of ordinary Logic: it is these principles that we must unravel in us, and it is, one must admit, something for which a common Philosophy is poorly equipped.*

Jean le Rond d'Alembert, Preliminary Discourse of the *Encyclopédie*
(Diderot and d'Alembert 2016: xxxi)

... for the love of truth is also a passion.

Condorcet, *Outlines* (1796 [1795]: 256)

Enlightenment writers frequently elevated 'reason' as a dominating epistemological and ethical concept, and rejected the passions as forces detrimental to the progress of humanity. This point is too well known to merit demonstration. Nevertheless, the same Enlightenment also placed explicit limits on the hegemony of reason through increasing recognition of the power and non-negotiability of the passions. This was the case even for Taylor's mainstream: Voltaire stated that the passions are the true 'wheels' driving human beings and that 'instinct, more than reason, conducts human life' (Rasmussen 2014: 71, fn. 99). Montesquieu had earlier prescribed conducting the nation by its passion rather than its reason since '[reason] never produces any great effect in the mind of man' (1777a [1748]: 411). Later, the founding 'ideologist' Destutt de Tracy collapsed the distinction between sentiment and reason altogether, arguing that 'thinking ... is feeling, and nothing but feeling' (1817 [1804]: 24). Other less 'mainstream' thinkers like Helvétius celebrated a final consensus about 'the necessity of the passions', and La Mettrie concluded the passions were 'as necessary to man as the air he breathes' (Riskin 2002: 50). Rousseau even contrasted – unfavourably – the 'reasoning and philosophical spirit' whose 'philosophical indifference' constitutes the 'tranquillity of death', with the 'great and powerful passion' of fanaticism (Rothschild 2001: 26).

Praise for the passions was almost always advanced in the context of a defence of national values or patriotism. This tendency went back at least as far as Montesquieu's *The Spirit of the Laws* (1748). Here Montesquieu asked, 'What is meant by virtue in a political state?' His answer was straightforward: 'Virtue in a republic is a most simple thing: it is a love of the republic; it is a sensation, and not a consequence of acquired knowledge' (1777a [1748]: 52). Diderot's *Philosophical Thoughts* (1746) followed up these comments with an unequivocal endorsement of the passions articulated in terms of a need for patriotic 'love'. The very first lines of the book provide a vigorous defence of the passions:

> *Thought no. 1*: People are for ever declaiming against the passions; they attribute to them all the pains that man endures, and forget that they are also the source of all his pleasures. ... [I]t is the passions alone, and strong passions, that can elevate the soul to great things. Without them, there is no sublime, either in morality or in achievement; the fine arts return to puerility, and virtue becomes a pettifogging thing. (1916 [1746–1751]: 27)

For Diderot, it was pointless if not insane to seek 'the ruin of the passions', for in doing so, man would 'end by becoming a monster'. Even 'sober' or 'deadened' passions merely made men commonplace, putting the safety of the nation at risk. The nation required patriotism, and patriotism required strong feelings of love: 'If I hang back before the enemy, when my country's safety is at stake, I am but a poor citizen. … If life is dearer to me than my mistress, I am a poor lover'. Although the passions had to be kept in 'harmony' in order to purge society of 'libertines', 'rufflers' and 'poltroons' (27–9), the passions were not mere props or instrumental means to a rationally derived end. Like Descartes, Diderot considered the passions 'the source of all pleasures', whose absence did not simply weaken the quest for morality or 'achievement' but emptied this quest of 'sublimity'.[17]

Helvétius likewise considered the passions 'the seminal element of the mind [*le germe productif de l'esprit*] and the powerful spring propelling men to great deeds' (1759 [1758]: 297). To stifle the passions would be to forgo the most powerful means of shaping and maintaining national sovereignty. Instead the legislator should, like a carpenter who 'from a tree-trunk can make a God or a bench' (220), exploit and mould the raw material of popular passions into models of civic virtue. The passions were 'necessary in a nation', being 'its life and soul'. Those who had the strongest would always triumph, for it was not calm deliberation but imprudence and folly that ensured 'the preservation of empires and the duration of the world' (407, 583). Perhaps contradictorily, however, and unlike his fellow *Encyclopédistes*, Helvétius drew a line between fanaticism and patriotism, not because fanaticism was inherently problematic or dangerous, but because it would be ineffective in the long run. Whereas 'A fanatic courage quickly weakens and extinguishes', the courage born of patriotism has durability and hence is 'the only one with which a wise legislator should inspire his fellow citizens' (436).

Clearly, any modern secular association of emotion with religion, and rationality with secularism, was a distant and in many ways unthinkable prospect in the mid-eighteenth century, when the *philosophes* were as likely to attack religion for its repression or denigration of the emotions as for its excessive emotionality. It could be constructed both ways: as on one hand inducing excessive sensualism or fanaticism (coded to Oriental religion, usually Islam), and on the other a quietistic individualism, a *lack* of passion (also coded to Oriental religions, but Christianity, too), at odds with the social requirements for a healthy nation-state. Thus, Rousseau did not reproach Christianity for its emotionality but its otherworldly inwardness and slavish indifference to the interests of society. Christianity was 'a completely spiritual religion' narrowly focused on heavenly matters ('The homeland of the Christian is not of this world', 1986 [1762–1772]: 224) and therefore incapable of fostering the requisite affects and allegiances for a viable nation-state. It taught indifference, servitude and dependence, rendering its spirit 'too favourable to tyranny for tyranny not to take advantage of it at all times'. Christians were born slaves, yet were unmoved by this fact, for life had 'too little value in their eyes' (151).

Similarly, Constantin François de Chasseboeuf, Comte de Volney (1757– 1820) attacked Christian morality for being 'unfriendly to human intercourse' or 'a code of misanthropy, calculated to give men a disgust for life and society, and attach them to solitude and celibacy' (1795 [1791]: 306–7). Christianity deadened the passions – a deficiency counterposed by Volney to the excessive sensualism and passionality of Islam. Towards the end of *The Ruins* (1791), the Christian representative in Volney's imagined global assembly of religions explains the problem of 'religion' in terms of two extremes: Islam's 'fascination of all the passions' and Christianity's 'extinction of all the passions': '[The Qur'an] produces the attachment it requires, by every allurement of the senses, and the fascination of all the passions. How different is the character of the Christian doctrine! and how much does its empire, established on the wreck of every natural inclination and the extinction of all the passions, prove its celestial origin!' (1795 [1791]: 186).[18] Diderot, too, worried about the pernicious effects of excessive Christian enthusiasm on society – not because this would entail an excess of emotion but, on the contrary, because it might create 'a thousand pillars rising above the ruins of all social affections': 'a new race of Stylites stripping themselves from religious motives all natural feelings, ceasing to be men and becoming statues in order to be true Christians' (1916 [1746–1751]: 29).[19]

As noted above, Diderot, Montesquieu and especially Rousseau are ambiguous figures haunting the fringes of mainstream anti-emotionalism, thus Berlin's admission that Diderot was 'a major liberator of feeling and natural passion'. But what about the central representatives of the 'cold' and 'rational' Enlightenment accused by Berlin of uncritically repressing or seeking to destroy the passions, like Holbach?

The passions of Paul Henri Dietrich, Baron d'Holbach (1723–1789)

Hirschman has helpfully listed three Enlightenment strategies for dealing with the passions, all stemming from concerns to formulate an effective model of statecraft. First, 'coercion and repression', whereby the state was entrusted with the task of regulating the passions. According to Hirschman, 'This solution did not survive the detailed analysis of the passions in the seventeenth century' (1977: 15–16). Second, the 'harnessing' of the passions, whereby the state or society, no longer acts as 'a repressive bulwark', but a 'transformer' or 'civilizing medium' (16). Thus Vico argued for the channelling of the three vices of 'ferocity, avarice, and ambition' into the requirements of 'national defence, commerce, and politics', hoping to foster virtues of 'strength, wealth, and wisdom' in the new republic (17). Third, the principle of the 'countervailing passion': the idea, first formulated by Bacon and Spinoza, that the passions could only be fought with passions (22–3).[20]

Holbach shifted constantly between all three positions. He occasionally advocated repressing the passions, as, for example, in his eleventh *Letter to Eugenia*: 'If we reflect for one moment on the effects of the passions, we shall perceive the necessity of repressing them ... Everyone must perceive that in giving a free course to unbridled desires, he becomes the enemy of society, and then it is the part of the laws to restrain him who renounces his reason' (1857 [1768]: 249). Quite predictably, the passions here formed one facet of a negative cluster also made up of 'imagination', 'dangerous enthusiasm', 'superstition' and 'fanaticism' – all of which were opposed to reason and the well-being of the nation-state.

> A morality conformable to the good of the state ... would not form men who would hate each other for speculative opinions, nor dangerous enthusiasts, nor devotees blindly submissive to the priests. It would create ... a body of inhabitants submissive to reason and obedient to just and legitimate authority. In a word, from such morality would spring virtuous men and good citizens, and it would be the surest antidote against superstition and fanaticism. (1857 [1768]: 209)

According to Holbach, 'Truth ... is only conformity to reason' (30) and we therefore had to 'Let reason be our guide' (261). Moreover, the passions were closely linked to religion, which tended to unleash them and so compromise the autonomy of reason: 'The more we respect [religious] errors, the more play they give to our passions, the more they disturb our mind, the more irrational they render us, the greater influence they have on the whole conduct of our lives' (1889 [1770]: 263). From one perspective, Holbach was as thoroughly rationalist as one would expect for the 'cold' Enlightenment.

Yet Holbach was a many-sided thinker and his rationalistic attacks on the passions, enthusiasm and fanaticism were considerably nuanced, if not contradicted, by a number of statements in his monumental *Système de la Nature*

(1770). Here Holbach no longer sought to 'repress' or destroy the passions for reason's sake, but – like Senault and Descartes – to redirect or 'canalize' them towards the good of society (Hirschman's second strategy). Following the *Système*, man should abandon 'the vain project of destroying passions' and try, instead, to 'direct them towards objects that may be useful to himself and to his associates'. The passions should be given 'free course' whenever they led to 'real and durable advantages to society', and were dangerous 'only because everything conspire[d] to give them an evil direction' (72).

> [Man] is indeed incessantly exhorted to resist these passions; to stifle and root them out of his heart: but is it not evident they are necessary to his welfare, and inherent in his nature? ... [I]s it not easy to be seen, that these passions well directed ... would necessarily contribute to the substantial and permanent well-being of society? The passions of man are like fire, at once necessary to the wants of life, and equally capable of producing the most terrible ravages. (99)[21]

For Holbach, drawing on Pierre Bayle, it was futile to repress the passions, since 'it is not the opinions of man which determine his acts, but his passions' (309). To create passionless men was to create men who did not act – a critique which ironically extended to religion itself, the great unleasher of emotion. Indeed, although Holbach criticized religion for 'authorizing' and 'unchaining' the passions (104), he also criticized it for 'tell[ing] the sensible being to have no passions, to be an insensible mass, or to combat his propensities by motives borrowed from the imagination, and variable as itself' (280). It was not the *philosophes* but the priests who 'endeavoured to put to the rout all his passions, without any distinction even of those which are the most useful to himself, the most beneficial to those beings with whom he lives' (154). Again echoing Senault and Descartes, Holbach railed against the Stoics, 'those passionless philosophers', who were 'willing to smother this great, this noble spring of his soul' (134). By 'desiring [man] to stifle his desires, to combat his propensities, to annihilate his passions', the Stoics did nothing but straightjacket man in 'sterile precepts, at once vague and impracticable' (157). Christianity merely furthered Stoicism, transforming the people into 'herds of ignorant slaves' subjected to the arbitrary will of an absolute despot (313).

As well as seeking to repress and unleash the passions, Holbach also supported the third of Hirschman's three strategies: the strategy of the 'countervailing passion'. Parroting Diderot, Holbach claimed that it is 'upon the equilibrium of the humours that depends the state of the man who is called *virtuous*': 'his temperament seems to be the result of a combination, in which the elements or principles are balanced with such precision, that no one passion predominates over another' (75, emphasis original). The second and third strategies were sometimes combined within the same sentence: e.g. 'Passions are the true counterpoise to passions; then, let him not seek to destroy them, but let him endeavour to direct them; let him balance those which are prejudicial, by those which are useful to society' (158).

Holbach did not only seek to balance and moderate the passions, however. On one hand, he can be taken to endorse a kind of middle-way between excessive emotion and passionless torpor, since fanaticism made men dangerous and apathy made men socially redundant. On the other, his revolt against emotional suppression could extend even to moderate passions. Although occasionally insisting upon emotional equanimity, e.g. in his counsel to 'restrain his passions within those just bounds which experience and reason prescribe' (72)[22] or let nature 'moderate' the passions (280), Holbach agreed with Diderot that even to moderate desire was to place an artificial and hence negative restriction on human nature. Once more, it was not secularists who sought to moderate the passions but religion:

> The greater part of the precepts inculcated by religion, or which fanatical and supernatural morals give to man, are as ridiculous as they are impossible to be put into practice. To interdict passion to man, is to desire of him not to be a human creature; to counsel an individual of violent imagination to moderate his desires, is to advise him to change his temperament – to request his blood to flow more sluggishly. (158)

Strong desire was not itself a problem. On the contrary, 'The man who is of a sanguine, robust constitution, must necessarily have strong passions' (75). As for Descartes, these strong passions simply required directing towards the proper ends, e.g. universal human happiness: 'Reason by no means forbids man from forming capacious desires; ambition is a passion useful to his species, when it has for its object the happiness of his race' (149).

Of course, it may be argued that Holbach valued the passions only insofar as they served an expedient function, as instruments towards the final, rationally derived telos of mutual benefit or universal happiness – the basis of a shift towards pure immanence, according to Taylor. As already noted above, however, Holbach (one-third of the 'radical Enlightenment') did not simply jettison appeals to the highest or transcendence but reframed these in national or civic terms. Properly directed, enthusiasm for 'transcendent virtues' itself conduced to moral excellence, since it excited in man 'that rapidity of motion which is approved when good results' (64). Holbach understood nationalism as itself a transcendent virtue and, like Senault and Descartes, considered the passions constitutive of the good itself. To reach the end goal and give up the passions which led us there would mean surrendering a fundamental aspect of what makes us human, where humanity was itself a matter of visceral, emotional, national commitment.

Cartesian influence

Holbach was highly critical of Descartes throughout the _Système_, and often for the very reasons levelled by Taylor against the mainstream Enlightenment: because Descartes advocated a distancing from and devaluation of the body. According to Holbach, Descartes 'assured us, that the body went absolutely for nothing in the sensations or ideas of the soul; that it can feel – that it can perceive, understand, taste and touch, even when there should exist nothing that is corporeal or material exterior to ourselves' (76). Holbach repeatedly attacked the doctrine of innate ideas and seemed unfamiliar with the nascent empiricism of Descartes's later work. If he had read the _Passions_, he did not admit it.

Yet it is unnecessary to postulate an undisclosed debt here, since Holbach explicitly links the _Système_ to Senault's _De l'Usage des Passions_ (1641), thereby establishing at least a secondary link between Holbach and the later Descartes. In a footnote to the _Système_, Holbach writes: 'Theologians themselves, have felt, they have acknowledged, the necessity of the passions: many of the fathers of the church have broached this doctrine; among the rest Father Senault has written a book expressly on the subject, entitled, _Of the Use of the Passions_' (99). Holbach's debt to Senault is obvious throughout the _Système_, not only through his general treatment of the passions, which parallels _De l'Usage_ exactly, but also through more or less direct reproductions of certain passages, e.g. on the Stoics. Compare for example Holbach's warning that 'To interdict passion to man, is to desire of him not to be a human creature' (158), with Senault's that 'to [destroy the passions] a man must destroy himself' (1641: 20–1, 129).

What makes Holbach's debt to Senault doubly interesting is that, having read _De l'Usage_, Holbach would have been well aware of the capacity for what he calls 'religion' to absorb such emotionalist work. Unlike the _Système_, _De l'Usage_ was not proscribed by the Catholic Church and was not placed on the Index. The _Système_'s theory of the passions was in fact representative of at least one orthodox strand of thought _within_ the religious fold. Holbach would have known this, and so it is difficult to avoid the conclusion that Holbach very deliberately misrepresented the religious stance to emotion, likely under two pressures: first, the pressure of his (and other *philosophes'*) negative socio-political project to disestablish the Catholic Church in France; but also, I suggest, to give weight to his positive project of not destroying but reorienting the passions towards the imagined community and values of the emerging nation-state in freedom from the clutch of 'religion'. By tying religion to an inadequate conception of emotionality, Holbach was able to justify its redundancy to the project of building up the necessary structure of affects for a viable nationalism.

I will turn to this problem shortly but must first examine a facet of Enlightenment thought that is essential to understanding why Holbach and others insisted so strongly on the importance of emotion during the eighteenth century: the rise to predominance of Lockean empiricism.

Worldly bodies: Empiricism, free will and temperament

It is now generally understood that if a single epistemology were taken as definitive of the eighteenth-century Enlightenment, this would not be rationalism but Lockean empiricism. According to the *Stanford Encyclopaedia of Philosophy*, Locke's *Essay Concerning Human Understanding* (1690) 'exerts tremendous influence on the age', primarily through Condillac's *Traité des Sensations* (1754).

> Despite the confidence in and enthusiasm for human reason in the Enlightenment … the rise of empiricism, both in the practice of science and in the theory of knowledge, is characteristic of the period. The enthusiasm for reason in the Enlightenment is not for the faculty of reason as an independent source of knowledge (at least not primarily), which is actually put on the defensive in the period, but rather for the human cognitive faculties generally; the Age of Reason contrasts with an age of religious faith, not with an age of sense experience. (Bristow 2017: unpaginated)

It is simply false that, as Berlin argued, the Enlightenment endorsed an anti-empiricist closure of the self from its surroundings, the senses, or man's physical environment. Locke was read and appreciated by all the *philosophes* without exception. Voltaire's pioneering work of science-fiction, *Micromégas* (1752), explicitly cites Locke as the pinnacle of modern philosophy, superseding Aristotle, Descartes, Malebranche and Leibniz.[23] The opening pages of d'Alembert's famous 'Discours Préliminaire' laid down the axiom that 'All direct knowledge is reducible to what is received through the senses; whence it follows that it is to our sensations that we owe all our ideas' (Diderot and d'Alembert 2016 [1751–1782]: I. ii). According to Holbach, '[man's mind] can understand either well or ill only those things which it has previously felt' (1889 [1770]: 84). Reason was 'the fruit of experience' (158; 1790: 37) and truth the product of a 'faithful relation' to the senses:

> At each moment of his existence man gathers experience; every sensation he has furnishes a fact that deposits in his brain an idea, which his memory recalls with more or less fidelity: these facts connect themselves, these ideas are associated, and their chain constitutes *experience* and *science*. Knowledge is that consciousness which arises from reiterated experience, of the sensations, of the ideas, of the effects which an object is capable of producing, either in ourselves or in others. All science must be founded on truth. Truth itself rests on the constant and faithful relation of our senses. (1889 [1770]: 64, emphasis original)

Condorcet began his *Outlines of an Historical View of the Progress of the Human Mind* (1795) by declaring 'Man is born with the faculty of receiving sensations' (1796 [1795]: 9) and later praised Aristotle for handing down the idea that 'OUR IDEAS, EVEN SUCH AS ARE MOST ABSTRACT, MOST STRICTLY INTELLECTUAL ... HAVE THEIR ORIGIN IN OUR SENSATIONS' (1796 [1795]: 91, capitals in original).[24] The *Encyclopédie* stated that 'there is nothing innate except the faculty of feeling and thinking: all the rest is acquired' (Vyverberg 1989: 42). For Diderot (a close acquaintance of Condillac), empiricism was the foundation of morality, since 'our virtues depend on the sensations we receive, and the degree by which we are affected by external things' (1916 [1746–1751]: 81–2).[25] As Riskin sums up the situation, insofar as the Enlightenment centred around a 'single ideal', this could be summed up in terms of our 'receptiveness to a world outside the mind, a world that imposed its claims through the senses' (2002: 10).

A shift towards the senses was, of course, a shift towards the body. Reflecting on the relation between metaphysics, morality and the senses, Diderot added: 'As to me it has always been very clear that the state of our organs and our senses has a great influence on our metaphysics and our morality, and that those ideas which seem purely intellectual are closely dependent on the conformation of our bodies' (1916 [1746–1751]: 80). For Buffon, only physical touch could convey a 'complete and real knowledge' of the outer world and convince us we were not alone; this is why he thought 'animals who have hands seem the most spiritual' (Riskin 2002: 48). Similarly, Montesquieu poked fun at contemporary Stoics or 'neo-Stoics' for ignoring the power of the body to condition the soul. Unlike

Europeans, canny 'Asians' did not resort to Seneca and other Stoics to manage their travails, but to chemical concoctions. They altered the body to alter the mind: 'When some ill fortune befalls a European', says Usbek, Montesquieu's fictionalized alter-ego in *Lettres Persanes*, 'he can do nothing except read a philosopher called Seneca: but Asians, being more sensible … take concoctions capable of making man happy, and enchanting the recollection of his woes' (1973 [1721]: 108). Like the later Descartes, Montesquieu-Usbek considered the soul profoundly joined to, and therefore affected by, the body:

> The soul, united to the body, is ceaselessly tyrannized by it. If the blood's movement is too slow, if the spirits are not purified enough, if there are too little of them, we fall into despondency and misery: but if we take concoctions that can alter the disposition of our body, our soul regains its ability to receive joyful impressions, and it feels a secret pleasure at seeing its machine regain, so to speak, its motion and its life. (108)[26]

Thus, he concluded: 'It is much better to withdraw the spirit from its reflexions, and treat man as sensible, instead of treating him as reasonable' (108). Empiricism could not but force a confrontation with – and revaluation of – the body, its sense structure and the external world.

Mind–body dualism and the worldliness of reason

Holbach clearly considered himself an adversary of mind–body dualism. He strongly criticized 'those who still obstinately persist in making the soul a substance distinguished from the body' (1889 [1770]: 76). For Holbach the soul could not be distinguished from the body since it was itself an emergent property of the body and the arrangement of its parts:

> Is it not evident that the soul depends on the arrangement of the various parts of the body, and on the order with which these parts conspire to perform their functions or motions? Thus, the organic structure once destroyed, can it be doubted the soul will be destroyed also? … An organized being may be compared to a clock, which, once broken, is no longer suitable to the use for which it was designed. To say, that the soul shall feel, shall think, shall enjoy, shall suffer, after the death of the body, is to pretend that a clock, shivered into a thousand pieces, will continue to strike the hour, and have the faculty of marking the progress of time. (119)

This was a basic reiteration of Descartes's late theory of the soul and his claim that '[the soul] is related solely to the whole assemblage of the body's organs'

(1985a [1649]: 340). Nevertheless, Holbach went further than Descartes in collapsing the gap between soul and body. For him, the soul did not simply depend on the body but was of the same nature: 'man has made himself double, has distinguished his mind from his body, supposed it of a nature different from all known beings' (1889 [1770]: 159) – an ontological conflation typically understood in terms of a materialist reduction. For Holbach, 'the wants of the mind, as well as those of the body, are purely physical' (160): 'the interior organ of man, which is called his *soul*, is purely material. He will be enabled to convince himself of this truth, by the manner in which he acquires his ideas; from those impressions, which material objects successively make on his organs, which are themselves acknowledged to be material' (76, emphasis original). Holbach's identification of soul and body stemmed from his empiricism, which threw the soul into contact with the body and its sense impressions. The idea that the soul could 'perceive, understand, taste and touch, even when there should exist nothing that is corporeal or material exterior to ourselves' was absurd. As for Descartes, the apprehensions of the soul depended absolutely on the presence of external objects that 'beat on the senses', and the soul could not 'move itself ... without being determined to such action by any exterior object' (76). Indeed, a natural extension of Holbach's empiricism and reembodiment of soul and mind was a recognition of the extent of environmental influence on the formation of temperament.

> It is from nature – from his parents – from causes, which from the first moment of his existence have unceasingly modified him, that man derives his temperament. It is in his mother's womb that he has attracted the matter which, during his whole life, shall have an influence on his intellectual faculties – on his energies – on his passions – on his conduct. The very nourishment he takes, the quality of the air he respires, the climate he inhabits, the education he receives, the ideas that are presented to him, the opinions he imbibes, modify this temperament. (61)[27]

The causal linkage of external reality and soul entailed not only a materialist reduction of spirit to flesh, and a consequent externalization of sources of the good (more on this below), but a revaluation of the body as a constitutive element of the soul and its 'ideas'. Holbach rejected out of hand the claims of 'Descartes and his disciples', who deceived us into thinking 'the body went absolutely for nothing in the sensations or ideas of the soul' (76). The body was central to our interactions with the world and hence to our ideas, 'opinions' and even 'reason', which emerged as a secondary product of experience.[28]

The source of [man's] errors arises from this, that he regards his body as gross and inert, whilst this body is a sensible machine, which has necessarily an instantaneous conscience the moment it receives an impression, and which is conscious of its own existence by the recollection of impressions successively experienced; memory, by resuscitating an impression anteriorly received, by detaining it, or by causing an impression which it receives to remain, whilst it associates it with another, then with a third, gives all the mechanism of *reasoning*. (79, emphasis original)

Taylor's association of the Enlightenment with a 'stance of disengagement' wherein 'The body tends to fall away' (2007: 288) in proportion to the elevation of reason clearly makes no sense here. It is not simply that 'rationalists' like Holbach or Diderot consistently sought to rehabilitate the body and passions at the centre of the Enlightenment's 'discourse of pure reason'. Eighteenth-century empiricism dictated that reason and the body could not be understood in isolation from each other; the body and the external world were essentially, not contingently, imbricated in processes of reasoning. For Holbach and others, thought itself was the action of 'receiving or retracing the impressions left by external objects or organs of the body upon the self' (1790: 25).

Free will and the alteration of temperament

The reembodiment of reason had critical implications for the autonomy of the will, since the tracing of reason to externally acquired sense data led Holbach to the same issue confronting Descartes in the *Passions*, namely, where to situate agency. Unlike Descartes, however, who still equivocated on the impossibility of free will – sometimes insisting that reason or the will dictated the passions, sometimes that the passions could influence the will – Holbach pushed his materialist determinism to a radically fatalistic conclusion: since the will was determined by a multiplicity of external objects whose cumulative effect was beyond calculation, man was not – could not be – free. Insofar as agency existed at all, Holbach situated it in 'Nature', not man.

The errors of philosophers on the free agency of man, have arisen from their regarding his will as the *primum mobile,* the original motive of his actions; for want of recurring back, they have not perceived the multiplied, the complicated causes which, independently of him, give motion to the will itself; or which dispose and modify his brain, whilst he himself is purely passive in the motion he receives. (1889 [1770]: 94, 62)

While 'speculators ... shut their eyes to the necessary and continual correspondence which is found between the mind and the body', Holbach insisted that the will, the activity of the passions and 'the continual regeneration of desires' arose out of 'that activity which is produced on the body by material objects which are not under [the mind's] control, and that these objects render it either happy or miserable, active or languishing, contented or discontented, *in despite of itself and of all the efforts it is capable of making to render it otherwise*' (160, emphasis mine). In his later *Éléments de la Morale Universelle, ou Catéchisme de la Nature* (1790), Holbach discussed the question of whether the passions always determined the will or actions. His answer was that they do not, not because reason or the will ultimately dominated the passions, but because the passions could be opposed by contrary passions. For Holbach, 'choosing' was never the act of a sovereign, decision-making self, but a matter of domination by the stronger of two or more passions, which carried or 'dragged' the will along with it:

> Q.   Does a passion always determine man's will, or always make him act?
> A.   It always makes him act when its effect or impulse is not blocked by another passion; in the opposite case, his will is not determined, and the action is therefore suspended. ...
> Q.   What is choosing?
> A.   It is to be determined by the stronger of the passions; it carries the will along. (1790: 8–11)

Holbach's strict determinism is completely incompatible with the hegemony of reason or will endorsed by the Stoics/neo-Stoics and – according to Taylor – definitive of the eighteenth century. The power of environmental context and education to alter man's dispositions or temperament entailed that man's choices were generated and restricted by the unique historical circumstances in which he developed. For Holbach, 'our thoughts are always involuntary': 'Man is not ... for one instant, the master of his ideas, which are every moment excited by objects over which he has no control, and causes which depend not on his will or exertions'. He cites Augustine to this effect: '"There is not," says he, "one man who is at all times master of that which presents itself to his spirit"' (1857 [1768]: 261–2).

Belief in 'the God of Nature' (279–80) did not entail that man was entirely powerless to shape his destiny, however. On the contrary, recognizing the importance of environmental context and the body's insertion in that context was the first step towards a viable theory of cultivated virtue based on a reorganization of man's total environment: physical, social and intellectual. In an almost verbatim repetition of Descartes, Holbach speculated that, just as animals had passions that could be 'modified', man's temperament – utterly devoid of innate qualities – was infinitely capable of correction and modification by 'causes as physical as the matter of which it is constituted' (1889 [1770]: 62). Thus,

> We are all in some measure capable of forming our own temperament: a man of a sanguine constitution, by taking less juicy nourishment, by abating its quantity, by abstaining from strong liquor, etc., may achieve the correction of the nature, the quality, the quantity, the tendency, the motion of the fluids, which predominate in his machine. A bilious man, or one who is melancholy, may, by the aid of certain remedies, diminish the mass of this bilious fluid; he may correct the blemish of his humours by the assistance of exercise; he may dissipate his gloom by the gaiety which results from increased motion. (62)

Never completely in control at the singular moment of the decision, man could nevertheless predispose himself to virtue indirectly, by a long process of self-fashioning through the manipulation of external factors. Temperament, agency and indeed reason itself, emerged from historically contingent material and ideological structures that preceded and disciplined the 'autonomous' will; for Holbach as much as for Augustine, 'It was not the mind that moved spontaneously to religious truth, but power that created the conditions for experiencing that truth' (Asad 1993: 35).

Imagination

As noted earlier, Berlin, like so many before and after him, considered the Enlightenment absolutely antithetical to imagination. 'Phantasms' or 'chimera' of the imagination were almost by definition opposed to Enlightenment 'facts' and tied fundamentally to religion. A similar point is made by Asad when opposing the pre-modern, religious worldview to the modern secular, in an attempt to refine Benedict Anderson's theory of secular homogeneous time:

> What needs to be emphasized beyond Anderson's famous thesis is that the complex medieval Christian universe, with its interlinked times ... and hierarchy of spaces ... is broken down by the modern doctrine of secularism into a duality: a world of self-authenticating things in which we *really* live as social beings and a religious world that exists only in our imagination. (2003: 194, emphasis original)

For Berlin and Asad, the 'modern doctrine of secularism' evinces a clear-cut rejection of the imagination as fundamentally tied to religion. For the former, it took a Counter-Enlightenment revolt against ahistorical reason to rehabilitate the imagination as a central aspect of national identity and revolutionary self-determination. For the latter, the idea that 'the imagination and reason have little commerce with each other' was typical of the Enlightenment (2003: 28, 44).

There is indeed a rich discourse attacking the imagination at all levels of the Enlightenment. Condorcet railed against the establishment of the Church, since in this act 'we observe advancing ... the art of deceiving men in order to rob them, and of assuming over their opinions an authority founded on the hopes and fears of the imagination' (1796 [1795]: 34). Holbach himself suggested that 'To combat the religious opinions of men, is to combat with their imagination' and 'The more imagination men have, the greater enthusiasts will they be in matters of religion, and reason will be less capable of undeceiving them of their chimeras' (1889 [1770]: 294). Religious imagination was particularly tied to fear, since 'Fear has made Gods', which in turn exacerbated the incompatibility of imagination and reason, since 'it is impossible to reason when we tremble' (297).

Imagination was also a foundation for intersubjective inscrutability and dispute, since it denoted an internal condition wherein 'the phantoms which are presented to [man's] imagination are incapable of being considered in the same light by all who contemplate them' (74). The content of imagination was, however, fixed by *external* conditions – conditions masterfully manipulated by the priesthood, who placed frightening and enchanting pictures before man's eyes:

> [To erect the empire of fanaticism and imagination] with more certainty, [the perfidious ministers of religion] have unceasingly terrified mortals with hideous paintings, have astonished and seduced them by marvels and mysteries, embarrassed them by enigmas and uncertainties, surcharged them with observances and ceremonies, filled their minds with terrors and scruples, and fixed their eyes upon a future, which, far from rendering them more virtuous and happy here below, has only turned them from the path of true happiness, and destroyed it completely and forever in their bosoms. (1857 [1768]: 5)[29]

There is no doubt that, at one level, imagination was a serious adversary in the fight against religion. To direct men away from religion would entail a total overhaul of their lived environment, the erasure of fearful religious objects and representations, and, potentially, the blanket destruction of all imagination in favour of reason and the raw, objective – i.e. intersubjectively certifiable – facts of experience.

Yet precisely because the imagination was so powerful, it was not necessarily the case that it could or even should be destroyed. As Vyverberg notes, the imagination could play a positive role in the Enlightenment, e.g. in the *Encyclopédie*'s prescription for the collaboration of reason with 'the faculty of imagination' – a point which Vyverberg reads as 'quite in line with the Enlightenment in general' (1989: 36–7). Just as the passions and habits could usefully be redirected towards secular ends (the ends of the nation-state), so could the imagination. Thus Holbach did not seek to destroy the imagination any more than he did the passions, for the imagination was 'by far the most lively faculty of the mind' (1857 [1768]: 257). Not only was the imagination a fundamental component of thought itself, allowing the recollection and synthesis of images impressed on the mind by the senses,[30] but a vivid imagination was characteristic of good health: it marked the difference between a vigorous and a torpid constitution.[31] Predictably, the imagination, like enthusiasm or fanaticism, was defended for its power to buttress national sentiment, or *love of country*:

> *Imagination,* when it wanders, produces fanaticism – religious terrors – inconsiderate zeal – frenzy – the most enormous crimes. When imagination is well regulated, it gives birth to a strong predilection for useful objects – an energetic passion for virtue – an enthusiastic love of our country – the most ardent friendship: the man who is divested of imagination, is commonly one in whose torpid constitution phlegm predominates over that sacred fire, which is the great principle of his mobility, of his warmth of sentiment, and which vivifies all his intellectual faculties. (1889 [1770]: 64)

Fifty years before the *Système*, Montesquieu prescribed 'imagination' and 'education' as primary means of 'modifying' the passion of glory 'engraved' on the heart (1973 [1721]: 213). Twenty years later, Charles Maurice de Talleyrand-Périgord's (1754–1838) *Rapport sur l'Instruction Publique* (1791) criticized the reason-imagination opposition, arguing that the 'ancient divisions' between 'Memory', 'Imagination' and 'Reason' were no longer viewed as fixed (*irrévocablement fixées*) but 'incomplete and arbitrary' (1791: 14). More recently, Landy and Saler have linked mid-eighteenth-century theories of imagination to the birth of modern fiction, or 'the possibility for experiencing fiction as the site of a disenchanted enchantment, one which is "real" only as long as the story lasts' (2009: 11–12). Yet for many of the *philosophes*, including those most typically associated with 'cold rationalism', imagination was part and parcel of the politics of everyday life and a key ingredient of man's general 'intellectual faculties'.[32]

Historical assemblages: Opaque selves and the chaos of history

'In all [history] we see the operation of one principle, namely human reason, which endeavors to produce unity out of multiplicity, order out of disorder, and out of a variety of powers and designs one symmetrical and durably beautiful whole'. These rationalistic lines, written by the Counter-Enlightenment philosopher Johann Gottfried Herder in *Outlines of a Philosophy of the History of Man* (1803 [1784]: 294), were, by the end of the eighteenth century, radically at odds with the Enlightenment's understanding of affect, habit and political power. Many Enlightenment philosophers, and especially the *économistes* (Turgot, Condorcet, Adam Smith, etc.), underlined the contingency of social forces and their resistance to rational ordering and prediction. For Turgot, economic life was 'a system of sentiments', a 'multitude of obscure facts', a 'mass of unknown causes' which 'combine with one another and change the prices of things which can be bought and sold'. Condorcet resisted the idea that economic relationships are 'susceptible of the order or regularity of "absolute and precise truths," or of "general principles of mechanics,"' for economic life is rather a 'mass of operations carried out, in an independent manner, by a large number of men, and directed by interest, the opinion, by the instinct, so to speak, of each of them' (Rothschild 2001: 236).[33] According to Rothschild, this is 'an unpromising territory for the spirit of system, which is "dazzled by an idea or a principle" and which "wishes to know everything, explain everything, arrange everything"' (236). It is closer to Nietzsche's naturalized ontology – an ontology that, in Cox's words, 'explains all entities on a single model, as assemblages of "dynamic quanta," the incessant change and transformation of which is the result of successful and unsuccessful attempts by each assemblage to extend its control over environing assemblages' (Cox 1999: 79).

For Holbach, too, the eruption of great historical figures or events, e.g. Genghis Khan, stemmed from a quasi-random 'assemblage' of forces – pre-cognitive, affective, historical. Just as a single spark could set alight 'millions of other contiguous grains, of which the united and multiplied powers, terminate by blowing up mountains, overthrowing fortifications, or converting populous cities into heaps of ruins', so 'imperceptible causes, concealed in the bosom of nature until the moment their action is displayed, frequently decide the fate of man'. The 'happiness' or 'wretchedness' of individuals or whole nations were attached to powers man could not foresee, appreciate or stop. 'Perhaps, *at this moment*', Holbach speculated, 'atoms are amassing, insensible particles are combining, of which the assemblage shall form a sovereign, who will be either the scourge or the saviour of a mighty empire' (1889 [1770]: 116, emphasis original). In this radically unpredictable world, even a good book, 'by touching the heart', could influence a prince and determine the destiny of the human race (101). Forces fluctuated, disassociated and rejoined in assemblages of power channelled through environmental conditioning factors (social pressure, discourse, etc.) and habits. Man could not 'answer for his destiny one single instant' (116) but was enmeshed in a network of habits and affects beyond consciousness and calculation that occasionally gave rise to great political turmoil, as in the case of Alexander or Muhammed:

> An idea, which is only an imperceptible modification of the brain, gives play to the organ of speech, which displays itself by the motion it excites in the tongue: this, in its turn, breeds ideas, thoughts, passions, in those beings who are provided with organs susceptible of receiving analogous motion; in consequence of which, the wills of a great number of men are influenced, who, combining their efforts, produce a revolution in a state, or even have an influence over the entire globe. It is thus that an Alexander decided the fate of Asia; it is thus that a Mahomet changed the face of the earth; it is thus that imperceptible causes produce the most terrible, the most extended effects, by a series of necessary motions imprinted on the brain of man. (79)[34]

Man's historicity not only undermined the possibility of complete motivational and causal transparency; it was a further check on the doctrine of free will, since connections between his feelings, ideas and actions were both out of his control and lost to memory. Man was fundamentally opaque to himself: 'he is not master of recalling to himself his ideas at pleasure; their association is independent of him; they are arranged in his brain in despite of him and without his own knowledge, where they have made an impression more or less profound' (93).[35] Holbach's self was traversed by forces outside its control, driven by hidden passions and the contingencies of circumstance. His understanding of character formation was thoroughly embodied, not to say Pavlovian, in its insistence on the power of conditioning and experiential association to shape temperament, character and agency. If people moved around and acted upon things, this was not because the mind moved the body, but the body the mind: the latter was prompted by the former '*frequently without [the mind's] own cognizance, and often in despite of itself*' (160, emphasis mine), having been conditioned to react before the event by long histories of association and habituation.[36] This is very far from the immanent clarity and autonomous reason that Taylor takes to define Modern Exclusive Humanism.

Conclusion

There is a tendency now to think of secularization or modernity as entailing the
domination of reason and immanent self-clarity over the regressive forces of
religion and especially religious 'passions'. On this understanding, secularization
was contingent on the erasure or repression of emotions, since emotions were
almost by definition incompatible with the secular foregrounding of pure
reason, and this especially in the realm of political contestation labelled the
'public sphere'. Kant is important here. Towards the beginning of *A Secular Age*,
Taylor cites Louis Sébastien Mercier (1740–1814) to the effect that:

> Good books depend on enlightenment in all classes of the people; they adorn
> the truth. It is they who already govern Europe; they enlighten the government
> about its duties, its shortcomings, its true interest, and the public opinion to
> which it must listen and conform: these good books are patient masters that
> wait for the state administrators to awaken and for their passions to subside.
> (2007: 189)

Immediately after this passage, perhaps significantly drawn from Habermas's
The Structural Transformation of the Public Sphere (1989), Taylor notes that
'Kant famously had a similar view' (189).

This view clearly construes the public sphere as a rational entity: 'By going
public, legislative deliberation informs public opinion and allows it to be
maximally-rational'; the public sphere is 'a locus in which rational views are
elaborated which should guide government' (189). The Kantian or neo-Kantian
(Rawlsian, Habermasian) take-away message is clear: secularization means
rationalization and rationalization means the deadening or 'calming' of the
passions. This elevation of reason can then be projected onto the 'mainstream'
Enlightenment if not the Enlightenment as a whole and understood as a motive
force behind the secular emancipation from religion that culminated in the
French Revolution – perhaps *the* founding moment of secular modernity.

As the foregoing has shown, however, between 1750 and 1790 a growing
recognition of the force of the passions and culturally embedded processes of
habituation significantly altered the way French philosophers discussed and
problematized religion. During this time, the 'calming of the passions' which
Taylor and Habermas associate with secularization could be – and usually was –
linked to religion. Insofar as a 'public sphere' emerged out of the Enlightenment,
the *philosophes'* own perception of this sphere was fundamentally non- or
postrational. Public opinion or the public will were conceived in terms of a

constant and unpredictable flow of passions, against Christianity, and against the 'elite' and idealistic program of neo-Stoicism.[37]

In the following chapter, I consider some of the practical implications of this more 'baroque' past (Riskin 2002: 10). How did the *philosophes* envisage putting these theories into action or translating them into policy? How would they seek to reorient people's dispositions away from religion and towards the nation-state? According to Asad, the eighteenth-century unification and essentialization of the self helped subjects become 'object[s] of social discipline' (2003: 74). But what forms of governance stemmed from a *de-essentialization* of the self under the radical Enlightenment? How exactly were secularism and nationalism to be cultivated and inculcated in an already postrationalist context?

Enlightened bodies II: The crafting of a secular-national subject

Thus success, as all history proves, constantly attends the people who are animated by strong passions: a truth too little known, the ignorance of which has opposed the progress that might otherwise have been made in the art of inspiring the passions: this art is at present unknown even to those politicians of reputation who calculate pretty justly the interest and strength of a state, but have never perceived the singular resources, which, in critical conjunctures, might have been drawn from the passions, when people have the art of exciting them.

Claude Adrien Helvétius, De l'Esprit (1759 [1758]: 217)

Introduction

Historically, the contrast between universal Enlightenment and particular tradition has functioned as a well-known imperialist device, legitimizing the expansion of Western 'secular' civilizations into colonized territories, a device which today thrives in the context of anti-immigration and a perceived confrontation between our Enlightenment 'values' and their 'culture' or 'customs'.[1] Former Volkspartij voor Vrijheid en Democratie (People's Party for Freedom and Democracy) leader and European commissioner Frits Bolkestein has warned about 'the dire consequences of accepting too many Muslim immigrants, whose customs [clash] with "our fundamental values"' (Buruma 2006: 29). On this account, joining the Dutch national majority is construed as a process of jettisoning regionally specific, contingently sedimented habits in favour of timeless European values or principles, since the former – unlike the latter – are historically cultivated and therefore indecipherable to and unregulatable by a secular logic of unmediated rational speech acts in the public sphere. Secularism demands that culture give way to 'principle', or the unchanging, universal demands of the natural unconditioned being – a being usually attributed to the Enlightenment. As Ayaan Hirsi Ali explains to Ian Buruma, 'the great thing about the Enlightenment ... is that "it strips away culture, and leaves only the individual"' (Buruma 2006: 168). Similarly, anthropologist Clifford Geertz claimed that '[Anthropology and the Enlightenment] endeavour to construct an image of man as a model, an archetype, a Platonic idea or an Aristotelian form. In the Enlightenment case, the elements of this essential type were to be uncovered by stripping the trappings of culture away from actual men and seeing what was then left – natural man' (1973: 50). For some, Enlightenment universalism presented the ideological equivalent of a get-out-of-jail card; for others, it acted as a veil on the ongoing power of the symbolic and affectual, and sanctioned the spread of Western bullets and bacillus across the globe. Both supporters and critics of the Enlightenment agree that it entailed a rejection of culture. But how exactly did the Enlightenment bring about this process of cultural exorcism, particularly given its recognition, examined in the previous chapter, of the non-negotiability of the body?

Emma Rothschild and Albert Hirschman have highlighted the close relation between Enlightenment thought on the passions and eighteenth-century projects to construct and make over the secular nation-state. Enlightenment discourses of emotion were not simply about forming 'morality and religion' but managing the general will or public opinion; in other words, *statecraft*.[2] Drawing on Tocqueville, Rothschild explains that the role of the state for *Économistes* like Adam Smith or Denis Diderot was '"not only to command the nation, but to shape it in a certain way"; to "form the spirit of the citizens," to imbue them with the "ideas" and "sentiments" which the state itself deems "necessary"' (2001: 34). As she concludes,

> One crime of the enlightenment was to have led other people into sin; but the crime of wishing to reconstruct the minds of other men was in a different version more sinister. For it was to make a religion out of irreligion. A subset of the 'sect of philosophers' were in Lammenais's description 'apostles of impiety'. Voltaire was for them 'the priest of reason'; they were willing, in their 'blind fanaticism', to sacrifice entire societies to their principles. This was the quasi-religious spirit of the *Économistes* or Physiocrats, for Tocqueville, and the spirit of the Jacobin principles. It was the spirit of Robespierre's religion of the Supreme Being, and of the revolutionary project (Talleyrand's project, in his revolutionary period) of a public education which would 'imprint, for ever, new sentiments, new morals, new habits'. (2001: 35)

According to Hirschman, the rehabilitation of the passions during the eighteenth century did not stem from a new ethic or 'new rules of conduct for the *individual*' but from 'a new turn in the theory of the *state*' aimed at 'improving statecraft within the existing order' (1977: 12, emphasis original).

This chapter points to ways in which empiricism and theories of the passions shaped practical guidelines for the cultivation of virtue in the French, pre- and post-revolutionary state. Focusing on a range of documents, from Holbach's *Système de la Nature* (1770) to Talleyrand's *Rapport sur l'Instruction Publique* (1791), I argue for an intimate relationship between Enlightenment empiricism, pedagogy and statecraft in mid- to late-eighteenth-century France, suggesting that the diversity of Enlightenment ideas surrounding people's education cannot be understood in isolation from the project of building up a French national imaginary on solid, affective foundations. This was an inherently cultural project, in which the limits of reason were acknowledged and embraced by the very 'rationalist' proponents of Enlightenment criticized by Berlin and Taylor in the previous chapter.

To emphasize the heavily nationalist dimension of French educational reform, I begin by dispelling the popular myth of Enlightenment 'universalism' according to which the Enlightenment was opposed in principle to the regressive and parochial force of the national particular. I show that, on the contrary, a heartfelt sense of historical, geographical and racial belonging was an essential ingredient of the French Enlightenment, while universalism was routinely attributed to its principal enemy, Catholic Christianity. I then provide a critique of Talal Asad (2003) and Saba Mahmood's (2009) 'habit-blind' understanding of the secular, considering various ideas advanced by enlightened reformers that leaned upon the habits and emotion as the cruxes of a sound education. Not only did the eighteenth-century French Enlightenment *not* reject the habits, but it actively fostered and regulated them, provided they supported the national project. I end with a brief discussion of Immanuel Kant and his retroactive, rationalizing effect upon the Enlightenment, suggesting that intellectual histories of the West, and especially genealogies of the secular like Taylor's, must look beyond Kant to grasp the full scale of the Enlightenment's engagement with the body.

Universal Enlightenment

The opposition between universalist Enlightenment and particularist Counter-Enlightenment (or religion) is now part of the standard discourse on the genealogy of modernity. In 2010, Owen and Owen still alleged that 'universalism is constitutive of the Enlightenment, asserting the priority of reason and a common human nature over tradition and custom' (2010: 8). According to Jonathan Israel, 'the Enlightenment ... effectively demolished all legitimation of monarchy, aristocracy, woman's subordination to man, ecclesiastical authority, and slavery, replacing these with the principles of universality, equality, and democracy' (2001: vi). Isaiah Berlin similarly argued that the Enlightenment's emphasis on 'unchanging laws' and abstract, universal reason generated a blindness in principle to the power of the particular, e.g. particular cultures, habits, communities and nations. While Voltaire, Diderot, Helvétius, Holbach and Condorcet, with their obsessive attachment to unchanging values, transcendental norms and generalized knowledge systems, envisaged 'only universal civilization, of which now one nation, now another, represents the richest flowering', Herder and other Counter-Enlightenment figures insisted on an irreducible 'plurality of incommensurable cultures' and a basic human need to 'belong to a given community, to be connected with its members by indissoluble and impalpable ties of common language, historical memory, habit, tradition and feeling' (Berlin 1979: 12). Seen in this light, Enlightenment 'cosmopolitanism' entailed 'the shedding of all that makes one most human, most oneself' (12).

Charles Taylor (2007) similarly sees rational disengagement and the rise of science as entailing a shift of perspective from the local to the universal. According to him, the Enlightenment entailed 'a rise out of base, sensual self-absorption into a broader, higher, purer perspective' – one defined by 'Enlightenment and science'. Indeed, 'Science by its very nature involves our taking an objective, and in this sense universal perspective on things. To see human life in the view from nowhere, to use a term of the epoch, from the standpoint of the "impartial spectator," is to think in universal, and no longer parochial terms' (2007: 254). Taylor predictably plots a direct link between Descartes and the Enlightenment: 'Enlightenment universalism followed in [Descartes's] footsteps' (694). Against this Cartesian enlightened universalism, Taylor positions the Romantics. For these, the human good is 'in its very essence sensual, earthly' and 'whoever identifies a transcendent goal departs from it, betrays it'. Whereas the Enlightenment tended to mutilate humanity through its insistence on the autonomy of reason, the separation of mind and body, and man's separability from his physical environment, the Romantics believed 'we are in an order of "nature"' and 'part of this greater whole'. Organicist nationalism was just one step away: 'One side of this attraction is the sense of belonging, being part of our native land' (547).

Universal Christianity/particular Enlightenment

As Vyverberg (1989) and Rothschild (2001) have shown, the Enlightenment evinced a complex and often contradictory approach to the universal/ particular distinction, frequently appealing to the value and non-negotiability of historically acquired, cultural differences. Although reason's basis in the nature of things seemed to imply a universal standard of truth applicable across boundaries of nation or race (e.g. in Diderot's claim that 'Truth, independently of my caprices, should be the rule of my judgments', 1916 [1746–1751]: 29; or Holbach's that man's duties and virtues 'are the same for all those who inhabit this globe', Vyverberg 1989: 43), rationalistic universalism was matched in the Enlightenment by a parallel discourse on cultural and ethical heterogeneity, stemming from at least two factors: (1) empiricism, which forced a reckoning with irreducible differences across sensed environments; and (2) new discoveries about other countries – especially the Orient – that put increasing pressure on generalized statements about mankind as a whole. These two factors worked in tandem: if environmental context varied from place to place (as it patently did), and everything, including morality, was based on the senses and acquired through that varying context, there could be no 'universal morality'. Despite its frequently declared universalism, the Enlightenment could not ultimately suppress 'the implications of empirical observations on the diversity of mankind' (Vyverberg 1989: 55).

Although 'tradition and custom' were sometimes degraded by the Enlightenment as a distortive ideological influence on otherwise universal, rational or objective knowledge,[3] they could also be reclaimed from the dilatory power of the universal as a necessary form of parochialism. Consider for example Hume's response to Fontenelle, on the ethical implications of astronomic science. Fontenelle claimed that 'Nothing can be more destructive to ambition and passion for conquest, than the true system of astronomy' since astronomy reveals the insignificance of the world against 'the infinite extent of nature'. Against such claims, Hume first dismissed Fontenelle for the loftiness of his ideas ('This consideration is evidently too distant ever to have any effect'), then worried about its implications for nationalism, since it would 'destroy patriotism as well as ambition' (1987 [1742]: 26). Mathematicians were particularly prone to this issue:

> Mathematicians tell us, that the whole earth is but a point, compared to the heavens. To change one's country then is little more than to remove from one street to another. Man is not a plant, rooted to a certain spot of earth: All soils

and all climates are alike suited to him. These topics are admirable, could they fall only into the hands of banished persons. But what if they come also to the knowledge of those who are employed in public affairs, and destroy all their attachment to their native country? (47)

Fascinatingly, Christianity was routinely criticized by the *philosophes* for *not being particularistic enough* – in other words, for expanding the circle of identification too far, skipping the nation to reach universal humanity. Boulanger and Holbach, for example, railed against religious emphases on universal equality which, in their attempt to make man more than man, 'soon made humanity disappear' (1762 [1761]: 150).[4] For these, the 'imaginary picture' of celestial happiness generated 'false ideas concerning liberty, equality and independence' and reduced man to nothing by creating a 'god-monarch so great, so immense' that it 'caused him to loathe and voluntarily subjugate himself' (146). Religion destroyed humanity by offering two equally extreme and destructive conceptions of the self: 'on one hand, man wanted to be more than he could, or should be, on earth; on the other, he degraded himself below his natural state. Thus true man was no longer to be seen, and in his place appeared the savage and slave' (146). Even democratic rule put forward unrealistic demands on human sociality, since it insisted on replicating the *religious* case for equality:

> The Republicans only reestabished a primitive Theocracy ... Since it was imagined that a universal equality, which a thousand physical and moral factors have and will always distance from Earth, being made only for Heaven; since it was imagined, I say, that such equality was the essence of liberty, all the members of the Republic made themselves equal, all became kings, all became legislators. (250)

For Boulanger and Holbach, only a secularized (non-Christian) nationalism could provide a realistic and natural environment for the flourishing of virtue. For 'Nature' did not tell man to love 'everyone', as Christians believed. Rather, it told man 'to *love the country which gave him birth*, to serve it faithfully, to blend his interests with it against all those who shall attempt to injure it' (Holbach 1889 [1770]: 281, emphasis original).[5]

Vyverberg reads Enlightenment thought on the relation between universalism and particularism, or rationalism and empiricism, as a discourse of cooperation and harmony. According to him, 'For the mainstream of the French Enlightenment, the cooperation of reason and empiricism ... was a virtually unquestioned assumption. How, indeed, could a contradiction between rationalism and empiricism exist? The universe itself was rational' (1989: 53). True as this may be in terms of the Enlightenment's aims and self-understanding, it is not always clear how this cooperative model played out in practice. A particularly stark example is provided by Holbach's thoughts on moral sentiment and especially the sentiment of 'love'. On one hand, Holbach insisted on the necessity of replacing the particularistic 'morality of religion' with a universal 'morality of reason' (1857 [1768]: 243).[6] Since this rational morality was founded on 'sentiments inherent in our nature', it would be 'stable and equal for all men, never varying with time or place' (1889 [1770]: 358). On the other, it is not clear how these sentiments could be 'inherent in our nature' given Holbach's commitment to empiricism. Like everything else, the capacity to love was acquired: 'Those sentiments of love, which fathers and mothers have for their children; those feelings of affection, which children, with good inclinations, bear towards their parents, are by no means innate sentiments; they are nothing more than the effect of experience, of reflection, of habit, in souls of sensibility' (1889 [1770]: 81).[7] In other words, 'inherent' sentiments of care and duty towards society were not inherent, virtually ruling out the possibility of a universal morality. According to Holbach, 'All men have not the same eyes, nor the same brains; all have not the same ideas, the same education, or the same opinions' (1857 [1768]: 274). Although empiricism on one hand constituted the basis of agreement and social harmony (since, according to Holbach, men do not argue about 'objects that are cognizable to their senses, and which they can submit to the test of experience', 1857 [1768]: 275), what was cognizable to the senses (and shaped reason) varied from context to context, making men 'essentially different' (1889 [1770]: 61, 85).[8] Holbach was unequivocal on this point:

> There are not two individuals of the human species, who have precisely the same traits; who think exactly in the same manner; who view things under the same identical point of sight; who have decidedly the same ideas; consequently no two of them have uniformly the same system of conduct. The visible organs of man, as well as his concealed organs, have indeed some analogy, some common points of resemblance, some general conformity, which makes them appear, when viewed in the gross, to be affected in the same manner by certain causes; but the difference is infinite in the detail. The human soul may be compared to those instruments of which the chords, already diversified in themselves by the manner in which they have been spun, are also strung upon different notes: struck by the same impulse, each chord gives forth the sound that is peculiar to itself, that is to say, that which depends on its texture, its tension, its volume, on the momentary state in which it is placed by the

circumambient air. It is this that produces the diversified spectacle, the varied
scene, which the moral world offers to our view: it is from this that results the
striking contrariety that is to be found in the minds, in the faculties, in the
passions, in the energies, in the taste, in the imagination, in the ideas, in
the opinions of man: this diversity is as great as that of his physical powers:
like them it depends on his temperament, which is as much varied as his
physiognomy. (1889 [1770]: 60)[9]

For Holbach, humanhood was less a universal and integrated state than a
condition of radical plurality in which assemblages of sensual 'chords' emerged
in harmony with their environment and varied from context to context. Holbach
did not advocate an abstract 'cosmopolitanism' entailing 'the shedding of all that
makes one most human, most oneself', but was deeply sceptical of *Christian*
attempts to make man other than what he is: an eminently localized and
therefore particular being, reared, shaped and conditioned by the contingencies
of lived experience.

The fact that human differences were 'infinite in the detail' and intrinsically
bound up with their lived environments had radical implications for emerging
theories of statecraft. From the mid-eighteenth century, appeals to underlying,
unifying principles were superseded by a more realpolitik approach to
subjectivity and agency, in which the work of governance became less a
matter of convincing people through good reasons, than of manipulating their
conditioning environments for the national good. Key to this development was,
once again, the concept of 'habit'.

Virtuous habits

Yet habit – strange thing! what cannot habit accomplish?
Herman Melville, *Moby-Dick* (1967 [1851]: 240)

Momentary interests, rooted habits, public opinion, have much more power
than imaginary beings, or than theories which themselves depend upon the
organization of man.
Holbach, *Système de la Nature* (1889 [1770]: 134)

In 'Techniques of the Body' (1934), Marcel Mauss developed the notion of
'*habitus*' as 'the techniques and work of collective and individual practical
reason', distinguishing the term from pre-existing concepts of 'habitude',

'habit', 'custom' or '*exis*', the '"acquired ability" and "faculty" of Aristotle' (1973 [1934]: 73). He argued that *habitus* differed from the latter since it varied not only between 'individuals' but between 'societies, educations, proprieties and fashions, prestiges' (73). Pierre Bourdieu later adopted and refined the term as 'systems of durable, transposable dispositions, structured structures predisposed to function as structuring structures, that is, as principles which generate and organize practices and representations that can be objectively adapted to their outcomes without presupposing a conscious aiming at ends or an express mastery of the operations necessary in order to attain them' (1990 [1980]: 53). *Habitus* and *schesis* have been used more recently by Talal Asad (2003: 95) and Saba Mahmood (2009) to flesh out an understanding of religious virtue opposed to secular reason. For Asad, a paradigmatic instance of a *habitus*-based understanding of morality is provided by the Myth of Oedipus, since within this myth, Oedipus's actions on discovering what he has done (beginning with 'self-punishment') arise from 'an embodied capacity that is more than physical ability, in that it also includes cultivated sensibilities and passions, an orchestration of the senses' (2003: 96). Whereas a secular framework of attribution and blame tends to construe the self in essentialist terms, as 'a single subject with a continuous consciousness in a single body' (a subject that shares much in common with Taylor's 'buffered self'),[10] Oedipus shows that moral actions do not necessarily depend on the decisions of an autonomous actor, or 'a sequence of natural causality to which "responsibility" can be attached'. The complex array of events or 'accidents' leading to the myth's tragic denouement both addresses and *constitutes* Oedipus's morality, dispersing agency into the network behind Oedipus's particular *habitus* – a *habitus* which, though contingent, is largely non-negotiable:

> *Habitus* ... is not something one accepts or rejects, it is part of what one essentially is and must do. ... Oedipus puts out his own eyes not because his conscience or his god considers that he deserves to be punished for failing to be responsible – or because he thinks he does – but because (as he says) he cannot bear the thought of having to look his father and his mother in the eyes when he joins them beyond the grave, or to see his children, 'begotten as they were begotten'. He acts as he does necessarily, out of the passion that is his *habitus*. (96)

This virtue-centred understanding of agency and pain is inherently historical. It would be impossible for Oedipus to feel and act as he does without the precedence of a long and particular history of events and practice shaping his present *habitus*. The tragedy of Oedipus is therefore an object lesson in 'how the past – whether secular or religious – constitutes agency' (98), but it can also be *contrasted* with a secular self-perception of temporal immediacy. According to Asad, whereas secular approaches to the good have tended to rely upon ahistorical principles removed from the contingencies of affect and corporeality (e.g. in their emphases on absolute freedom), religious actors (notably Muslims) tend to treat the materiality of the living body as 'an essential means for cultivating what they define as virtuous conduct and for discouraging what they consider as vice'. In this view, not only are 'fear', 'hope', 'felicity' and 'pain' central to ethical cultivation but 'the more one exercises a virtue the easier it becomes' and 'the more one gives in to vice, the harder it is to act virtuously'. In other words, from a religious, specifically Islamic, point of view, virtue unfolds within time and therefore cannot easily be undone: 'Time is not reversible' (89).

Asad and Mahmood take these ideas as the basis for a critique of modern secular approaches to religious subjectivity, particularly the problem of translating religious needs and demands into the logocentric, Protestant idiom of the public sphere. According to them, this problem of translation deepens the divide and exacerbates tensions between embodied (non-Western) religion and disembodied (Western) secularity, e.g. by rendering certain forms of Islamic subjectivity illegible to liberal-democratic sensibilities. I have already explored ways in which the habits infiltrate Descartes's later work, *Les Passions de l'Âme* (1649), softening the binary between disembodied secularity and embodied pre-secularity structuring *A Secular Age*. Broadly speaking, the same arguments apply to Asad and Mahmood. But how does a 'dehabituated' understanding of the secular stand up in the context of the eighteenth century – i.e. precisely the point at which 'secularity' takes on its modern meaning, as the disestablishment, absence or negotiability of religion?

Enlightenment habits

According to Rousseau, the task of the reformer – as of the child tutor – was not, as is commonly understood, to allow free reign to man's untainted 'nature' (verified by observations of the noble savage) but to train the raw mass of human sentiments into alignment with nature, so 'artificially' allowing our 'natural' propensities to flourish. Artifice or education in this case involved a careful crafting of the scope and form of man's habitual formations, treading a fine line between freedom and coercion. Paradoxically, liberty was both antithetical to and dependent upon the cultivation of habits. Although 'The only habit the child should be allowed to contract is that of having no habits' (1921 [1762]: 30), habit formation could be redefined as a 'natural' process and therefore reinstated as the crux of a sound education:

> Nature, we are told, is merely habit. What does that mean? Are there not habits formed under compulsion, habits which never stifle nature? Such, for example, are the habits of plants trained horizontally. The plant keeps its artificial shape, but the sap has not changed its course, and any new growth the plant may make will be vertical. It is the same with a man's disposition; while the conditions remain the same, habits, even the least natural of them, hold good; but change the conditions, habits vanish, nature reasserts herself. Education itself is but habit. (6–7)[11]

Although Rousseau on one hand advised the tutor to 'Prepare the way for [the pupil's] control of his liberty and the use of his strength by leaving his body its natural habit', he also insisted that 'As soon as the child begins to take notice, what is shown him must be carefully chosen' (30). This was so because 'what is shown' would determine the sensual, passional and intellectual structure of annexation underpinning the child's character and carried into adulthood. For Rousseau as for Descartes, this structure was fundamentally a matter of sense impressions – impressions especially susceptible to annexation in 'the dawn of life', when a child's sense experiences are still 'the raw material of thought'. At this time, sense experiences should be presented to the child 'in fitting order, so that memory may at a future time present them in the same order to his understanding' (31).[12]

In *Esquisse d'un Tableau Historique des Progrès de l'Esprit Humain* (1795), the 'cold rationalist' Condorcet argued that man is capable of converting 'momentary impressions' accompanied by pleasure or pain into 'durable sentiments of corresponding nature' and hence of 'experiencing these sentiments either at the sight or recollection of the pleasure or pain of beings sensitive like himself' (1796 [1795]: 10). This was the basis of empathy. It was also the basis of nationalism, since it was only natural that man attach himself to opinions received 'in infancy' and to 'the customs of his country'. Following the same logic, climate, habit and 'the sweets annexed' to a 'state of almost complete independence' explained what he described as the 'mental stagnation of Oriental peoples' (36). Later, Destutt de Tracy drew on the example of 'Mr. Pinel' and his experiments on the clinically insane to argue that 'the art of curing demented people is none other than the art of manipulating their passions' and 'forming their habits' ('former leurs habitudes'; 1817 [1804]: 299–300, fn. 1).

Holbach's habits

It would be easy to conclude from certain comments that Holbach deployed the concept of habit in order to attack it. For example, he claimed 'it is to habit, consecrated by time, that [man] owes those errors into which everything strives to precipitate him, and to prevent him from emancipating himself' (1889 [1770]: 67). He also criticized those who are 'inebriated by their passions, or hurried along by the torrent of habit' (157).[13] Habits generated pernicious 'customs' and 'prejudices' that tenaciously resisted the advances of 'reason', 'experience' and 'good sense'. They were opposed to 'the clearest demonstrations', which could 'avail nothing against those passions and those vices which time has rooted in [man]'. This, precisely, was 'the source of that obstinacy which man evinces for his religion' (63).

Very similar views were later expressed by Kant, in his *Anthropology from a Pragmatic Point of View* (1785). According to Kant, habit 'deprives even good actions of their moral worth because it impairs the freedom of the mind and, moreover, leads to thoughtless repetition of the very same act (monotony) and so becomes ridiculous'. Kant drove home this point by emphasizing the animality of habitude. 'The reason why the habits of another stimulate the arousal of disgust in us', he claimed, 'is that here the animal in the human being jumps out far too much, and that here one is led instinctively by the rule of habituation, exactly like another (non-human) nature, and so runs the risk of falling into one and the same class with the beast' (2006 [1785]: 40). There was nothing essentially enlightened, nonreligious or 'secular' about such ideas. Already in the fourth century CE, Augustine argued that passion and the formation of habits distorted the will and created 'a chain' or 'harsh bondage' that 'held man under restraint' (1992 [397–400]: 140). For him, habit was a 'treadmill' (146) and sin 'the violence of habit by which even the unwilling mind is dragged down and held, as it deserves to be, since by its own choice it slipped into the habit' (141).[14]

Yet unlike Kant and Augustine, Holbach did not reject the habits entirely. He could not, because the habits alone attached man 'either to virtue or to vice' and were in themselves morally neutral. Habits were simply 'mode[s] of existence – of thinking – of acting, which [man's] organs, as well interior as exterior, contract by the frequent reiteration of the same motion, from whence results the faculty of performing these actions with promptitude and with facility' (1889 [1770]: 67). What mattered was not their presence, which was non-negotiable since 'To tell a man to renounce his habits, is to be willing that a citizen, accustomed, to clothe himself, should consent to walk quite naked' (178), but their character or direction. And habits did indeed need directing, for man was no more 'naturally good' for Holbach than for Rousseau. Although Holbach frequently insisted on the need to jettison human artifice, i.e. religion, and surrender to nature's natural benevolence, religion was, contradictorily, both the source of unnatural habits and a mere veneer on unchanging human character: 'Religion leaves men just such as nature and habit have made them' (1857 [1768]: 253). The problem (from one side of Holbach's multi-facetted attack on religion) was precisely that religion did *not* alter the course of nature and thus did not intervene in the formation of virtue.

Moreover, against Taylor's 'higher goods' theory of secular disenchantment (see previous chapter), Holbach linked the habits very specifically with 'the ideas which man forms to himself of happiness', i.e. an ethical sense of the higher. Habits generated virtually every aspect of a person's consciousness, including their sense of moral direction:

> If things be attentively considered, it will be found that almost the whole conduct of man, the entire system of his actions, his occupations, his connexions, his studies, his amusements, his manners, his customs, his very garments, even his aliments, are the effect of habit. He owes equally to habit the facility with which he exercises his mental faculties of thought, of judgment, of wit, of reason, of taste, etc. It is to habit he owes the greater part of his inclinations, of his desires, of his opinions, of his prejudices, of the ideas, true or false, he forms to himself of his welfare. (1889 [1770]: 67)

Just as enthusiasm could produce both 'good results' and 'disorder' depending on the aims to which it was directed, habits could 'make [man] either reasonable or irrational, enlightened or stupid, a fanatic or a hero, an enthusiast for the public good, or an unbridled criminal' (75). They generated man's 'system of opinion' (1857 [1768]: 256) and were listed by Holbach as one among four factors providing man with 'a taste for morals' (the others were 'experience', 'reflection' and 'reason'; 1889 [1770]: 141). The habits were particularly useful as guards against an impending threat to the post-religious order: concealed crime.[15] Moral habituation acted as a reliable guarantee against private wrongdoing, providing the necessary constraints where traditional, religious systems of morality were abandoned. Just as a man who 'from his infancy contracted a habit of cleanliness' would be 'painfully affected at seeing himself dirty, even when no one should witness it', so 'He who has formed to himself a habit of practising virtue ... abstains even from concealed crimes, since these would degrade him in his own eyes' (1889 [1770]: 141). Habit clothed the body, or even *parts* of the body, with good or bad dispositions. According to Holbach, 'The arm which [man] has received from nature is neither good nor bad' yet its use could become criminal if the habit was contracted of 'using it to rob or to assassinate' (72).

Slow reform and the intractability of childhood habits

A consequence of thinking through man's 'habitual' nature concerned the length of time required to instil good habits, particularly those geared towards the national good. For many of the *philosophes*, the process of mental and practical reform had to be gradual.[16] Voltaire insisted that the emergence of a nation depended upon an extended process of conditioning: 'For a nation to be assembled into a body of people, for it to be powerful, experienced and wise, a prodigious length of time is necessary' (1878 [1756]: 8). 'Sovereigns', Hume wrote, 'must take mankind as they find them and cannot pretend to introduce any violent change in their principles and ways of thinking' (1987 [1742]: 260). A similar point was made by Rousseau: 'It takes a long time for ideas and sentiments to change to the point where men can bring themselves to take other men as masters' (1986 [1762]: 142).

For Holbach, likewise, virtue stemmed not from a coercive imposition of rationally derived rules by the will or pure reason, but a process of gradual conditioning and adjustment. A good example is provided by his account of a person's fall into crime:

> Experience proves that the first crime is always accompanied by more pangs of remorse than the second; this again, by more than the third, and so on to those that follow. A first action is the commencement of a habit; those which succeed confirm it: by force of combating the obstacles that prevent the commission of criminal actions, man arrives at the power of vanquishing them with ease and with facility. Thus he frequently becomes wicked from habit. (1889 [1770]: 67)[17]

Men could not simply change their mental and ethical habits at will. Stuck in the ruts of habit, their 'customs of thinking' were as difficult to change as their bodily habits.[18] 'Deep rooted prejudices' were virtually indelible and the mind had as much trouble disengaging itself from familiar patterns of thought as the body did 'remain[ing] quiescent after [being] accustomed to exercise'. Religious prejudices in particular were like 'snuff': one could only renounce them with 'extreme pain', since habit made them 'a sort of want we cannot dispense with' (1857 [1768]: 256). Changing people's opinions was almost as hard as changing their language (1889 [1770]: 63) and the longer these opinions were engrained, the harder the task ('there is nothing more difficult than to efface the notions with which we are imbued during our infancy'; 1857 [1768]: 9).

Importantly, childhood marked the earliest stage in the formation of habits and was therefore a particularly sensitive time for establishing life-long associations – a well-known fact among the *philosophes* and a key line of attack against the Catholic appropriation of young and pliable souls. Early in life man's organs were 'extremely flexible' (1889 [1770]: 68).[19] The infant mind was particularly disposed to 'receive whatever impression is made upon it' and the priests therefore cynically 'seized upon the youth to inspire them with ideas that they could never impose upon adults' (1857 [1768]: 6).[20] A great burden was then placed on the educator to form not only the youth's knowledge, but 'the habits, the opinions and the modes of existence adopted by the society in which he is placed'. Children's guardians provided them with their 'first impulse', an impulse which determined 'his condition, his passions, the ideas he forms to himself of happiness and … his virtues and his vices': 'Under the eyes of his masters, the infant acquires ideas, and learns to associate them – to think in a certain manner – to judge well or ill. They point out to him various objects, which they accustom him either to love or to hate, to desire or to avoid, to esteem or to despise' (1889 [1770]: 68). Through a gradual process of annexation and habituation, the student's mind would 'by degrees [saturate] itself with truth' (69).[21]

Gradualism was not the only model for acquiring habits, however. A single, intense experience could determine man's disposition decisively, bringing about a one-off re-configuration of sensations to thoughts and passions. Just as Descartes argued that the motions of the gland may be separated and re-annexed through 'a single action', e.g. coming upon 'something very foul in a dish we are eating with relish', so Holbach noted that '[A] single word frequently suffices to modify a man for the whole course of his life; to decide for ever his propensities'. Similarly, an infant who burned his finger on a flame was warned against similar actions in the future, while 'a man once punished and despised for having committed a dishonest action, [was] not often tempted to continue so unfavourable a course' (99–100).

It should be clear from the foregoing that any notion of an integrated subject with a continuous consciousness is explicitly dismantled by Holbach's disaggregated conception of the self – a self whose agency (insofar as 'agency' makes any sense at all in the Holbachian universe) is located not only in the body but its individual components (e.g. an arm that has contracted the habit of stealing). Holbach also considered virtue to be a matter of training over time, so that 'the more one gives in to vice, the harder it is to act virtuously'; time was no more reversible for him than for Sophocles or Augustine. Moreover, Mauss's distinction between *habitus* and 'customs' or 'habits', on the basis that *habitus* varied between 'societies, educations, proprieties and fashions, prestiges', whereas customs and habits only pertained to individuals makes little sense in a context where the latter were understood as the structuring conditions for different societies around the world and their different religions. If Indian society differed from French society, this was precisely because its habits were differently configured and grew out of (climatic, geographic, dietary, etc.) variations specific to the subcontinent as a whole. These factors all tended to shape temperament or dispositions at a sub- or unconscious level. The Holbachian understanding of the habits did not presuppose 'a conscious aiming at ends or an express mastery of the operations necessary in order to attain them' since mastery was ruled out in principle, along with the freedom of the will. In short, much of what has been discovered or rediscovered with regard to *habitus* or *schesis* was already common knowledge in the eighteenth-century French Enlightenment and used as the theoretical foundation of good governance.

Enlightened bodies

Given this context, it should not be surprising to find that the body occupied a central role in the transmission of patriotic sentiments and civic virtues, or what might be called the 'enculturation' of Enlightenment. In *Lettres Persanes* (1721), Montesquieu's alter-ego Usbek cites the discourse of a military general overheard in the streets of Paris, which explains the power of music upon the emotions. Although this general's troops have recently been defeated, he reassures his interlocutors that it is easy to remedy this failure, since he possesses 'six couplets of song' which will 'put everything back in order'. The general claims he has chosen 'several very clear voices, which, coming from the cavity of certain very strong chests, [will] move the people beautifully', and that the melodies are in a key that carries 'a very particular effect' (1973 [1721]: 252). Later, in *De l'Esprit des Lois* (1748), Montesquieu speculated about the effects of music upon the temperament, noting that the magistrates of the Greek republics found employment for idle citizens in athletic and military exercises, which had 'a natural tendency to render people hardy and fierce' (1777a [1748]: 50). Since hardiness and fierceness were not sufficient for civil society, there was a need to temper such exercises with 'others that might soften their manners'. Music, which influenced the mind by means of 'the corporeal organs', was well suited to this task, since it offered unparalleled opportunities to 'inspire the soul with a sense of pity, lenity, tenderness and love'. Those 'moral writers' who declaimed against the stage, concluded Montesquieu, 'sufficiently demonstrate the power of music over the mind' (39).[22]

Other Enlightenment thinkers followed suit, speculating about the precise means of manipulating the body to change emotions and ideas. In his private letters, Helvétius's emphasized, first, that virtue was a matter of the senses and emotion, and second, that the anticipation of physical pleasure was as effective as the anticipation of fear for cultivating virtue. According to him, a good example was provided by a 'moral ballet' he witnessed being danced by schoolchildren at Rouen. 'I may have observed', wrote Helvétius on 24 September 1758, 'the means by which pleasure leads men to virtue':

> I cite as proof a moral ballet danced by the students of Rouen in 1750 for the distribution of awards given by the parliament of Normandy following *Périande and Thémistocle*, tragedy in which pleasure leads young people, through dance, to the practice not only of civil and military virtues, but even virtues proper to religion. (2009 [1737–1772]: unpaginated)

In the aftermath of the French Revolution, the sentimental empiricists of the Committee of Public Instruction opposed the use of technical language and books in teaching, instead calling for a pedagogy that 'operated by the moulding of pupils' sensibilities through the careful management of their sensory experiences' (Riskin 2002: 14). Establishing a new system of public education and state-sponsored research, the Committee suggested that the 'whole art of instruction' could be distilled to the 'linking of sensations', for it was through sensation and *only* through sensation that virtues and vices 'entered the heart' (14–15). Jean-Paul Rabaut, a speaker before the National Convention, argued for 'education' over 'instruction', explaining that, while instruction rested on 'books, instruments, calculations, methods', education focused on cultivating the 'body and heart' through 'circuses, gymnasia, weapons, public games' and was thus a more durable and reliable support of the nation-state (264). Destutt de Tracy routinely emphasized the close relation between minds and bodies by reference to the learning process. 'Think about what happens when you read a book', he asked his students towards the beginning of *Élémens d'Idéologie* (1804), 'There is no doubt that when you learnt to read, you needed a distinct and felt knowledge [*connaissance distincte et sentie*] of the figure of every letter, of the sound that represents it in isolation, of how to join and fuse it with others in order to form syllables and words'. When reading later became a habit, it was possible to believe one only concentrated on the 'meaning' of the words. But in fact one merely pushed the work of analysis to a subconscious level.[23] This last point was crucial, for it was a fact that 'the more a movement is easy and rapid, the less it is felt, so that it often produces no sensation, and is absolutely invisible'. When one began dance or clavecin lessons, for example, the teacher had to convey the different volitions and stages of movement required of legs and fingers, and the proper order for their execution. Over time, however, intellectual operations became as easy and fluid as mechanical operations, and the whole process took on a life of its own. Only when intellectual operations ran smoothly and without effort did one have 'the dance step in the leg or the clavecin piece in the hand' ('mon pas de danse dans la jambe ou ma pièce de clavecin dans la main'). If, on the other hand, one's intellectual operations suffered a disturbance, confusion or hesitation, then one's mechanical operations would become irregular and poorly executed. Thus all our actions, even the most mechanical, carried 'the imprint of the state of our intellectual faculties' (255–6).

Notes on education

Eighteenth-century theories of the imagination, desire and recompense were not restricted to the rarefied atmosphere of philosophical elites, but could percolate into official government policy. There is a straightforward connection between French programmes of reform, especially concerning alterations to the educational apparatus, and Enlightenment thought on the necessity of awakening the right passions through empirical means. As Riskin has noted, Diderot's thoughts on the imperviousness of the blind to sensual experience had crucial implications for the shape and content of their education. Since blind people could not be conditioned through images (literal and metaphorical), they had to be trained towards virtue in dedicated institutions following a specially crafted curriculum. These institutions came to inform discussions of 'the sensory and sentimental bases of social harmony' (2002: 11) and fed into the official reports and 'notes on education' of the late eighteenth century. Charles Maurice de Talleyrand-Périgord's (1754–1838) *Rapport sur l'Instruction Publique, Fait au Nom du Comité de Constitution à l'Assemblée Nationale, les 10, 11 et 19 Septembre 1791* (1791) is exemplary in this regard. Although this document was only partially adopted into governmental policy, it serves as a key witness of the intimate relation between the postrationalistic theories of the late-eighteenth-century Enlightenment and formal programmes of education put into place during and after the Revolution.

For Talleyrand, the 'French scene' should become an 'auxiliary power of the revolution', and the pedagogical talents of the people, which until then had only 'polished the surface of customs [*moeurs*]' should henceforth 'correct the depths', serving both 'morality and fatherland [*patrie*]'. This political 'regeneration' would spread to the domain of the arts and 'through illusion, exert the most powerful of empires' (1791: 106). Given their immense power, the arts should not be feared but, on the contrary, valued and exploited as core elements of a 'new catechism for childhood' (11) to be taught even in the smallest schools of the kingdom:

> The Nation, far from doubting the influence of the arts, will therefore wish to cover itself in their glory: it will encourage them; it will honour them; it will entrust its interests to them; finally, it will place them in education as the surest means of treasuring morality. Sparta did not need to banish from its institutions the practice of the lyre; it only censured certain chords whose over-sentimental sound could enervate the soul and feminize customs [*efféminer les moeurs*]. (109)

Earlier warnings against religious imagery could thus flip into an endorsement of secular imagery for purposes of character cultivation; the artistic representation of great events and the energetic portrayal of the passions was and always would be 'a fertile means of instruction'. Although it was true that despotism had appealed to the power of art for sustenance, it was also true that the same art had deposited in Frenchmen the seeds of the revolution and was thus a potent means of 'reigniting and perfecting' French patriotism. Indeed, this was the end towards which art should 'direct all its power' (105).

Predictably, the arts were most effective directed at the youth, for it was in infancy that images made their most powerful and long-lasting impression. It was then that one had to 'sow the first grains of morality' ('jetter les premières semences de la morale') since it was well established that 'impressions dating from this first age of life are the only ones that time never erases' (99). Young people were 'disciples of everything surrounding them', but especially so when sensations first became annexed to ideas and physical impressions began to influence the 'affections of the soul'. 'Let us not be surprised to hear invoked *the arts* as props for morality', wrote Talleyrand, for 'To preserve precious memories, to eternalize actions worthy of remembrance … therein, without doubt, lies the teaching of virtue' (emphasis original). The imagination, which 'blazed' ('s'enflamme') at the sight of a masterpiece, mixed within this 'enthusiasm' the 'perfect imitation which enchants it, and the sublime line that delights it'. Early infancy was a particularly propitious time for the 'alliance of sensations and ideas', since it was then that sense impressions produced 'the most vivid and durable effects' (108). All the fine arts, music, spectacles, fights and prizes 'set aside for these glorious days' would, according to Talleyrand, help the people become 'happier and better' (108). They would nurture memories among the elderly, a sense of triumph among the youth and hope among children. Such sentimental 'effects' were especially important because a vigorous and long-lasting nationalism could never be built on an abstract assent to (constitutional) propositions alone. Government had not only to formulate a constitution but instil the appropriate feelings, customs and habits for the nation. 'Would the constitution truly exist if it existed only in our code', asked Talleyrand, 'if, from there, it did not send out roots into the soul of all Citizens; if it did not permanently imprint new sentiments, new customs and new habits?' (4–5).

These ideas were at least as old as Holbach's *Système*. For Holbach, the regulation of imagination would take place through two principal mechanisms: the educational apparatus (with 'education' defined as 'the true art of disseminating, the proper method of cultivating advantageous passions in the heart of man'; 1889 [1770]: 158), and later in life, through offers of 'recompense' and threats of 'crime and punishment', which would instil respectively 'hope of a true welfare' and 'the fear of real evil' (159). Since politics was 'the art of regulating the passions of man, and of directing them to the welfare of society' (69, 345), civic virtue and patriotism could not be learnt through subscription to sets of abstract moral principles but had, instead, to be inculcated through a kind of 'stick-and-carrot' framework for the shepherding of individuals towards authentic citizenship.[24] Good government simply consisted in directing men towards those objects of desire most conducive to national well-being and prosperity, through the careful establishment of nationalistic trophies and anti-nationalistic objects of fear.

> Government, by holding the magnet, has the power either of restraining [the passions], or of giving them a favourable or an unfavourable direction. All [man's] passions are constantly limited by either loving or hating – seeking or avoiding – desiring or fearing. These passions, so necessary to the conservation of man, are a consequence of his organization, and display themselves with more or less energy, according to his temperament: education and habit develop them, and government conducts them towards those objects which it believes itself interested in making desirable to its subjects. (72)

Because childhood was a particularly sensitive time in the formation of character, Holbach prescribed '[kindling] the imagination of the citizen' in early life. For this was 'the true means of obtaining those happy results with which habit should familiarize him, which public opinion should render dear to his heart, for which example ought continually to rouse his faculties' (159).

Talleyrand outlined three principal methods for the instillation of civic virtue: first, to train children, through the artificial methods outlined above; second, to 'relentlessly multiply around every individual and according to their affections, the strongest motives for doing good'; and third, 'to strike the senses and faculties of the soul with virtuous and profound impressions, in order that morality, which at first seems only an abstract product of reason or a vague result of sensibility, becomes a sentiment, a happiness, and, as a result, a strong habit [*forte habitude*]' (1791: 98). Emotion-imbued rhetoric was a fundamental means of instilling these sentiments and habits. Teachers dealing with such 'noble subjects' should not 'remain cold amidst students simmering with youth and courage', for

> it is to these new and pure hearts that the saintly enthusiasm of patriotism and liberty can be communicated with ease. How many touching speeches could animate these lessons and spread enchantment [*charme*] and interest! How much is the history of the Fatherland [*Patrie*] usefully tied to the teaching of its constitution! How this history speaks to the soul in a free country! What sweet tears it spreads! (44)

Such touching speeches would achieve their effect through a polychromatic seduction of the senses based on the ancient wisdom of the rhetoricians. According to d'Alembert's 'Discours Préliminaire', men communicated their passions primarily through 'eloquence', which 'speaks to sentiment as Logic and Grammar speak to the spirit'. The power of eloquence to give a single person control of an entire nation explained 'the superiority of one man over another' and if there was anything surprising about this, it was that one could have believed it possible to supplement 'such rare talent' with rationally derived rules in the first place. For d'Alembert, this was tantamount to the reduction of genius to 'precepts' (2016 [1751–1782]: I. x). Similarly, for Talleyrand,

> Man feels, he thinks, he judges, he reasons, he invents, he communicates his ideas through gestures, through sounds, through written and spoken discourses; he communicates his affections through the harmony of verses, of sounds, of shapes and colours; he consecrates them through monuments; he enquires into the nature of these beings, his own nature, what he owes, what is owed to him, what he can [do] and what he was. (1791: 57)

Through a careful manipulation of students' 'affections', the educational apparatus would eventually instil in reason 'this habit of seeing without effort what is, and this constant aim towards truth which thus becomes the dominant and often exclusive passion of the soul' (88). Such affections would later be amplified through the offering of nationalistic prizes – a branch, an inscription, a medal – ensuring that 'what is best' or 'most useful' is always guarded against indifference and immortalized for future generations. The timing for prize-giving ceremonies would naturally be chosen to maximize the solemnity of the occasion: 'Each place shall choose the most solemn moment to honour the triumph of talent. This day will be everywhere a day of celebration, and all those invested with a function by the people's will, shall have to assist [the celebrations] as the most immediate organs of public recognition' (84). Years would be punctuated by national days, wherein spirits would be drawn towards and enchanted by 'ancient festivals'. Here, in the midst of 'games, wrestling and all the emotions of a universal joy', the 'love of Fatherland' would, as in ancient times, be exalted 'to the degree of enthusiasm' (106).

For Condorcet, likewise, love of truth was a passion (1796 [1795]: 256) and the inculcation of civic virtue a matter of 'sentiment' as much as 'knowledge' (1847 [1791–1792]: 173). His *Cinq Mémoires sur l'Instruction Publique* (1791), published in the same year as Talleyrand's *Rapport*, contain detailed instructions on the contents of a national pedagogy at different stages of education. Although Condorcet at one point criticizes the *philosophes* for turning truths into prejudices by 'seizing man from his first moments' and assailing him with 'images indestructible by time' – images which 'attach him to laws [and] to his country's constitution by a blind sentiment' and 'lead him to reason only through the bedazzlement of imagination and the stirring up of passions' (215) – his own model of civic indoctrination did not depart radically from this model. Condorcet's earliest educational stage involved 'moral stories' designed to awaken 'the first moral sentiments' ('les premiers sentiments moraux') and thereby instil the germ of a fully developed civic habitus. This element of a child's education would incorporate 'short moral stories, appropriate for fixing their attention on the first sentiments which, following the order of nature, they should feel' (e.g. feelings of pity for humans and animals). At this stage, they should be given no 'maxims' or objects of 'reflection' but should simply be guided to 'reflect upon their sentiments' (234–5). As Rothschild notes, for Condorcet, reading novels was the best way to understand how actions influenced people since it was the 'domestic virtues' that had 'the greatest influence on the general happiness of society' (2001: 200).

Conclusion

As Nussbaum (2013: 5) observes, Kant reacted to Rousseau by warning against the dangers of political emotion since this could lead to a counterproductive and unethical unleashing of republican violence. He had history on his side. The post-revolutionary Reign of Terror is among the bloodiest episodes of Western history. Yet I argue Kant's consequent rejection of affect and rationalistic sublimation of political nation-building to the realm of the supersensible did not just alter the trajectory of secular thought; his work (and its later elaboration in Rawls and Habermas) actively obscures an alternative history underwriting the foundation of modern nation-states – an *affective* history at odds with the Kantian self-perception of a viable nationalism founded on the pure autonomy of reason.

This obscuration matters because the substantial work of establishing a national community and its 'imaginary' (Anderson 2006) out of the substance of Christian sentiment had arguably been done by the time Kant made a significant contribution to political thought. The major works of the Republican canon were published twenty years before Kant's *Critique of Pure Reason* (1781) and the American constitution created in 1787, more than ten years before his *Anthropology from a Pragmatic Point of View* (1798) (which, we will recall, forms the basis of Charles Hirschkind's history of secular thought). These are the same documents – more or less unchanged – still undergirding modern constitutional states (Rothschild 2001: 48). Yet it is well known that the Founding Fathers built on Montesquieu and his intellectual descendants, who themselves drew on Locke, not Kant. As Vyverberg explains:

> The Enlightenment defended again and again an approach to the world that combined rational, sometimes quite abstract thought, with empirical observation of earthly phenomena. The voice of Immanuel Kant, proclaiming a radical separation of the world of phenomena from that of eternal ideals – the one perceived in part by the senses, and the other the object of a special insight – sounded only late in the century and was heard not at all in the circle of Voltaire, Diderot and d'Holbach. (1989: 53)

If a single stream of thought can be taken as definitive of early formulations of post-religious political power, it is the theory of the 'countervailing passion', which, as Hirschman observes, was imported into America from France and England 'as an important intellectual tool for the purposes of constitutional engineering' (1977: 28). It is *this* and other theories of the passions that define early approaches to public power and representation, not Kant's rationalistic theory of the supersensible or a postulated neo-Kantian public sphere of rational deliberation. The Kantian notion of a free and 'maximally-rational' public sphere had little or nothing to do with the French Enlightenment, for whom the fundamental ingredients of political life – the passions – were understood to disperse and intensify by force of rhetoric and eloquence, not the abstract interplay of rationally derived 'good reasons'.[25] A French emphasis on eloquence was, if anything, read as a discovery that superseded a *presecular* faith in the autonomy of reason; the *philosophes* did not seek to repress discourse that manipulated the passions, but – at least in a restricted sense – to rehabilitate it *against* the perceived rationalism of the past:

> Is it necessary to excite the passions through eloquence? Question today decided in the affirmative, but which has not always, nor everywhere, been so. The famous trial of the Areopagite regarded this resource among orators as a form of trickery, or, if we like, as a veil suitable for obscuring truth. (Diderot and d'Alembert 2016 [1751–1782]: XII. 147)

According to the *Encyclopédistes*, the 'latin eloquence' underlying modern democratic governance not only 'admitted' the passions but 'required' them. The passions were 'the soul of discourse' and 'the means by which the orator exert[ed] upon his listeners an absolute empire [*empire absolu*]'. Even the 'gentle passions' had to be stimulated without 'study or affectation', using external appearances, gesture, tone and style to 'breathe something soft and tender that comes from heart and goes straight to the heart [*qui parte du coeur and qui aille droit au coeur*]' (XII. 147). If Kant's 'two-world metaphysic' ensured 'the autonomy of the moral will' by 'circumscribing the role of the passions and habits to the sphere of sensible life' (Hirschkind 2011: 637), the mid- to late-eighteenth-century *philosophes* saw 'sensible life' as the very basis of communicative reason. For them, there could be no such autonomy, for the will was subject to the power of orators to inspire 'whatever feelings they pleased' (Diderot and d'Alembert 2016 [1751–1782]: XII. 147).

As Finbarr Curtis has recently noted, drawing on Benedict Anderson and Rogers Brubaker, the construct of an 'American people' necessarily precedes the establishment of democratic institutions, since these institutions depend on a pre-existing national body whose interests they are taken to represent. In his words, 'there is no stable group of people that exists prior to political discourse', for 'democratic institutions depend upon an already constituted people that democratic processes cannot themselves bring into existence' (2016: 58–9).

This is why early populist appeals, in order to be effective 'had to resonate with some sense of shared participation within an American nation'. This sense of shared participation was affective as much as it was reasoned; it could also – paradoxically – reinforce the very collective boundaries that democratic egalitarianism promised to undo: 'much of populist rhetoric was geared toward identifying the American people. This meant that although populist sympathy blurred the spiritual and corporeal boundaries between individual human beings, it often intensified the social boundaries that divided collective subjects from each other' (58–9). The work of intensifying these social boundaries could then disappear in a retroactive attempt to legitimize the state on a foundation of pure, universal reason, a gesture that ironically increased the latter's entitlement to privilege (e.g. of colonizing other territories, monopolizing the means of violence, etc.) by (a) representing the nation-state as a 'natural' outcome of the historical progress of reason; and (b) switching the grounds of Western exceptionalism from an inherent essence of 'Westernness' to the West's position in world time, since good reasons – unlike good customs or habits – were both universal and universally accessible, yet the fiduciary possession of a West which got there first.

The absolute dependence of a 'rational' democracy on the imagined or 'pre-rational' construction of the people is brought out by Taylor himself in his discussion of the shift from a transcendentally justified system of law – e.g. one drawing on divine command – to a post-transcendental legislature built on the sheer immanent force of communicative rationality (2007: 185–96). According to Taylor, a radical transformation took place in understandings of legitimacy during the American Revolution: what began with an appeal to 'the idealized order of Natural Law, in the invocation of "truths held self-evident" in the Declaration of Independence' (or, in other words, some sense of pre-existing laws true from time immemorial), gradually mutated into the self-legitimizing discourse of the newly minted public sphere (197). Eventually, the will of the people dispensed with the need for pre-existing laws and enthroned itself as the source of its own constitution. But crucially, Taylor points out, there was no shortcut to this endpoint. The transition to the constitutional state was necessarily carried out in two steps, with the first retroactively denied by the new order.

> The new social imaginary comes essentially through a retrospective re-interpretation. The revolutionary forces were mobilized largely on the basis of the old, backward-looking legitimacy idea. This will later be seen as the exercise of a power inherent in a sovereign people. The proof of its existence and

legitimacy lies in the new polity it has erected. But popular sovereignty would have been incapable of doing this job, if it had entered the scene too soon. The predecessor idea, invoking the traditional rights of a people defined by its ancient constitution, had to do the original heavy lifting, mobilizing the colonists for the struggle, before being relegated to oblivion, with the pitiless ingratitude towards the past which defines modern revolutions. (2007: 198)

As Benedict Anderson writes, 'All profound changes in consciousness, by their very nature, bring with them characteristic amnesias', the amnesias of nationalism being particularly vulnerable to 'voicing over' (2006: 204, xv).

My point, however, is that Taylor, like so many others, *contrasts* this reading with the self-understanding of the Enlightenment, as though the affective construct of the nation were something exclusively to be excavated through a critical reengagement with our secular past, a reading between the lines or 'against the grain' of intellectual history. Such a retroactive disavowal of the history of sensual empiricism in secular (or anti-religious) discourse can be compared to the modern evisceration of Victorian sexuality examined by Foucault in his *History of Sexuality* (1976–84). Just as the liberal flourishing of sexual freedom was contingent on the retroactive construction of a sexually suppressed Victorian society, so the current 'liberation' of affect from the shackles of secularity and its discovery in the seams of Western intellectual history is contingent upon a constructed history of secular aversion to the passions and sentiment that, in fact, never existed in undiluted form and never stood apart from the Enlightenment project of building up the nation-state.

According to William Mazzarella, 'politics in practice always involves an ongoing and inconclusive mediation between, on the one hand, claims to finite and located identification, and, on the other, an aspiration to universal relevance' (2009: 305). This tension can itself be understood in terms of what Mazzarella calls 'the pragmatics of institutional practice' – a pragmatics wherein 'abstract [universalistic] institutional demands seek [particularistic] affective resonance and [particularistic] affective appeals reach for [universalistic] legalistic justification' (299). With regard to the Enlightenment, it is easily forgotten that the fight *against* religion was from its inception a simultaneous fight *for* the nation-state. Thus, Holbach wrote in *Le Christianisme Devoilé* (1766):

Many men without customs have attacked religion because it went against their inclinations; many wise men have held it in contempt because it seemed ridiculous; many people have seen it as irrelevant because they did not feel its bad effects: as a citizen, I attack it because it seems to me damaging to the wellbeing of the State, enemy of the progress of the human spirit, opposed to the healthy morality from which political interests can never be separated. (1776 [1766]: xxxi–xxxii)

To the extent that secular affects are ignored in favour of a Kantian liberalism that takes 'polite conversation' (or a Habermasian sphere of deliberative rationality) as the basis of national consciousness, it will be impossible to grasp 'what makes nations tick', since it is a fact of history that national formations have relied on the 'religious' language of love and desire first, and the rationalistic language of political deliberation second. We cannot, therefore, unproblematically think of Enlightenment as generating or even slotting into a great narrative of 'disembedding' (Taylor 2007). The Enlightenment did not necessarily entail the closure of the self, but perhaps more accurately brought about *new* kinds of embeddedness, new modes of porousness, linked especially to the imagined values and community of the emergent nation-state. Today we cannot but inhabit a space already shaped by this secularizing project. Nationalism – a doctrine of social allegiance founded fundamentally on the right kinds of emotion, not reasons – was *the* frame in which European secular propagandists developed their alternative theories of the social. This applies as much to the central figures of the 'cold', 'rational' Enlightenment, like Diderot, Holbach, Helvétius and Condorcet, as to proto-Counter-Enlightenment figures like Montesquieu or Rousseau.

As I will show in the following chapter, the ideological and phenomenological shift which Taylor takes as a defining feature of our (Western) emancipation from religious power – the Enlightenment's disembodiment of the self – was, insofar as it existed at all, bound up with a very specific problem: the West's confrontation with Oriental religions, especially Islam. If Christian 'enthusiasm' could paradoxically mark a move away from the body, a stilling of the senses, or a deadening of the passions, Islamic 'fanaticism' almost invariably stood for the opposite: an excessive sensualism and passionality detrimental to the interests of the nation-state. Insofar as 'disengaged reason' can be taken as representative of a general Enlightenment attitude to subject and agency, it was, by the mid- to late-eighteenth century, deployed in the specific context of a racist anti-Islamism, not anti-religion in general. To this context I now turn.

The ritual mask of oriental despotism: Wonder and superimposition in Montesquieu's *Lettres Persanes* (1721) and *De l'Esprit des Lois* (1748)

Nations having given the name of genius only to such assemblages of ideas
as were of use to them, and despotism having in almost all Asia prohibited
the study of morality, metaphysics, civil law, politics … the orientals must,
consequently, be treated as stupid barbarians by the enlightened people of
Europe and eternally become the contempt of free nations and of posterity.
Claude Adrien Helvétius, *De l'Esprit* (1759 [1758]: 233)

To priest-rid Spain repair, or slavish France;
For Judas' hire there do the devil's task,
And trick up slavery in Religion's mask.
Mr. Havard, Prologue to *Mahomet the Impostor* (Voltaire 1773 [1744]: unpaginated)

All children are afraid of masks.
Rousseau, Émile (1921 [1762]: 30)

Introduction

In *Why I Am Not a Christian*, Bertrand Russell off-handedly comments that the origins of 'the concept of God' are traceable to 'the ancient Oriental despotisms' (1957: 17). It is a brief and unexplained remark, sandwiched between a progressivist endorsement of scientism and an attack on the 'dead past'. But it lights up an intellectual track reaching back to Nicolas Antoine Boulanger's work of speculative history *Recherches sur l'Origine du Despotisme Oriental* (1761) and the broader field of eighteenth-century Enlightenment thought. Boulanger's friend and publisher Holbach described God as 'a real sultan from Asia' (1768: 14) and the New Testament as an 'Oriental novel' (1770: xii). The very term 'Oriental despotism' was coined by Helvétius in his atheistic tract *De l'Esprit* (1758). This confluence of atheism and Orientalism demands an explanation. Why was a strong link between religion and Oriental despotism forged at this time? And what lay behind its extraordinary reproducibility, so that it could be presented, mid-twentieth century, without further elaboration?

The foregoing chapters have traced some of the ways seventeenth- and eighteenth-century philosophers thought about the passions and emotions. I have argued that French thinkers from Descartes to Holbach were more attuned to the body and its power to shape the public will than Taylor's *A Secular Age* suggests. By the mid-eighteenth century, they sought not to erase or even dominate the body or passions, but to channel these into the appropriate avenues for a viable nation-state, generating a 'baroque' (Riskin 2002; Kahn 2006; Wolff 2017) more than a 'rational' politics of Enlightenment. This was not a matter of clearing out emotion from the Republic of Letters or a Habermasian public sphere of mutually intelligible, free-floating good reasons, but of strategically manipulating the passions in the national interest. Transcendence and traditional concepts of virtue were likewise reconfigured in nationalistic terms. The *philosophes'* insistence on the deferral of reason to the passions, and an empiricist epistemology that emphasized the power of external circumstances and experience, especially among the youth, provided a powerful model for the creation of national subjects. As we have seen, late-eighteenth-century emphases on the formative power of the imagination and imagery were central to the pedagogical style of post-revolutionary France, when the careful management of schoolchildren's imaginative and 'felt' universe became key factors in the nationwide cultivation of civic virtue.

The following chapters examine a recurrent trope of the Enlightenment – the figure of the Muslim Oriental despot – as a pedagogical tool for two simultaneous, eighteenth-century projects: to fight against religion and build up the national imaginary on secure emotional foundations. While existing discussions typically focus on the despot as a metaphor, sign or symbol for the monarch or pope (e.g. Althusser 1972) – a cautionary measure to avoid persecution in a context where not believing still carried significant risks – such semiotic readings miss much of what made this figure such a powerful and ubiquitous motif of Enlightenment thought. In line with eighteenth-century theories of emotion, representation and habituation, and drawing on Victor Turner's theory of the ritual mask in his seminal essay 'Betwixt and Between' (1964), I suggest the Oriental despot functioned affectively to disturb traditional valuations of religion and conceptions of sacred and profane by overlaying a historical figure of fascination and aversion on the untouchable domain of religion, so reconfiguring or 're-annexing' the structure of affect surrounding formerly sacred figures and objects of worship. Racial tropes and especially the trope of the Oriental despot 'queered the habitual' by making strange a deeply rooted and hitherto invisible facet of Western culture, in a manner analogous to the defamiliarizing mask of the primitive rite.

This chapter also challenges the specific idea, recently put forward by Larry Wolff (2017), that Enlightenment representations of Oriental despotism in print and on the stage tracked the expansion of European empire. Explanations of such representations in terms of economic factors or Europe's relation to the Ottoman empire sidestep a crucial development in France towards the beginning of the eighteenth century, namely, the growing tendency to appeal to representations of the Oriental despot for a domestic critique of religious and political power. The Oriental despot, mapped onto the Islamic prophet Muhammed, provided a vital tool for the affective undoing of Catholic hegemony. This had little to do with colonialism, but reflects, rather, a canny attentiveness to the force of Orientalist, racial imagery for the formation of non-Catholic but not non-civic subjects. When European empire began to peak towards the end of the eighteenth century, the Enlightenment provided a ready template for the reinforcement of Oriental otherness based on racialized religious and behavioural attributes.

I begin by outlining Turner's theory of the ritual mask, then review existing scholarship on Oriental despotism, providing a brief history of the concept, both in the lead up to the eighteenth century and in the eighteenth century itself. I then question Wolff's 'expanding empire' narrative of Oriental despotism, suggesting other important currents were present in Europe towards the mid-eighteenth century, which made the Oriental despot an attractive tool of domestic, anti-Catholic polemics. I focus on two works in particular, Montesquieu's *Lettres Persanes* (1721) and *De l'Esprit des Lois* (1748), discussing different polemic strategies within these works, including Montesquieu's deployment of wonder and irony in the *Lettres'* superimposition of European and Persian worlds, and his categorization of Christianity and Islam as equivalent subcategories of religion in *De l'Esprit*. I suggest these works played a pivotal role in hitching long-standing notions of Oriental despotism to Catholicism via the emerging category of religion, a tendency that only intensified in the second half of the eighteenth century, from Helvétius's coinage of Oriental despotism to the *Encyclopédie*'s entries for 'Arabs' or 'Saracens', and Boulanger's virulent Orientalism in *Recherches*. Insofar as a change occurred in representations of the Oriental despot during the eighteenth century, it was from an ironic and superficially sympathetic portrayal of the religious and cultural other, to a straightforward aversive othering of the Oriental – a development which itself reflected increasing sensitivity to the polemic force of religion as a catch-all category of the secular, and growing concerns over its power.

The following points to a striking conclusion and a new set of questions concerning the genealogy of our secular age. If, according to Taylor, 'The sense of being menaced by fanaticism is one great source of the closure of immanence' (2007: 546), the latter was not brought to a close simply through the menace of fanaticism in general. Enlightenment attacks on religious fanaticism were almost always articulated in the narrow codes and affective tropes of Orientalism, creating a tripartite assemblage of despotism, Islam and secularism. Insofar as modernity is characterized by a stance of disengagement (from the body, transcendence, etc.), this disengagement was primarily secured through negative representations of the Muslim other. How might this alternative genealogy of the secular nuance our understanding of the secular body, recast as a contingent assemblage of affects and habits? What role did representations of religious, racial and cultural otherness in print and on stage perform in the construction of secular-national subjectivities during the eighteenth century? And can we travel upstream to uncover a history of the secular body that is truly 'other-wise'?

'A man's head on a lion's body'

In 'Betwixt and Between: The Liminal Period in *Rites de Passage*' (1964), Turner suggests that (1) the period of margin or liminality demarcated by van Gennep in his tripartite theory of religious ritual is an 'interstructural situation' in which the social lifeworld of participants is reconfigured to suit their new status, and (2) this reconfiguration is facilitated by the use of 'monstrous masks' and other sacred articles or *sacra*, which themselves perform two functions: they act as physical props for the generation of abstract thought, and serve to defamiliarize the habitual by tying images, ideas and concepts together in unusual ways. For Turner, the liminal stage is one of tense potential, in which old patterns of thinking are thrown into question and reassessed in the light of profound ritual experiences. Liminality 'breaks ... the cake of custom and enfranchises speculation'. It is a realm of 'pure possibility' or 'primitive hypothesis' whence 'novel configurations of ideas and relations may arise' (48), and where one finds 'a promiscuous intermingling and juxtaposing of the categories of event, experience, and knowledge, with a pedagogic intention' (53).

Ritual implements or *sacra* are fundamental to the pedagogy of the liminal. These *sacra* are always simple; indeed, their simplicity is a condition of their multivocality and power: 'It is [the sacred articles'] interpretation which is complex, not their outward form' (51). Addressing the peculiar 'disproportion', 'monstrousness' and 'mystery' of the *sacra*, Turner interprets the simplistic exaggeration of certain features (e.g. the head, nose, phallus, etc.) as fundamental building blocks for speculative thought: 'It seems to me that to enlarge or diminish or discolor in this way is a primordial mode of abstraction. The outstandingly exaggerated feature is made into an object of reflection. Usually it is not a univocal symbol that is thus represented but a multivocal one, a semantic molecule with many components' (51). The reduction of outward complexity is a move towards abstraction that in turn enables the elaboration of complex thought, as the reduced item becomes ideologically detachable and recombinable across a range of semantic fields. The monstrous mask does not just facilitate abstract thinking but serves to rewire patterns of aversion and desire in prescribed ways. Turner here draws on Williams James's 'law of dissociation by varying concomitants' to explain how monsters teach neophytes 'to distinguish clearly between different levels of reality':

> Here, I think, Williams James's so called 'law of dissociation' may help us clarify the problem of monsters. It may be stated as follows: when *a* and *b* occurred together as parts of the same total object, without being discriminated, the occurrence of one of these in a new combination *ax*, favors the discrimination of *a*, *b*, and *x* from one another. As James himself put it, 'What is associated now with one thing and now with another, tends to become dissociated from either, and to grow into an object of abstract contemplation by the mind. One might call this the law of dissociation by varying concomitants'. (52–3)

Continuing, Turner points to the power of these disassociations and reassociations to unsettle previously accepted, and therefore invisible, phenomena. The 'grotesqueness and monstrosity' of liminal *sacra* serve to dislodge key elements of the taken-for-granted lifeworld of ritual participants and make neophytes 'vividly and rapidly aware of what may be called the "factors" of their culture':

> [In ritual masks] elements are withdrawn from their usual settings and combined with one another in a totally unique configuration, the monster or dragon.

Monsters startle neophytes into thinking about objects, persons, relationships, and features of their environment they have hitherto taken for granted. … [M]onster- or fantasy-making focuses attention on the components of the masks and effigies, which are so radically ill-assorted that they stand out and can be thought about. The monstrosity of the configuration throws its elements into relief. Put a man's head on a lion's body and you think about the human head in the abstract. (53)

In the following, I will suggest that 'despotism' ('the first monster', according to Foucault; 2003 [1975]: 94) and especially *Oriental* despotism can be seen as analogous defamiliarizing devices aimed at throwing into relief and undermining the papacy, Catholicism and/or religion in the first stage of Turner and van Gennep's tripartite theory of rite. The despot's simplified, 'mask-like' features were equally exaggerated, caricatured, made into objects of reflection, and thus adaptable to a range of discourses for different purposes. By putting the head of Islam on the body of religion, or the Oriental despot on the pope/monarch (and vice versa), Enlightenment writers from Montesquieu to Helvétius encouraged people to think of religious or papal charisma and power in the abstract. But more than that, they forced a desacralization of religious authority by 're-wiring' religious affects of love and devotion, drawing them away from Catholicism and towards a secular ideal of true religion and/or republican principles of civic commitment and democratic love, exactly congruous with eighteenth-century theories of mass manipulation.[1] In order to contextualize the emergence of Oriental despotism as a tool of secular power, I begin with a brief history of the idea, as it has percolated through European discourse from Ancient Greece onwards. This will serve as a useful basis for unpacking the uses of the despot in the eighteenth century and beyond.

A brief history of Oriental despotism

Insofar as what we now understand as modernity, secularity and the nation-state emerged out of political reconfigurations in Europe during the eighteenth and nineteenth centuries (Asad 2003: 181–204), it is difficult to overestimate the importance of Oriental despotism to this genealogy. Perhaps no other concept has been so consistently deployed and instrumentalized across discourses at the dawn of modern political theory. If despotism was the first great 'ism' of the West (Sawer 1977: 12), Oriental despotism was its master variant and archetypal representative in the geopolitical cosmology of the Europe and

America. Whenever despotism is mentioned in European discourse, whether favourably or (more often) unfavourably it is usually prefixed or suffixed with 'Oriental', 'Asiatic', 'of the East', etc. The East was, and in many ways still is, the go-to geographical location for the ideal form of despotic government.[2]

Like any ideal, Oriental despotism was put to various uses. As Minuti explains, 'The classical scheme was not merely reproduced, but enriched with particular articulations and specific values which were connected to different exigencies and contexts'. So, in fifth-century Greece, the concept acted as 'an effective tool of automatic recognition of Greek identity and superiority over other "barbarous" nations, mainly the great Persian enemy', whereas in eighteenth-century revolutionary literature it became a discursive instrument for the articulation of emerging political models against fears of absolute monarchy (2012: unpaginated; Grosrichard 1979). Marian Sawer's *Marxism and the Question of the Asiatic Mode of Production* (1977) provides an in-depth survey of European uses of the concept through the last two millennia, tracing its role in domestic issues of government and its eventual elaboration in Marx's comparative economic theory. Lucette Valensi (Valensi and Denner 1993) has likewise argued that early modern Venetian literature on the Ottoman empire was composed, at least partly, in response to European fears of despotism. In contrast, Joan-Pau Rubiés (2005) and Michael Curtis (2009) have argued that European representations were not mere reflections of European concerns, but rooted in empirical evidence brought back by seventeenth- and eighteenth-century travellers like Jean-Baptiste Tavernier (1605–1689), François Bernier (1620–1688) and Jean Chardin (1643–1713). According to Rubiés and Curtis, the Oriental despot was never a simple figure of alterity but a powerful exemplar of the possibilities and pitfalls of despotic government, a kind of thinking tool for the elaboration of republican and democratic political theory that nevertheless had an independent existence outside the European political sphere.

From Aristotle to Bernier

The idea of a politico-economic system distinctive to Asian or Oriental countries and contrasted unfavourably with European systems is at least as old as Aristotle (Sawer 1977; Grosrichard 1979; Rubiés 2005; Minuti 2012). Aristotle was the first to systematize Western and non-Western forms of political organization, drawing for his historical knowledge on the polemical outpourings of centuries of Greek-Persian conflict. He divided forms of governments into three basic types: tyrannic, despotic and democratic. The key difference between tyrannic and despotic governments was that the first is established by force, whereas the second is established by consent, with the helping hand of a slavish disposition endemic to 'barbaric' and 'Asian' peoples. The *Politics* presents the distinction as follows:

> There is another sort of monarchy not uncommon among the barbarians, which nearly resembles tyranny. But this is both legal and hereditary. For barbarians being more servile in character than Hellenes, and Asiatics than Europeans, do not rebel against a despotic government. Such royalties have the nature of tyranny because the people are by nature slaves. (Sawer 1977: 5)

After Aristotle, the idea of Asiatic despotism receded into the background, before reviving, first, with the twelfth-century crusades (e.g. in the writings of Anglo-Norman historian William of Malmesbury), then in the thirteenth century with the rediscovery of Aristotle and translation of *Politics* into Latin.[3] By the fourteenth century Oriental despotism was used by Marsilius of Padua and William of Occam to attack the power of the papacy (Sawer 1977: 6). At this point the concept became tightly linked with the concept of private property: this was seen as lacking in Asia and especially parts of the world subject to Islamic law (7).

By the sixteenth century, codifications were solidifying and representations of the Asiatic despot condensed in the figure of the Turkish sultan or 'Oriental prince'. Machiavelli illustrated the difference between 'hereditary nobility' and 'service nobility' by linking the first to the Persian kingdom of Darius. Jean Bodin also tied Aristotle's Asiatic despot to the Sultan of Turkey in order to flesh out his own tripartite political system. According to Bodin, there exist three main types of kingship: royal, tyrannical and seigneurial (despotic). Whereas the royal monarch 'respects the laws of nature and hence respects the liberty and property of his subjects', the seigneurial monarch (found in Turkey, Muscovy, Tartary and Ethiopia) 'is master of both the persons and the property of his subjects' (7–8).

Ample material for speculation about Oriental governments was provided by a flourishing of travel writings in the sixteenth and seventeenth centuries. The burden of the reports about these 'previously semi-fabulous regions' was that 'Asia was dominated by absolute monarchies' (9). Central figures like Jean Baptiste Tavernier (1605–1689) and François Bernier (1620–1688) continued to build on negative representations of Oriental systems, in particular its putative rejection of private property. Bernier claimed this rejection lay behind the observed decline and backwardness of the Orient, issuing a warning to French finance minister Colbert against the encroaching power of Louis XIV and rumours that he and his minister were about to appropriate all land in France. When nineteenth-century economists explained the Oriental system as a result of the absence of land property, 'Tavernier and Bernier were cited copiously' (10).

The Oriental despot in the eighteenth century

Representations of the Orient and Oriental despot multiplied across all genres – philosophy, history, political theory, theatre, opera, etc. – from the end of the seventeenth to the beginning of the eighteenth century. During this time, Oriental despotism was primarily used by feudalists to 'discredit the supporters of absolutism by identifying them with the infidel Turks and otherwise inferior Asiatics' (Sawer 1977: 12) As French absolutism progressed under Mazarin and Louis XIV, so did anti-monarchic pamphleteering: the French monarchy was repeatedly compared to Eastern despotisms or the Turkish sultanate. The point of this propagandizing was usually not to undermine the monarchy altogether, but to emphasize the importance of a separate body of power – the aristocracy or nobility – which would have a tempering effect on sovereign power, an idea developed earlier by Machiavelli. In *Il Principe* (1532), Machiavelli had described two basic modes of political rule found throughout history: either despotic rule by a single prince, reducing all other persons to servants (exemplified by the Turkish emperor); or rule by a prince and barons empowered by their own noble birth (exemplified by the French monarchy). In the latter case the prince was subject to laws existing independently of himself and kept in check by the independent power of the nobility; in the former, he had unlimited power over his subjects, who were essentially slaves (Rubiés 2005: 117; Curtis 2009: 55). Rousseau later described *Il Principe* as 'the book of Republicans' (1986 [1762–1772]: 78).

Eighteenth-century representations of the Oriental despot were not always negative. According to Sawer, this period saw the concept of Oriental despotism emerge for the first time as a positive model of enlightened governance.[4] In particular, Jesuit missionaries in China propagated a more flattering image of the Orient, as an idyll of interreligious peace and tolerance (1977: 18). Wolff (2017) has recently traced the complex interactions between European history and the changing face of the Oriental despot, as he appeared in operatic and other stage productions, from Molière's *Le Bourgeois Gentilhomme* (1670) to Rossini's *Le Siège de Corinthe* (1826). According to him, the 'singing Turks' of the eighteenth century 'were not simply the manifestations of fantasized, exotic

Otherness, produced by imperial projects of mastery, but rather reflected a sense of intimacy, and even identity, between Turks and other Europeans, between the singing subjects and the listening public' (2017: 7). The Orient also became attractive enough to *sell*, providing some of the first tropes of early modern Gallic advertising. According to Christopher Todd, French poster art really took off in the nineteenth century, transforming advertising into 'an attractive minor art form' (1989: 547). But already in the eighteenth century:

> There were to be found appeals to the exotic and slightly erotic, reflecting the literary taste for the Orient, as in the *Pâte de Guzellik, ou Ekmecq Turc, pour la Propriété, à l'Usage du Sérail*, the *Eau Sultane du Sieur Pagnon de Constantinople*, the *Eau de Roxelane, Cosmétique Orientale*, the *Opiat Turc*, or the *Opiat Royal* which is 'le même dont on use au sérail du Grand Seigneur'. (543)[5]

Such positive evocations cannot simply be interpreted as the result of a more generous or sophisticated engagement with the Orient, however. For Wolff and Sawer, the Oriental despot's changing fortunes demonstrate he was less a reflection of empirical observations than a kind of theatrical raw material used by Europeans to '[explore] what it meant to be European' (Wolff 2017: 2). This altered constantly in response to changing historical circumstances. Although the Oriental despot was, towards the beginning of the eighteenth century, configured in almost exclusively positive terms, Wolff traces the consequent devaluation of the despot to the emergence of full-blown colonialism at the beginning of the nineteenth century. A need to dominate rather than converse with the Orient made it difficult to sustain a subtle and multifaceted engagement with racial and cultural otherness, and the Oriental despot was either forgotten or portrayed as the corrupt leader of an ailing empire:

> The Ottoman empire finally became the object of consummated imperialist aggression in 1830 with the French occupation of Algeria, and one might argue that this also inaugurated the age of high Orientalism in French culture, with Eugène Delacroix arriving in 1832, right behind the occupation. This was, however, the very moment that European operas on Ottoman subjects ceased to play a major role in the repertory ... In other words, far from being produced as a cultural consequence of European Orientalism, these operas could no longer flourish in an age of high Orientalism, the age of European colonization of Ottoman territory, the age of the Ottoman empire as the Sick Man of Europe. (8)

Lucette Valensi (1993) has similarly linked the late-eighteenth-century devaluation of the Oriental despot to the gradual transition of power from the Ottomans to Europe.

Combining Sawer and Wolff's analyses together, a two-way movement can thus be traced in the quality of despotic representations, from the seventeenth to the nineteenth century: the Oriental despot first evolves from a negative to a relatively positive example, as philosophers and political speculators appealed to the Orient for existing models of 'enlightened despotism', valour and powerful passions (perhaps, among other things, reflecting nostalgia for the old 'honour ethic' on the wane since the seventeenth century);[6] then from a positive to a negative example, as colonialism began to peak at the beginning of the nineteenth century. As colonial violence increased, it became harder to recognize the colonized, and necessary to paint their systems of government in increasingly broad and darker brushstrokes.

This model is elegant but does not add up entirely since, as Wolff himself admits, even authors and composers who initially seemed sympathetic to the Orient frequently reverted to reductive and negative caricatures within their own work – and this well within the eighteenth century. Mozart's *Die Entführung aus dem Serail* (*The Abduction from the Seraglio* or *Il Seraglio*, 1782) portrays a pasha 'wrestling with his own dark side – perhaps his Turkish side, or perhaps simply his sense of his own absolute power'. The pasha forces himself upon the embodiment of European virtue, Konstanze, threatening her with 'tortures of all kinds' if she does not submit. As Wolff writes,

> His barbarous threat becomes the point of departure for her dazzling musical acrobatics, a triumph of vocal ornamentation that anticipates the certain triumph of her European virtue. He possesses absolute power over her, but she demonstrates her defiance by showing in the extraordinary range, length, and ornamentation of the aria that she can do something that he can never do: she can sing! ... The clash of civilization between Turkey and Europe here appeared in its starkest outlines, represented as an inseparable chasm between barbarous menace and brilliant civilization, the latter expressed in a vocal display of operatic mastery. (2017: 197)

Similarly, Mozart's 1788 *Beim Auszug in das Feld* (*On Leaving for the Front*) portrayed the Holy Roman Emperor Joseph II as 'a hero of the Enlightenment' facing off against backward and intolerant Turks, who 'sink many a lovely land ... in waste and horror' and know 'no duty but murder'. As Wolff himself concludes, Mozart's opera showed from at least one angle that 'the Turks were the one people more than any other who needed to be taught, by military force, the lessons of the Enlightenment' (220–1).

These more negative representations suggest the vagaries of the Oriental despot through European discourse do not track perfectly the expansion of

European colonialism. Other factors seem to have been involved that made the Oriental despot an attractive figure for domestic polemics in different areas of political culture. In fact, as Sawer points out, one stream of writers alongside Montesquieu consistently employed Oriental despotism as a negative model for Europe, 'the epitome of all that was to be avoided at home' (1977: 16). Intriguingly, this stream consisted almost entirely of figures registered under Taylor's label of 'radical Enlightenment', including two of the most famous atheists of the eighteenth century, Helvétius and Holbach:

> One of the earliest of these was Helvétius, who agreed with Montesquieu's use of the concept as a means to attack native French absolutism, but disagreed with the alternatives to absolutism put forward by Montesquieu. Where Montesquieu wished to preserve aristocratic privilege as a counterbalance to the monarchy, Helvétius wished to initiate a limited and secular monarchy, uncluttered by such a multiplication of petty despotisms. It is in Helvétius's *De l'Esprit* (1758) that the phrase 'Oriental despotism' appears, probably for the first time. (16–17)

According to Sawer, although Helvétius coined 'Oriental despotism', the term really entered common currency with the publication of Boulanger's anti-religious polemic *Recherches sur l'Origine du Despotisme Oriental* (published in 1761 by Baron d'Holbach). The concept, if not the term, was in fact widespread through virtually all anti-monarchic and/or anti-Catholic Enlightenment literatures, from *De l'Esprit des Lois* (1748) to the *Encyclopédie* (1751–1782). These works often articulated their attacks through hierarchical racial classifications in fashion at the time. *De l'Esprit* described 'ancient Persians' as 'the vilest and most cowardly of all people' (1759 [1758]: 386), repeatedly contrasting the slavish submissiveness, vileness and cowardliness of 'Orientals' with the spirit of Europeanness, which came closer to 'the heroism of the Greeks' (399). The *Encyclopédie*'s entry for 'Arabia' was brief and to the point: 'Arabs are Muslims; they are governed by emirs or sheikhs, each independent from the others but all dependent on the Sultan. Arabs are thieves and thugs' (Diderot and d'Alembert 2016 [1751–1782]: I. 570).[7]

I do not think this convergence of eighteenth-century Orientalism, racism and secularism is coincidental. In order to understand the persistence and ultimate rise to predominance of the monstrous Oriental despot, it is important to recognize not just the colonial background of Enlightenment culture but the mutual imbrication of Oriental despotism and the Enlightenment's sharpening challenge to the category of religion. Even before the advent of high colonialism, the Oriental despot was being put to work to both define and fight against religion: on one hand by undermining Christian notions of religious and civilizational uniqueness; and, on the other, by yoking profane Islam and sacred Christianity to the same religious taxon. It is not by accident that Helvétius attacked religion in two stages, first through a critique of Islam and only then through a critique of 'all nations' ('What I have said of the Arabs and Saffrians may be applied to all nations influenced by the motives of religion'; 1759 [1758]: 429). Such specific appeals to Oriental otherness for an assault on religion in general marked the culmination of a way of thinking about representation, the emotions and the body in currency since at least the late seventeenth century, and lend weight to Mahmood's (2010) argument that our 'secular age' was, at its roots, intrinsically dependent on representations of other cultures.

In order to deepen analysis of the relation between representations of the Orient and eighteenth-century secularism, and – crucially – to show that such representations did not emerge from a vacuum but were reflective of the empiricist context in which they emerged, I turn to two works in particular that had a formative impact on eighteenth-century thought as a whole and established a foundation for the development of high-colonial discourse: Montesquieu's epistolary novel *Lettres Persanes* (1721) and his later work of political theory *De l'Esprit des Lois* (1748). I examine the *Lettres* particularly for its form and narrative technique, and *De l'Esprit* for its theoretical framework, which, I argue, concretized a number of elements already present in the *Lettres*. I will suggest that both works deployed Oriental despotism as an affective trope connecting European religion to Eastern abjectness, in order to bring about a Cartesian and/or Turnerian reconfiguration of European affects and sensibilities. Whilst neither *Lettres* nor *De l'Esprit* are the most Orientalist or racist works of the eighteenth century, their sophistication makes them an exceptionally interesting examples of the secular-Orientalist mindset, and how subtly this could shape eighteenth-century discussions of religion.

Wonder and difference in *Lettres Persanes* (1721)

> *It seems to me, Usbek, that we never judge things except through a secret return upon ourselves.*
>
> Montesquieu, Lettres Persanes (1973 [1721]: 156)

Lettres Persanes traces the fortunes of two Persian noblemen, Usbek and Rica, as they leave Persia for Europe and settle in France in 1712. The story is told through a series of letters, mainly by Usbek, to acquaintances back in Persia and a seraglio of five female captives, Zashi, Zéphis, Fatmé, Zélis and Roxane. The bulk of these recount Usbek and Rica's encounters with European culture: their discoveries, surprises, pleasures and disappointments, as they navigate their way through French society and reflect upon what they hear and see. Usbek is portrayed, on one hand, as an idealized man of the Enlightenment, coolly detached from his observations and quick to highlight the contradictions and conceits of French society; and on the other, as a petty tyrant still unable to relinquish control over his five wives, or even recognize his own despotic tendencies. Usbek's relation to the seraglio sours as the narrative progresses, since his distance from Persia makes it difficult to retain the control he wielded at home. Despite his appeals to the head eunuch, Usbek is unable to prevent the seraglio's descent into chaos and his wives' consequent death. These events mark the end of Usbek's enlightened aspirations and his eventual return to Persia.

According to Isaiah Berlin, '[Montesquieu's] vignettes of characters and situations are not stylized, neither caricatures nor idealizations in the manner of his century' (1979: 137). This is certainly untrue of *De l'Esprit des Lois*. But the case of the *Lettres Persanes* is more complex. In order to draw out the subtleties of this 'foundational work of the Enlightenment' (Wolff 2017: 8), it is necessary to dig below the surface level of representation, to reveal the tacit structure of irony underlying the work. Drawing especially on Jean Starobinsky's (1973) analysis of the *Lettres*, I suggest there is an intimate link between the work's narrative device of presenting France through the eyes of travelling Persians and contemporaneous theory on the power of the passions. A reframing of the *Lettres* in these terms suggests the superficial generosity of Montesquieu's engagement with Persianness and Oriental despotism testifies less to a genuine concern with anthropological fairness or accuracy than to a maximization of the *Lettres'* polemical force, in line with ambient theories of the emotional subject.

Epistemic framework: from empiricism to despotism

The *Lettres* is an empiricist work. At one point, Usbek describes an ideal society – articulated in terms of a fictional group of 'Troglodyte' breakaways – that directly echoes Descartes, Locke and Grégoire's theories on the cultivation of virtue through the senses. According to Usbek, this society raised its children to virtue by 'ceaselessly' placing the tragic example of its compatriots' misfortune (i.e. the misfortune of the abandoned Troglodytes) 'before their eyes'. The breakaways were thereby made to 'feel' ('sentir') that 'the interest of the individual always rests in the interest of the group [*l'intérêt commun*]' and the society thrived as a result.

Its people entered a feedback loop of increasing reproductivity and virtue, since the greater number of moral 'examples' led to increasing virtue, which in turn led to increased reproductivity: 'virtue, far from diluting in the multitude, was, on the contrary, strengthened by the greater number of examples' (Montesquieu 1973 [1721]: 71).

The *Lettres* also evinces a distinct ambivalence regarding the power of locally acquired habits and dispositions. As Starobinski explains, Montesquieu everywhere alludes to the superiority of the universal, through the ironic proliferation of cultural particularities (1973: 8–9). The more he references specific cultural institutions, the more contingent, ridiculous and extraneous they seem. For example, the shift to a universal plane of enlightened 'love', 'charity' and 'humanity' comes through a devaluation of the external, material and ritualistic aspects of religion, which always divide and particularize, and whose adoption is anyway a matter of historical contingency. As Usbek writes to Rhédi: 'one must choose the ceremonies of one religion over those of two thousand [others]' (Montesquieu 1973 [1721]: 126–7).

Yet Montesquieu on occasion seems to take up a less universalist position, that recognizes the force of habit and raises unsettling questions about reason's subservience to historically contingent, conditioned desires. At one point Zélis writes to Usbek:

> I cannot agree with these mothers who only confine their daughters when they are on the point of giving them a husband; who, condemning rather than devoting them to the seraglio, make them violently embrace a way of life they should have inspired in them. Must one expect everything from the force of reason and nothing from the gentleness of habit? It is pointless to speak to us of natural subordination: it is not enough to make us feel it; one must make us practise it, so that it sustains us at this critical time when the passions start to grow, and encourages us towards independence. (160–1)

On one hand, this passage may be read as a straightforward endorsement of 'the force of reason', coded in patriarchal terms and foregrounding the will as the pivot on which subordination and freedom turn (answering 'yes' to Zélis's rhetorical question). On the other, it may be a warning about the way free choices and desires are conditioned before the act of will, and beneath the surface level of consciousness. Zélis supports neither liberation nor forceful imprisonment for her fellow captives, but their wilful subjugation, the re-orientation of their desires. Her friends should be 'inspired' through a process of early habituation to freely choose the life of the seraglio. Their subjugation is not a matter of the freedom of the will itself but of the way the will is pre-conditioned to swing one way or another – a process connected to the body since, for Zélis, not only must subordination be felt, but practised and developed into a habit.

Montesquieu clearly intended the above passage as a caution concerning the power of habitual conditioning. But whether he sought thereby to discredit the habits in general, or merely to warn about the bad uses to which the habits could be put is unclear, and, I would suggest, deliberately so. The main question stemming from his position is not whether we could escape our contingently acquired habits – an impossibility on empiricist grounds – but who or what had privileged access to the sensual input of the unformed human.

This experience- and power-sensitive conception of the subject anticipates two related developments of the eighteenth century: the turn towards 'soft' methods of statecraft examined in the previous chapter, and the elaboration of Oriental despotism as the ideal form of corrupt power. Whereas, in the sixteenth century, Francis de la Noue (1531–1591) could still describe the Turkish kingdom as 'a terrible tyranny', Çırakman argues this coercive model was superseded in the eighteenth century by the softer model of despotism (2001: 53) – a trend which echoed emerging insights into the power of sensual conditioning.[8] If the figure of Oriental power was, as Sawer, Rubiés and others have argued, a 'thinking tool' for the elaboration of Western political thought, the nature of this figure could not but alter in accordance with evolving theories of socialization. Increasing concerns over the political ramifications of empiricism would naturally foster the creation of a sensually manipulative Oriental despot, accused of controlling our surroundings to his advantage.[9] Nicolas Boulanger later used precisely this assumption for his own attack on Oriental despotism, claiming that '[young Asiatics] kiss their chains' because surrounding objects impress on their minds that 'they are slaves and ought to be so' (1762 [1761]: 20, 26).[10]

If the content and theory of the *Lettres* showcased a complex, tripartite interaction between empiricism, religion and power that reflected the broader context of French thought on the manipulation of people and passions, how was this reflected in the form of the work? How did the *Lettres* and particularly its device of a Persian gaze function as an empirical, anti-Catholic weapon in its own right? I will suggest that the *Lettres* did so in two ways: first, by inducing a sense of peculiarity or strangeness around common objects of perception associated with religion; and second, by superimposing Oriental symbols on these objects, so reconfiguring the structure of affect linked to formerly sacred objects of worship.

Surprise/wonder

For Starobinksi, the Persian attribution of the *Lettres* fulfils a number of purposes besides protecting Montesquieu's anonymity. Since it would not, in fact, have been difficult for authorities to uncover Montesquieu, Starobinski argues the intended effect has less to do with authorship than 'the constitution of the work itself'. On one hand, it confers on the 'found' documents an authority they would not have otherwise, since it bestows upon them 'the prestige of an origin external to any literary tradition' and thus frames the content of the letters as a matter of fact rather than creative elaboration (1973: 7–8). On the other, the 'outsider' perspective provides rich opportunities for satire, as it renders peculiar what is otherwise absorbed into the background of European life and therefore invisible. The conceit of a foreign gaze provides the necessary distance to draw out commonplace aspects of European life and recast them in the experiential terms of the naïve and detached Oriental other, for example, by allowing Montesquieu to focus only on those aspects of French society that *stand out* for the foreign visitors. The fictional mode privileges those aspects of French culture found 'striking' and 'singular' by the 'Oriental spectator', and which therefore mark a considerable 'gap of ignorance' ('écart d'ignorance') between observer and object. The effect is to 'renew' aspects of French culture and society that are commonly taken for granted and left unquestioned.

> Ideas, propositions ... are thought and traced for the first time; whoever states them clearly feels the pleasure of surprise derived from formulating them. The fiction of the travelling Persian is therefore rejuvenating, not only for the external objects he describes ... but the truths he brings to light. Certain great principles, well known, too well known, forgotten, can therefore be recalled, by their attribution to a newcomer who exposes them at the very moment his reason perceives them. (10–11)

By reflexively taking up the standpoint of the geographical and cultural outsider, Montesquieu provides a veritable anthropology of Europe or reverse Orientalism, allowing French readers to distance themselves from their own background and customs: 'In the erotic imaginary, Persia is close; in the observational irony, France, anonymous and caricatured, becomes a distant continent' (14). All the usual terms are inverted: East becomes West, Muslim becomes Christian, savage becomes civilized. Rica reassures Ibben that 'no kingdom has suffered from as many civil wars as the kingdom of Christ' (Montesquieu 1973 [1721]: 102). Islam is defended precisely for its non-violence: 'The sacred religion ... defends itself by its own truth; it has no need of such violent ways to sustain itself' (104).

In a striking inversion of nineteenth-century anthropology and imperialism, none of the people encountered by Usbek and Rica are named. Under the Persians' gaze, 'the individual, stripped of all personal identity, exists only through stereotyped gestures and speech, which characterize them as representative of a category: the eclipse of the [individual] name lays bare the social role, the function, the generic behaviour' (13). Moreover, like early anthropologists, the Persians are continually struck by the extraordinary words and practices of the self-same-other. Unaware of the cultural connections linking European ideas, customs and practices, they weave a picture of eighteenth-century France that is radically disjointed, almost pointillist, in its exclusive attention to the unexpected. This picture provides a disaggregating hermeneutic for readers to conceptualize, and therefore abstract themselves from, core facets of their own surrounding culture (14). Usbek's blindness to the cultural connections underwriting his experience of French society brings into the relief the logical lacunae and contradictions at the heart of the West and recasts them as the end point of an accumulated and oppressive tradition: 'Close connections do not exist or are no longer operational … [the] unprepared gaze becomes wise to lacunas and ruptures. … *Non sequiturs* become apparent' (15). Disaggregated facets of the West may then become the object of a second-order game of reassociation, in which successive singular images are combined incongruously, even sacrilegiously (e.g. a gossipy letter about Suphis follows a letter on the attributes of God), making surprise intrinsic to the structure of the *Lettres*. As Starobinski writes, 'The reader's thought process is forced to undergo sharp movements [*déplacements*], which are not without reward, by virtue of their incongruity. … Surprise … is the state of mind towards which the very tone of the *Lettres* constantly throws us' (10).

Recall that Montesquieu saw himself standing in the tradition of Descartes (to Isaiah Berlin's puzzlement). And indeed, Montesquieu's polemic construction closely mirrors Descartes's seventeenth-century views on wonder. According to Fisher, *Les Passions de l'Âme* is distinguished from other seventeenth-century works by its foregrounding of wonder (*admiration*) as the 'master' of and secret key to the other the passions. For Descartes, our entire experience is contingent on the wonder of the unexpected, the unordinary, or that which 'was not always already there' (Fisher 1998: 20). Descartes denies the possibility of 'feeling' the ordinary; experience of anything depends on 'a definable moment of a special kind that might be noticed, remembered, formulated in description, something discrete within the flow of time, something clear, self-contained, separable from what came before and after' (20). For objects to exist for us, they must bring about a rupture in the texture of lived experience; they must stand out.[11]

Part of my argument here is that the self-reflexive wonder of the *Lettres* functions to simultaneously pick out, isolate and critique an increasingly sharply defined category of the eighteenth century: religion. Religion emerges through the wonder that is constructed or performed around the Persians' naïve observations. What was hitherto absorbed into the background as another strand in the fabric of daily experience is here unravelled and subjected to the penetrating gaze of the Oriental other, thereby enacting the first stage in Descartes's declension from raw experience to objectification. If it is true, following W. C. Smith, that the eighteenth-century Enlightenment saw religion conceived for the first time as 'a generalization, abstracted, of something in which other people are involved' (22), the device of a foreign perspective was crucial to this process since it provided unparalleled opportunities for extracting religion – especially 'external' religion – from the habitual, making it strange and therefore real.

Superimposition

There is, then, a persistent tendency throughout the *Lettres* to place old facts before rejuvenated eyes and make them the object of a fresh judgement. This tendency is in line with the thrust of seventeenth- and eighteenth-century thought on affect and the formation of virtuous bodies. But the 'outsider' perspective also allows Montesquieu to reframe the habitual in radically other terms, thereby warping the *substance* of the Persians' objects of experience. The 'mythological mask' (Starobinski 1973: 16) deployed by Montesquieu to navigate French censorship rules on one hand allows him to mention 'what would, under its true name, be taboo' and, on the other, forces a redefinition of familiar objects in

(a) empirical terms – Homer becomes 'an old Greek poet' (Montesquieu 1973 [1721]: 113), a rosary a collection of 'small wooden grains' (103), the French king a magician who 'turns paper into money' (91), and the pope the 'chief of Christians' or 'an old idol worshiped through habit' (101)

(b) the 'equivalent' terms of the other – Benedictine monks become 'dervishes', (151), church becomes 'mosque' (96, 105, 119) and the Bible becomes the 'Qur'an' of the English (240)

The Persians' 'voluntary aphasia' or 'rediscovered materiality' effectively 'desacralizes' heretofore sacred beings and objects, by 'reclaiming them in the language of profanity or that of a competing religion' (Starobinski 1973: 17). This language is profane in two senses. On one hand, the erasure of a common grammar encoding religious convictions leaves only religion's exterior aspect – bare, empirical descriptions of ritual gestures 'stripped of the justification they receive from the "chain" linking ceremonies, dogma and "other truths"' (17). By peeling back the aura of prestige surrounding objects of faith, the Persians leave only 'the thin surface, delivered to naïve perception' (17–18). On the other, by 'sliding beneath the image of France, that of the despotic Orient', Montesquieu produces 'an effect of superimposition' that makes apparent 'the risks of an *orientalization* of the French monarchy' (23–4, emphasis original).[12] This 'hyperbolic' effect of superimposition itself occurs in at least two ways: through Montesquieu's game of linguistic substitution and through the construct of Usbek's domestic despotism, which stands as 'an eroticized *figure* of the *political* despotism that prevails in the Orient' (36, emphasis original).[13] Analogies and ironies multiply, both through the Persians' 'translation' of European culture into the terms of the objectionable other, and the reader's grasp of the meta-analogy framing Usbek's own limited, historically contingent perspective.

Montesquieu's transposition of terms was not neutral, even in the eighteenth century. His substitutes ('dervishes', 'mosques', 'seraglio') were already negatively valenced as a result of centuries of pejorative discourse about the Oriental and especially Persian other. This is why it is difficult to agree with Joan-Pau Rubiés, that Montesquieu's ultimate aim was 'not to create a gulf between the despotic East and Europe, but rather to state that despotic tendencies were universal' (2005: 168). Rubiés assumes that Montesquieu merely sought to encode a universal set of principles without regard for national or cultural boundaries; on this reading, Usbek and Rica could have come from anywhere. Yet, if irony works in the *Lettres* by analogy, the movement from plane to plane – from Christianity to Islam, or from the French monarchy to Oriental despotism – was not purely semiotic or clean. For Orientalization to be understood as a risk and not an opportunity required an entire pre-existing system of references that would ensure the correct reception, emotional as well as semiotic.

On one hand, this pre-existing system was strong enough that Montesquieu did not need to make his warnings explicit, only spelling them out later in *De l'Esprit des Lois*. On the other, the Persians' radical otherness is preserved in the *Lettres* through a number of reversals, whereby Persian attributes are straightforwardly made to stand for the cultural flipside of civilized France: e.g. Usbek's petty despotism and the scenic construct of the seraglio shore up a narrative of degenerate Oriental eroticism that would become the stock-in-trade of high colonialism.[14] According to Starobinski, by reserving the 'passional register' ('registre passionnel') for the Orient, Montesquieu makes clear that 'A very precise dividing line separates the world of sentiments, this Orient of the soul, and the superficial busyness that abounds in France' (1973: 13). Whilst it is debatable that the Orient stands for the passional register generally, since there is little in the *Lettres* to suggest a blanket criticism of the emotions, Oriental or otherwise (and this, as we have seen, would be out of character with the wider French Enlightenment), the Orient is still delineated on the basis of certain emotional attributes. For example, Usbek and Rica – not Frenchmen – are the *de facto* vehicles of jealousy and anger.[15] Moreover, Montesquieu makes clear that the Orient still provides the best example of a despotic model driven by fear. Thus Rica complains that 'At home, temperaments are all uniform because they are forced: one does not see people as they are but as they are constrained to be. In this servitude of the heart and spirit, one hears only fear, which has only one language, and not nature, which expresses itself so differently, and appears under so many forms' (1973 [1721]: 162). Similarly, Usbek's earlier claim that Islam is a religion of non-violence is directly contradicted by the observations of a fictional Zoroastrian, embedded in the epistolary narrative of letter LXVII. This 'letter within a letter' tells the story of a travelling Zoroastrian who loses his sister to a seraglio, finds her indoctrinated by Muslim captors and attempts to undo her 'willing slavery'. He tells his sister that 'only chance ... introduced Mahometism [into Persia]' and that 'this sect was established there, not by persuasion, but by conquest' (174). That this is in fact the correct reading of Islam is later made clear in *De l'Esprit des Lois,* where Islam is described as '[speaking] only by the sword' (1777b [1748]: 162).

Moreover, Usbek remains a *personnage clivé,* torn between his commitment to the values of Enlightenment and his power over the seraglio – a fractured identity that ensures any criticism levelled by him at France inevitably boomerangs against himself. The irony of *Lettres Persanes* is bidirectional. Just as Usbek's outsider perspective paints a picture of French society configured in Oriental terms, providing a warning against absolute monarchy, enlightened Usbek himself remains blind to the despotic forces at play in his own tyrannic micro-state. The reader seizes the situation in a kind of double play of irony, where the Persian other is simultaneously elevated as a prophet of enlightened progress and dismissed as a hypocrite. This allows Montesquieu to co-opt the othering language of the other without compromising the absoluteness of French superiority, since it is the Frenchman who, in the end, has the widest possible angle of vision over the drama.

Finally, every direct criticism of Oriental despotism or Islam not only discredited the Persians' observations but multiplied the effect of their critique since it lowered the standard of the judger and gave new urgency to European uprightness and reform. The strategy of allowing French society to be criticized, not just by outsiders but by Persians, had pedagogical value in itself. As Usbek puts it, 'There is nothing more humiliating than the thought of scandalizing heathens themselves. We are therefore required to maintain an equivocal conduct' (Montesquieu 1973 [1721]: 158–9).[16]

Orientalism?

According to Wolff, the *Lettres* 'concerned the balance of difference and resemblance between Christian Europe and Muslim Persia, and served as an implicit model for later reflections on the Ottoman empire'. For him, it is evidence of the fact that 'many writers of the Enlightenment were both deeply interested in understanding different societies and notably self-aware of their own relative cultural perspectives as shaping their observations', and therefore that 'The anthropology of the Enlightenment involved an engagement with other societies that was not simply a matter of constructing a binary system of Self and Other' (2017: 8–9). The Enlightenment's 'non-binary' engagement with other societies is then taken by Wolff as the basis for a later entrenchment of the East-West distinction, following the advent of high-colonialism.

The foregoing has drawn out a number of issues with this type of assessment by focusing on the strategic construction of *Lettres Persanes* as a polemic document addressing exclusively European concerns. In this light, Montesquieu's 'sympathetic' engagement with the Orient testifies less to European writers' interest in understanding different societies than to the usefulness of the alien – especially Oriental – standpoint for reflecting on and critiquing European society and religion. Despite the superficial generosity of his approach, Montesquieu's irony combined with a number of outright, reductive reversals, ultimately preserves a stable binary of self and other that would have been clear to readers in the eighteenth century.[17] Indeed, the very stability of Persian inferiority allowed Montesquieu to construct a vicious attack on the Catholic Church while seeming to elevate non-European cultures in a spirit of ecumenity. The Persianness of the travellers operated as a Turnerian ritual mask in two ways: on one hand, it allowed Montesquieu to criticize the Church in relative safety. But it also allowed him to overlay the most abject and degenerate template for 'religion' writ large over the sacred Church, prompting a fundamental recalibration of religious affects, even while Islam was held up as the rational antidote to Western habits and customs.

As the eighteenth century progressed, Montesquieu's evolving thoughts on despotic government coincided with a sharpening critique of non-Protestant religions, resulting in a hardened ideological stance against the latter, especially the double entity Catholicism/Islam. The move from fiction to political theory brought about a calcification of categories as Montesquieu articulated explicitly what was earlier embedded in the background of the *Lettres,* abandoning the latter's subtle allusions in favour of reductive caricatures of the East or Arabs. The *locus classicus* for these developments is Montesquieu's seminal work of political theory and speculative Orientalism *De l'Esprit des Lois* (1748).

Orientalism and secularism in *De l'Esprit des Lois* (1748)

If Machiavelli first introduced the idea of limited monarchy, it was left to Montesquieu to develop it systematically into a complete theory of political organization. *De l'Esprit des Lois* became a fundamental reference point for all political thought during the eighteenth century and after. Almost every treatise of political philosophy produced in the following half-century makes implicit or explicit reference to its core ideas. It was extensively and approvingly quoted in the *Encyclopédie* (e.g. in its entry on 'Christianisme') and its theory of the separation of powers had a particularly important impact on liberal political theory and the Founding Fathers of the United States, who referred frequently to the work in their drafting of the American constitution (Curtis 2009: 79).

Like his predecessors, Montesquieu used the concept of Oriental despotism as 'a weapon against absolutism' (Sawer 1977: 13). Unlike the more radical republicans who would gain ascendancy over the century, however, he still favoured a monarchy, albeit one in which sovereign power was tempered by intermediary bodies. For Montesquieu, absolute monarchies were too imbalanced and republics too fragile; the only viable model was a compromise between the two whereby monarchy and aristocracy kept each other in permanent check. Montesquieu argued that the erosion of the feudal nobility led inexorably to despotism: the centralization of power in the single figure of the king, who ruled over 'an atomized mass of social nothings' (13). The primary example for this blew from the East. For him, Asia was 'that part of the world where absolute power is to some measure naturalized' (1777a [1748]: 79).

Accounting for this peculiarity of the East, Montesquieu appealed to his theory of the climatic variation of peoples.[18] According to him, the great differences in learning, economy and politics observable across different cultures was attributable to differences in the climate and geography of their respective countries. Oriental despotism was a natural result of two factors: on one hand, despotic government was necessary to rule over vast territories unbounded by natural barriers (e.g. land and sea);[19] on the other, Asia suffered from extreme variations in temperature and had no temperate zone. This led to an imbalance of power between cold and hot regions, since the former grew strong and easily overcame and enslaved the 'enervated' nations of the latter (1777a [1748]: 317).

Despite the physical determinism at the heart of Montesquieu's analysis, non-geographical factors like religion could also have an effect on political systems. In most cases religion existed in symbiotic relation with its climatic and political environment; according to Montesquieu, 'a moderate Government is most agreeable to the Christian Religion, and a despotic Government to the Mahometan' (1777b [1748]: 160). Since the 'Arabs' were 'a people addicted to robbery ... frequently guilty of doing injury and injustice' (173), a more oppressive and violent form of religion was needed. This was provided by Islam, a religion which 'speaks only by the sword' and 'acts still upon men with that destructive spirit with which it was founded' (162). Islam could also underpin (rather than merely complement) despotism: 'In Mahomedan countries, it is partly from their religion that the people derive the surprising veneration they have for their prince' (1777a [1748]: 76). Though Montesquieu here placed Christianity in general on the side of moderation, he later split the religion into Catholic and Protestant factions with the first now indexed to the despotic model (see below).

Religion could also act as a countervailing force against natural factors, although this was always in the context of a displacement of religion from its natural environment. The redemptive power of religion was illustrated by Christianity: 'It is the Christian religion that, in spite of the extent of the empire and the influence of the climate, has hindered despotic power from being established in Ethiopia, and has carried into the heart of Africa the manners and laws of Europe' (1777b [1748]: 161). This passage illustrates well the simultaneously particular and universal thrust of the Enlightenment. Christianity was both organically connected to the circumscribed geography of Latin Christendom and exportable to the world at large as the carrier of universal values, despite its incompatibility in principle with the Ethiopian climate. Already in the eighteenth century, Anquetil-Duperron accused Montesquieu of misusing the concept of Oriental despotism to rationalize the confiscation of native land (Sawer 1977: 23; Rubiés 2005: 114).[20]

Church conflicts

Although Montesquieu praised Christianity throughout the book, *De l'Esprit des Lois* was placed on the Index of 1751. It is not difficult to see why. In the first instance, and in line with the eighteenth century's insistence on the power of habits, Montesquieu tacitly criticized the Catholic Church through a Lockean demystification of 'external ritual' as that which attaches us to religion and blinds us to the oppressive ideology of a bloated clergy. Examples again came from the East:

> A religion burdened with many ceremonies attaches us to it more strongly than that which has a fewer number. We have an extreme propensity to things in which we are continually employed: witness the obstinate prejudices of the Mahometans and the Jews, and the readiness with which barbarous and savage nations change their religion, who, as they are employed entirely in hunting or war, have but few religious ceremonies. ... When external worship is attended with great magnificence, it flatters our minds and strongly attaches us to religion. The riches of temples and those of the clergy greatly affect us. Thus even the misery of the people is a motive that renders them fond of a religion which has served as a pretext to those who were the cause of their misery. (1777b [1748]: 185)

Since the clergy was 'a family which cannot be extinct' and its wealth was 'fixed to it for ever' (189), Montesquieu concluded, in proto-revolutionary style, that 'These men play against the people, but they hold the bank themselves' (191). Whereas the Northern (Protestant) climate was naturally conducive to an eternal 'spirit of liberty and independence', the Southern (Catholic) climate bred a dullness and slavishness of spirit that led inexorably to dependence on a 'visible head':

> When the Christian religion, two centuries ago, became unhappily divided into Catholic and Protestant, the people of the north embraced the Protestant, and those of the south adhered still to the Catholic. The reason is plain: the people of the north have, and will for ever have, a spirit of liberty and independence, which the people of the south have not; and therefore a religion which has no visible head is more agreeable to the independency of the climate than that which has one. (163)

The pope, or 'visible head', was explicitly presented as an analogue of the Oriental despot. According to Montesquieu, popes behaved like 'the princes of the East' who, 'being educated in a prison where eunuchs corrupt their hearts and debase their understandings', '[abandon] themselves in their seraglio to the most brutal passions; pursuing, in the midst of a prostituted court, every capricious extravagance' (1777a [1748]: 23).

Montesquieu's second point of conflict with the Church concerned Christianity as a whole. If religion was bound up with models of state, his theory of climatic variations implicitly relativized Christianity, since it made it at least partly the result of environmental factors rather than a *sui generis* belief system established through exceptional revelation. This was an inherently materialist perspective in which various religions could be placed alongside each other and explained by reference to their different conditioning factors – factors that often revealed the baseness and expediency of 'universally-binding' religious codes around the world. Thus, Islam forbade eating pork because hogs were rare in Arabia and spread disease; Hinduism forbade eating beef because cows were rare in India and needed for other functions. Christianity was (at least theoretically) no exception, making it difficult to justify its privileged position as the bearer of a unique and sacred truth.[21]

Finally, following Montesquieu's model, the link between political and ecclesiastical power was reduced to one of instrumental utility. Any conception of a necessary link between Catholic God and monarch was projected outwards onto the Oriental despot as a form of false conscience, severely weakening the relation between a church and state whose mutual support became a matter of expediency. Even if different religions grew organically and symbiotically out of their different environments, theological and political doctrine (or 'the principles of society') could be analytically separated and the former valued not just for its truth but its *utility* to the stability of the nation-state. Thus, 'The most true and holy doctrines may be attended with the very worst consequences when they are not connected with the principles of society: and on the contrary, doctrines the most false may be attended with excellent consequences when contrived so as to be connected with these principles' (1777b [1748]: 175). In short, doctrines could be 'false', yet still 'extremely useful' (155, 177), severing the link between religious truth and political morality, and instrumentalizing the church's salvational theology (and institutional base), which now became a mere appendage to the more important project of founding a stable national society – a society contrasted, naturally, with the ideal-type antithesis of a free republic, the Oriental sultanate.[22]

De l'Esprit des Lois thus underscored three fundamental features of the secular at the dawn of the modern nation-state: an anti-Catholic turn away from external religion and towards Protestantism as the natural ally of 'liberty and independence', articulated in terms of a rejection of 'corrupt', 'debased' and 'brutal' Oriental despotism; the relativization of Christian belief, since Christianity, like every other belief system (but especially Islam), grew and survived on the basis of a harmony between itself and its particular environment (a small section of an ever-expanding globe); and the conceptual separation of religious and political doctrine (mirroring an institutional separation of church and state), since their relation was no longer deemed necessary but one of expedient and mutual beneficence. In almost all cases the Orient and concepts of Oriental despotism served as a master symbol or ritual mask for the codification of secular values.

The strategy of linking negative representations of the Orient to a critique of religion gradually gained momentum, reaching archetypal form in the major anti-religious polemics of the mid- to late-eighteenth century like Helvétius's *De l'Esprit* (1758) and Boulanger's *Recherches sur l'Origine du Despotisme Oriental* (1761). These mixed anti-Islamic and racist stereotypes freely and affectively. Helvétius asserted that Christian domination over the Turks resulted from the 'Musulman's stupidity', since the Islamic religion was 'only fit to eternise the stupidity and haplessness of that nation' (1759 [1758]: 436). Muhammed himself was 'a mere merchant, without learning, without education' who fell prey to the very fanaticism he inspired and only composed 'the mediocre and ridiculous work named the Koran' with the help of Greek monks (479). If Europeans now looked down upon the nations of Asia, it was because time had 'subdued them to a despotism incompatible with a certain elevation of mind' (458). Oriental princes themselves could not escape 'the general ignorance of their own nation', for their eyes were 'covered with a thicker darkness than those of their subjects' (390). And so on.

Conclusion

Introducing his seminal work of religious theory *Imagining Religion* (1982), J. Z. Smith cites Frances Hutchinson on Shaftesbury's account of Western travel writing and 'the monstrous taste which has possessed both the readers and writers of travels'. According to Hutcheson, these are

> sparing enough in account of the natural affections, the families, associations and friendships of the [American] Indians ... Indeed, of all their normal pursuits. They say, 'These are but common stories. No need to travel to the Indies for what we see in Europe every day'. The entertainment, therefore, in these

ingenious studies consists chiefly in exciting horror and making men stare. The ordinary employment of the bulk of Indians ... has nothing of the prodigious, but a human sacrifice, a feast upon enemies' carcasses can raise a horror and admiration of the wondrous barbarity of the Indians. (xii)

According to Smith, this extract 'states with precision the most interesting dilemma of choice confronting the student of religion', namely, the question of whether one should focus on 'those things which "excite horror and make men stare"' (the exotic) or '"common stories," on "what we see in Europe every day"' (the ordinary). Smith sides with the latter. For him, the most productive approach for 'the development of history of religions as an academic enterprise' is to treat 'exotic' myths as 'common stories' and grant no 'privilege to myth or other religious materials'. From this perspective, 'There is no "other" – it is all "what we see in Europe every day"' (xii–iii).

Smith's concern to de-privilege the exotic in favour of the commonplace is turned on its head by the conceptual premise of *Lettres Persanes* and *De l'Esprit des Lois*, which sought to make the commonplace exotic, as part of a deliberate polemic strategy against the Catholic Church. A crucial methodological concern of the late twentieth century is thus adumbrated by an earlier awareness of the revolutionary potential of a cross-cultural comparison effected *in reverse* and the destructive potential of the Orientalist gaze turned against itself. This strategy was not simply negative, however. As Smith notes in an observation drawn from Victor Shlovsky, 'there is extraordinary cognitive power in ... "defamiliarization" – making the familiar seem strange *in order to enhance our perception of the familiar*' (xiii, emphasis original). I take this to imply that proper comparison is not simply about replacing the ordinary with the exotic in a new hierarchy of value, but establishing a conceptual relationship that is itself productive of meaning. Neither the ordinary nor the exotic generate religion as a self-standing category of the social, but the movement from one to the other and the 'magic' involved in drawing these previously incommensurate categories together – a dynamic that is particularly relevant to the Enlightenment, because, as W. C. Smith has argued, the abstract category of religion took shape or was 'reified' primarily *through* negative constructions of other religions and other places (1964: 43–9; App 2010). Religion did not emerge, then become a problem. It emerged *as* a problem, from within secular discourse and by means of Orientalist representations, in other words, precisely through the sorts of strategy found in *Lettres Persanes* and *De l'Esprit des Lois*.

It is now widely recognized that Oriental despotism was deployed as a 'safe' means of criticizing two established authorities, the monarchy and the Church, since it enabled the dissimulation of a vigorous anti-monarchism and anti-clericalism behind the veil of a neutral study of religions.[23] Althusser in particular claimed that representations of Oriental despotism in Montesquieu were intended as a closet attack on the French monarchy. He thought the 'Oriental despot' was a fiction, or 'scarecrow' ('épouvantail') of Western political thought intended 'to edify by its very horribleness' (1972: 83–4). To conclude, I suggest the concept of Oriental despotism performed at least three additional functions analogous to the ritual mask and its 'promiscuous intermingling and juxtaposing of the categories of event, experience, and knowledge, with a pedagogic intention'. First, it created an ideal foil for Christianity, which simultaneously relativized and diminished Christianity's stature, since both could be considered on the same plane, or part of the same taxonomy of religions, in turn facilitating the construction of religion as an abstract, overarching category tied to affective signifiers of barbarity, cowardliness, fanaticism, lasciviousness, quietism, irrationality, etc. Second, it 'queered the habitual' through a superimposition of extraordinary forms of life onto the ordinary, contiguous with ambient theories of behavioural and affective conditioning, in this way contributing to the break-up of pre-secular, spiritual porousness (Taylor 2007). (In Turner's words, the 'grotesqueness and monstrosity' of the despot made neophytes 'vividly and rapidly aware of … the "factors" of their culture'.) Finally, it generated and preserved the integrity of the national body or 'fatherland', since its compatibility with modern theories of racial and civilizational difference enabled a powerfully affective attack on universal 'religion' through the particular (and hence restricted) case of Islamic peoples (Persians, Saracens, Arabs, etc.). Such versatility may help explain the impressive reproducibility of Oriental despotism in secular discourse and shed light on the convergence of Orientalism, anti-religion and nationalism in the French Enlightenment. It also emphasizes the inseparability of Orientalism from the genealogy of our secular age, despite its absence in Taylor's work.

The following chapter examines an alternative public medium for the representation of Oriental despotism in the eighteenth century – theatre. As I will show, there are clear continuities between eighteenth century epistemology, ethics and nationalism, and negative representations of Oriental religion on the stage. A fertile gathering point is provided by Voltaire's work of anti-clerical propaganda *Le Fanatisme* (1741).

'A morbid impression': Race, religion and metaphor in *Le Fanatisme, ou Mahomet* (1741)

Reasons are no longer needed; what is needed is a stage production.
Denis Diderot, *Entretiens sur le Fils Naturel* (1821 [1757]: 161)

It may be the play provokes no demonstration or visible upset, but rest assured, its affective consequences will be very real.
Tariq Ramadan, Open Letter to Hervé Loichemol (1993: unpaginated)

Does this poem not make us love true virtue?
Anonymous, Preface of *Le Fanatisme* (Voltaire 1753b [1741] : unpaginated)

Introduction

After initial performances of *Le Fanatisme* in Lille in April 1741, Voltaire told his friend le Comte d'Argental, 'You may think I blaspheme when I say that Lanoue, with his ape-like physiognomy [*physionomie de singe*], played the role of Mahomet much better than Dufresne'. According to Voltaire, 'the little baron' Lanoue had improved so much since the first showing, and had 'such a natural playfulness, such passionate movements, so true and so tender', that everyone burst into tears 'as one bleeds from the nose' ('comme on saigne du nez', 1878 [1711–1778]: XXXVI. 53).

Race and racism have, in the last few decades, been pluralized and extended to cover non-biological as well as biological attributes. Tariq Modood argues there are not only 'colour or phenotype racisms' but also 'cultural racisms which build on colour a set of antagonistic or demeaning stereotypes based on alleged or real cultural traits'. According to Modood, 'The most important cultural racism today, at least in Western Europe, is anti-Muslim racism, sometimes called Islamophobia' (2007: 44–5). Similarly, Didier Fassin (2006) argues for the recent emergence of a 'racism without race' evident in terminological slippages between signifiers of religion and body. As Mayanthi Fernando writes, 'the classical biological basis of race has been culturalized; race, religion, and culture now intertwine to construct a reified notion of radical alterity that takes the signifier Muslim (*musulman*)' (2014: 18; cf. Mahmood 2009: 851).

While Modood and Fassin provide a critical expansion of the interface between race and religion post-9/11, they may be remiss in portraying the racialization of Islam as a predominantly twenty-first-century phenomenon. In doing so, they leave the door open for conservative politicians to disregard their concerns as a late-modern capitulation to 'snowflake' culture, and a concession to the demands of an increasingly strident Muslim community, who, by appealing to the language of tolerance for a defence of 'intolerant' practices and beliefs, are seen by some to turn European values of non-discrimination against Europe itself.[1] But the racialization of Islam is not new. As Fernando notes, 'It constitutes not an emergence so much as a reemergence, a reinstantiation of a much older process of interpellation, categorization, and differentiation':

> Race and religion have always formed a nexus. In colonial Algeria there was never a strict division between race and religion, and race referred to a community of values that were not necessarily biological but were no less intractable. Algerians were Arabs were Muslims. … [C]ontemporary designations of the Muslim as Other continue to draw on older figurations of alterity. (18)

Although it can be difficult to trace precisely the way in which Islam has interacted with race through Western intellectual history, partly because the concept of race is so modern (posing risks of anachronism), and partly because the term is so diffuse in the first place, one thing is certain: racial figurations of Islam went to the core of the French Enlightenment.[2] Cross-stitchings of religion and race could be implicit, as they were in Montesquieu's theory of the climactic variation of peoples.[3] But they could also be explicit, even strategic, as they were in Voltaire's portrayal of Muhammed. For Voltaire, Mahomet's power to strike the fear of religious fanaticism into his audience stemmed, at least partly, from his primitive physical alterity. Later elaborating on Lanoue's distinctive talent, Voltaire wrote 'that ape acts very well, and I know of no one else who can put the appropriate power and terror into Mahomet' (1878 [1711–1778]: XXXVI. 108).

This chapter analyses the interaction between race and religion on the eighteenth-century stage through Voltaire's characterization of Mahomet, connecting the latter to contemporaneous thoughts on the control of affect (or the Enlightenment body) through the theatrical subject. It suggests Mahomet's racial profile in *Le Fanatisme* is neither incidental to the play nor demonstrative of a hyperbolic excess of artistic license at odds with Enlightenment 'rationalism' but a carefully considered anti-religious device calibrated for maximum emotional impact, in line with ambient theories of the passions and their manipulation for purposes of statecraft. Islam did not just happen to map onto racial, cultural or ethnic images of alterity in Voltaire's work. It was intentionally configured as such, contiguous with prevalent understandings of emotion, representation, race and power. By using Islam and a stock array of affective, Orientalist tropes to delegitimize external religion (i.e. Catholicism) in favour of a secularized and nationalistic conception of virtue, Voltaire epitomizes a form of racist, anti-religious polemicism rooted in eighteenth-century empiricism and late-Cartesian approaches to the passions. He therefore provides an excellent example of Orientalism's historical connection to the modern secular, and a gateway to a more 'other-wise' secularism.

To unpack the complex set of assumptions and motivations behind *Le Fanatisme*'s racialization of Islam, I begin by examining Lanoue's physiognomic 'fit' with two key tools in Voltaire's polemic repertoire: established preconceptions concerning the degeneracy of Islam, and those concerning Oriental despotism. I then contextualize Voltaire's report that spectators 'burst into tears' following Lanoue's performance by discussing the role of eighteenth-century tears as public expressions and affirmations of virtue, emphasizing the close-knit relation between such expressions, the contemporaneous indexation of emotions and characters to peoples or nations in order to 'disambiguate' and intensify theatrical representations, and attendant approaches to the cultivation of citizenship through the body. Given Voltaire's self-conscious directorial power, candidly outlined in epistolary material of the time, I suggest the despotic figure of Mahomet can be seen, ironically, as a projection of Voltaire's own concerns regarding the subject-forming potential of theatre. I end by proposing that a strictly semiotic approach to *Le Fanatisme* is inadequate to grasp the sophistication of Voltaire's technique, which relied on theatrical bodies as affective, moral forces in their own right, rather than mere signifiers for an absent signified. Against contemporary supporters of the play see Introduction, the Islam of *Le Fanatisme* was not – or not simply – a metaphor for Catholicism, or subsumable into a system of 'ironic significations'. Mahomet's Islamicness and ape-like rendition were intrinsic to the play's message and emotional power.

The racialization of Mahomet

Le Fanatisme unfolds during Muhammed or 'Mahomet's' post-exilic siege of Mecca in 630, pitting him against the enlightened sheik and guardian of Mecca, Zopire. Unbeknownst to Zopire, two of his young protégées Palmyre and Séide are his long-lost children, kidnapped fifteen years earlier, raised in Mahomet's camp and recaptured but still under Mahomet's sway. Mahomet's desire for young Palmyre and his increasing jealousy of Séide inspire a Machiavellian plan to kill two birds with one stone, by first convincing Séide to kill Zopire as an act of religious devotion, then instructing his second-in-command Omar to denounce Séide and have him arrested. During the murder, Séide learns the truth concerning his father but it is too late: Zopire dies and Séide flies into a vengeful rage, drawing together a mob for Mahomet's punishment. Appearing before Mahomet, Séide wavers and falls to the ground apparently at Mahomet's command, but really succumbing to the latent effects of Mahomet's earlier poisoning. As her brother dies, Palmyre follows, renouncing Islam before throwing herself onto Séide's knife. The play ends with a frustrated soliloquy from Mahomet and his promise to 'reign the Universe as a God' (1753b [1741]: 105).

Lanoue fitted well into the skin of Mahomet because the latter was himself a compound of Orientalist tropes mixing racial, emotional and religious attributes. *Le Fanatisme* construes Muhammed as a lecherous, lascivious, jealous and deceitful fanatic who spreads 'fanatism and sedition' (4), an 'insolent Arab who strides with the authority of kings' (10) and an 'Impostrous Monster' (11).[4] To call anyone an 'Arab' during the seventeenth and eighteenth centuries was an insult in itself: Arabs were typically portrayed as bloodthirsty and rage-prone thieves (as Voltaire wrote elsewhere, Arabs were 'a population of brigands', who, before Muhammed, 'thieved while worshipping stars', and under Muhammed, 'thieved in God's name'; 1878 [1764]: XVII. 105). The play also reproduces a number of narrative and scenic tropes that give contextual depth to Mahomet's savagery, e.g. the idea that Muhammed and Fatima dwelled in caves (1753b [1741]: 17), that they spread Islam like poison (17), that Arabia is a dead and burning landscape (32) and that Islam is a religion of the sword, spread by force to subjugate humanity.[5] Thus, in Act 2, Scene 5, Mahomet says to Zopire, 'Le Glaive and l'Alcoran dans mes sanglantes mains,/Imposeraient silence au reste des humains./Ma voix feroit sur eux les effets du tonnerre,/Et je verrais leurs fronts attachés à la terre' (34–5).[6]

The 'brigand' Mahomet is predictably motivated by pathological sexual instincts – he loves a woman he has effectively raised himself – that reflected a general seventeenth- and eighteenth-century fascination with the exotic mysteries and perversity of the seraglio (Netton 1990). Mahomet's carnality formed a critical element in a 'set of characteristics that typified a fixed "Arab" psychology and physiology' and reinforced a sense of base, sexual predatoriness surrounding the mystic Orient (Hammerbeck 2003: 11). Such formulations were already commonplace by the early eighteenth century and would have been familiar to Voltaire's audience. Michel Baudier's 1631 *Histoire Générale du Sérail* dwelled heavily on the women's quarters of the seraglio: its title page, which depicts four naked women bathing the Sultan, 'frames Baudier's overriding interest in the carnal pleasures of the Sultan's palace' (Baudier 1631: iii–iv; Hammerbeck 2003: 11). The French medievalist Philippe Sénac has traced negative erotic portrayals of Islam to at least the ninth century, when Alvare and Euloge, two Spanish monks living in Umayyad Muslim Toledo, described Islam as 'A deceitful sect, founded by a nefarious man, a false prophet, a web of lies promising a polygamous and perverse paradise to its initiates'. In the same century, *Une Vie de Mahomet* (publication date unknown) identified the beast of the Apocalypse with Muhammed, since the latter was generally believed to have died in 666 (Sénac 1983: 28, 30–1). By the late Middle Ages, theologians such as Nicolas of Cusa (1401–1464), Denys van Leeuwen (1402–1471), John of Torquemada (1388–1468) and Alfonso a Spina (1412–1491) all emphasized the '"fraudulent" or "hypocritical" character of Muhammed's claim to prophesy'. Muhammed was portrayed as 'an ambitious schemer, a bandit and a lecher' whose religion '[fell] short of Christianity' since it relied on 'force' and encouraged 'private laxity in sexual matters' (Daniel 1993: 276). Mahomet's likeness to an ape in *Le Fanatisme* was undeniably intrinsic to his perverse sexuality. Voltaire later drew on Herodotus's accounts of Egyptian bestiality to suggest 'It is not unlikely that, in hot countries, apes subjugated young women' (1878 [1756]: 7).

Not only did the 'monolithic Other' (Spellberg 2004: 292) of Mahomet fit Lanoue's reduced, 'ape-like' features perfectly, but he was easily superimposed on the other great Other of the eighteenth century, the Oriental despot. As Hammerbeck writes, '[The] essentialization of the Prophet as a tyrannous ruler' paralleled the quasi-mythological figures of Xerxes, Salah ad-Din and Tamurlaine, who 'all served as cultural templates of the "eternal," despotic Other' – a template also 'indicative of inherent racial characteristics' (2003: 14). While Mahomet's first lines evoke the essence of tyranny, he does not rule principally by 'fear' or force.[7] His psychological hold over imprisoned Palmyre directly references the terminology of the seraglio, itself a miniature model of despotic government articulated, as in Montesquieu's *Lettres Persanes* (1721), through the epistemological framework of Lockean empiricism.[8] Having grown up in Mahomet's care, Palmyre and Séide are now 'in his chain' (1753b [1741]: 28, 31), but this chain is not physical or coercive. On the contrary, Palmyre and Séide have been conditioned from birth to 'treasure their irons' ('Sans parens, sans patrie, esclaves dès l'enfance,/Dans notre égalité nous chérissons nos fers'; 10).[9] Like Montesquieu, Voltaire associated despotic subjugation with a cynical control of people's sensual and habitual environment. Jealous of Palmyre, Mahomet asks 'Votre coeur a-t-il pu, sans être épouvanté,/Avoir un sentiment que je n'ai pas dicté?' (50). She answers, 'Esclave de vos loix, soumise à vos genoux,/Mon coeur d'un faint respect ne perd point l'habitude' (52).[10] This admission is later echoed by Mahomet, in his claim that 'La nature à mes yeux n'est rien que l'habitude,/Celle de m'obéir fut son unique étude' (70).[11]

Voltaire's choice to align a specifically religious figure of authority with the archetypal bogeyman of pre-modern political theory radically challenges Larry Wolff's claim that the early 1700s were still characterized by a 'sympathetic' engagement with Oriental despotism (see previous chapter). Wolff claims the 'despotic' antihero of Voltaire's *Zaïre* (1732), Orosmane, was 'by no means remote from enlightened European values' (2017: 45), supporting his general assumption that European stage-performances did not negatively misrepresent the Orient or Oriental despotism until the advent of high-colonialism. The extent to which Orosmane's unusual alloy of Orientalness and Enlightenment should be taken at face value is debatable.[12] Yet by the time *Le Fanatisme* was performed, just nine years after *Zaïre*, the Oriental despot has morphed into an unambiguously sinister figure of political and religious power, as remote from enlightened European values as one could imagine. This disambiguation reflects, I would suggest, two related developments: (1) growing interest in the religious and political consequences of empiricism, as the implications of Locke and the later Descartes's insights came to the surface; and (2) Voltaire's changing attitudes towards 'external', historically contingent forms of religion, particularly Catholicism. The period 1721–1741 is punctuated by two major works, *Lettres Philosophiques* (1734) and *Le Mondain* (1736), both of which marked a strengthening of anti-Catholic sentiment and an attendant need to simplify the figure of the Oriental despot for polemic purposes. The latter was already a convenient and powerful symbol of political otherness, due to centuries of elaboration about the dangers of tyrannic and despotic government. Voltaire deepened the 'savage slot' (Trouillot 2003: 7–28) of Oriental despotism by first tying the Oriental despot to the foreign, specifically Arab figure of religious authority, then cutting him down even further, caricaturing Muhammed in unprecedentedly reductive and racialized terms. The effects, if Voltaire's account can be trusted, were sensational.[13]

Tears of virtue and racialized bodies on the stage

Voltaire's celebratory boast that spectators of *Le Fanatisme* burst into tears before Lanoue 'as one bleeds from the nose' must be seen in the wider context of eighteenth-century codes for the public expression of emotion. In *Histoire des Larmes* (1986), Anne Vincent-Buffault has argued that, privately, in the sphere of the eighteenth-century family home, tearful exchanges between parents and children were considered 'beneficial' and 'evidence of the intensity of familial affection', while tears shed publicly at others' misfortunes or good deeds provided a positive signal for the expression of feeling and virtue (1991 [1986]: 20–1). Analogous standards applied to the theatre, where shared tears could be read as affirmations of the audience's inherent good nature, against the hierarchical and hereditary model of the old regime. According to Angela Pao, 'Spectators who could be moved to tears of joy or compassion were both exhibiting and refining their sensibilities – sensibilities that identified them as members of the new elite of innate worth which was to supplant the old elite of noble birth' (1998: 67). The 'communal shedding of tears' in theatres thereby constituted an opportunity for the public performance and affirmation of an eminently modern notion of virtue:

> The theatre as a setting for tears shared in mutual recognition, allowed everyone to prove his natural bounty through tenderness, and all to prove the excellence of their relationships which pushed them to fling themselves in each other's arms … The observation and the participation of others multiplied the moral effects. The tears which were shed revived the sensibility and were a commitment to virtue. (Vincent-Buffault 1991 [1986]: 67–8)

In this context, getting audiences to cry was not only a mark of great craftsmanship, but an ethical achievement of particular distinction. The 'aesthetic battle' was an 'ethical battle' (60) and moving the audience to tears was considered a 'moral triumph' (Pao 1998: 54).[14] Unsurprisingly, the theatre was sometimes seen as competing with the church as an institution of moral instruction. The influential philosopher and cultural critic Friedrich Melchior Grimm described spectators leaving one performance as having 'hated vice, loved virtue, cried in concert, and developed side by side what is good and righteous in the human heart'. According to him, 'one does not come out from a sermon feeling better disposed' (Vincent-Buffault 1991 [1986]: 67).

The uncanny parallel between religious and secular power in eighteenth-century theories of the stage was later developed into a full-blown programme for the co-optation of the former by the latter. Writing at the height of the revolutionary fervour that would shortly engender secular religions like the national Cult of Reason, the anonymous French translator of Johann Jakob Engel's 1788 work of stage theory *Ideen zu einer Mimik* (*Idées sur le Geste et l'Action Théâtrale*) suggests that, during ancient Oriental rites, the Canephores (ritual participants charged with carrying sacrificial gifts) 'had to harmonize their steps, their attitudes and their gestures' in order to endow ceremonies with the required solemnity and sense of unity to 'strike the multitudes' ('cet ensemble important et auguste qui devoit frapper la multitude'; 'Translator's Preface' 1794: 25–6). Since the movements of the body were, he suggested, direct reflections of 'the sentiments by which the soul is affected', and since the pagan gods were so numerous and diverse, one could speculate that 'the variety of cults, of ceremonies, of favours asked of the gods, could successively run through the whole circle of sentiments by which the human soul may be affected, and establish thereby every element of mime and gesture, and the attitude proper to every isolated affection or passion' (26). It was important to understand the structure of this gestural and emotional index because it provided a kind of key to the manipulation of the emotions on the modern stage, and a map for the seizure of religious gestures and affects by the secular. In more religious times, the translator wrote:

> Every prayer, every wish, every religious act contained one or more sentiments; therefore an analogous play necessarily manifested in the movements of the body, which, despite the modifications caused by each individual's particular properties, were able to transmit from generation to generation, until the progress of culture, the love of arts and the need for new pleasures caused the [art of] pantomime to seize and exploit them as the primary elements of its craft. (27)

In other words, just as religious sentiments were formerly indexed to specific religious actions and rites, and passed down from generation to generation, so the sentiments in general were indexed to particular movements of the body and, via an unconscious process of resonance, could be individually stimulated by reproducing the appropriate movement before one's eyes. Just as the passions manipulated the body, the body – properly represented – manipulated the passions. Corporeal movements and physiognomic attributes therefore became 'the primary elements' of the theatre director's 'craft' and it was the latter's task to understand them in order to speak the language of emotion powerfully and clearly (Vincent-Buffault 1991 [1986]: 69).

There is no doubt Lanoue's distinct physiognomy played a crucial role in Voltaire's triumph. It was taken for granted during the eighteenth century – as it would be now – that powerful theatrical effects should not, and could not, be secured through bare dialogue but the entire production: the stage sets, sounds, music, costumes and physical presence of the performers. As Pao writes, 'Nonverbal elements were called upon both to support the meaning of the verbal text and to exceed it in making an impact on the audience. ... One of the key sites for the projection of [non-verbal] signs was ... the actors' bodies' (1998: 19). The melodramatic body of the eighteenth century was, in Peter Brooks's words, 'a body seized by meaning' (1994: 18), one whose presence must unambiguously communicate the simple and powerful messages of the drama. This was particularly important during the eighteenth century because the body's semiosis was both ideally unambiguous and irreducible to language – a quality that carried certain benefits in an institutional milieu haunted by the risk of censorship. Unlike the voice, the body's distinctive gestures and features could transmit meaning in relative independence from 'psychic, social, or circumstantial' forms of repression, going where language failed or feared to tread (Pao 1998: 20).[15]

An important factor for the transmission of corporeal signs (and passions) was the actors' closeness of fit to a pre-established character-set with racial and national attributes. It was assumed that the truthfulness of plays relied on 'the exact reproduction of physical and visual details', including the close match of actors' physiognomy and character (38). According to the translator of *Idées sur le Geste*, the principal qualities demanded of actors were 'a fiery soul that feels and expresses the passions; a gentle and persuasive sentiment that captivates all who listen; a physiognomy that is their systematic and faithful interpreter' ('Translator's Preface' 1794: 11). Crucially, the figures used by theatre directors had to be well known for the correct message to get across. The translator of *Idées* insisted that, despite people's misconceptions, the 'signification' of theatrical gestures was not inherent in the gestures themselves but emerged through the presentation of a 'principal idea' that only became effective when it awakened and reinforced associated ideas already held by the audience (21–2).[16] It was therefore imperative that theatre directors restrict their art to 'known subjects' that would pre-empt any ambiguity of interpretation. In the translator's words,

> Pantomime must restrict itself to treating familiar subjects, in the same way that the music of lyrical drama must accompany speech: they can and must reinforce the sentiment. But if these two arts arrogate to themselves the right to express, by their own means, subjects that are completely unknown, the one will become a vague and insipid [form of] gesticulation, the other a succession of tones which, though well-ordered and enchanting of the ear, will have an equivocal meaning that everyone can vary and interpret according to their fantasies. ('Translator's Preface' 1794: 29)

In this context, the systematic indexing of character-types to peoples, in fiction and non-fiction, provided a powerful non-verbal code for the disambiguation of plot and meaning.[17] After seeing *Zaïre* performed in 1810, one critic praised Voltaire for his ability to 'oppose foreign manners one to the other and to our own with astonishing skill'. According to him, 'the brushes [Voltaire] uses to paint *Zaïre, Tancrède* and *Mahomet* are not the same; it is impossible to indicate the distinctive traits of Turkish, French, Chinese and Tartar, Spanish and Mexican customs more naturally than he does in *Zaïre* or *The Orphan of China* or in *Alzire*'. Voltaire's characters all achieved their aim because they spoke 'their proper language' ('le langage qui lui est propre') and reflected accurately 'the physiognomy and language of Orientals' (Pao 1998: 48–9). People's proper physiognomy and language were typically ranked hierarchically, with Europeans at the top and Orientals at the bottom, or at least below the French, casting a nationalistic aura over otherwise neutral works. In *Zaïre*, 'happier' France is frequently conjured as the antithesis even of Orosmane's enlightened Jerusalem. The rigidity of racial-national categories was such that Orosmane's virtuous nature could only be made believable through linguistic slippages that revealed a 'true' Scythian or French identity beneath the Oriental appearance: 'Le maître de ces lieux, le puissant Orosmane,/Sait connaître, seigneur, et chérir la vertu./ Ce généreux Français, qui vous est inconnu,/Par la gloire amené des rives de la France' (1877 [1732]: 574).[18] In all cases, the bodies and gestural repertoire of actors played a crucial role in defining and reinforcing not only the semiosis of the play but its emotional and ethical impact. For the translator of *Idées*, the successful exploitation of each actor's 'natural sensibility' and their ability to come across as more than 'automata' was essential to achieving 'the moral aim of the play' ('le but moral de la pièce'), where morality was by definition a matter of national commitment ('Translator's Preface' 1794: 3, 15).[19]

The racialization of Muhammed through Lanoue therefore fulfilled at least two core functions of eighteenth-century theatre. On one hand, Lanoue's physiognomy 'reflected accurately' the true nature of the primitive Oriental, acting as an effective 'kinaesthetic trigger' to awaken spectators' affective memories and entrench inherited assumptions of European superiority through the mechanics of a 'perfect illusion' ('Translator's Preface' 1794: 3). On the other, this awakening was intense enough to provoke an outward expression of spectators' natural sensibilities, in line with contemporaneous understandings of moral affirmation, performance and cultivation. To put it differently, Lanoue (a) had an appearance that aligned with pre-established categorizations of race and national character, allowing him to (b) trigger powerful emotional responses in his audience and (c) configure and cement a particular inhabitation of virtue that also shored up the imagined community of the French nation-state, either through explicit references to the superiority of the French or because virtue and national identity were so closely connected in the first place (as Rousseau and Porter put it, 'each society had its very own moral message'; 1990: 11). Voltaire's racialization of Muhammed is thus a paradigmatic example of the way early modern theories of emotion and image, or what passed 'before people's eyes', interacted with racial or national taxa to yield a powerful model of political manipulation that was simultaneously secular (insofar as it dealt with religion or religious categories, e.g. 'fanaticism'), nationalistic and rooted fundamentally in the body.

Voltaire = Mahomet

One must enchant the spirits of a proud people.
                    Mahomet to Omar, *Le Fanatisme* (Voltaire 1753b [1741]: 45)

I have been speaking in relatively loose terms about the *strategy* of using a racialized figure of Islamic authority for a domestic critique of religious power. To justify this term, however, it is necessary to show that Voltaire's characterization was deliberate and not simply a reflection of his and others' limited knowledge of the Orient at the time. How much did Voltaire know about Islam and Muhammed prior to composing *Le Fanatisme*?

By the time he began writing *Le Fanatisme*, Voltaire had 'more than a basic knowledge of Islam' (Gunny 2010: 97). His earlier plays *Zaïre* (1732) and *Zulime* (1739) both concerned Muslim characters, and he was familiar with Sale's 1734 translation of the Qur'an, as well as biographies of Muhammed by Boulainvillier and Gagnier (Badir 1974: 127). Correspondence with Cideville and Pierre Aunillon begins with the Islamic profession of faith 'There is no God but God', and he hoped to read Tavernier's *Voyages en Turquie, en Perse et aux Indes* (1676), Chardin's *Voyages en Perse* (1686) and d'Herbelot's *Bibliothèque Orientale* (1697) in 1742. Moreover, Voltaire was surprisingly aware of the pitfalls of Orientalist speculation. According to him, 'philosophers who build systems on the secret construction of the universe' are like 'our travellers visiting Constantinople and discussing the seraglio: they have only seen the outside, and pretend to know what the sultan does with his favourite [concubines]' (1753a [1741]: 112). Although Voltaire seems to have engaged in an earnest attempt to learn as much as possible about Islam and Islamic culture, however, *Le Fanatisme* 'evidences little of the riches offered by some of these books' (Gunny 2010: 97). As Grosrichard observes, 'At a point when the studies of Orientalists endow the person, the life and the teachings of Mahomet with an image increasingly in keeping with historical truth, it is surprising to see Voltaire still treating him as "a rogue, a rascal, and a fool"' (1998: 107).

Napoleon famously reproached *Le Fanatisme* for failing to represent Muhammed as a 'great man'. Voltaire, said the Emperor,

> has departed both from nature and history. He has degraded Mahomet, by making him descend to the lowest intrigues. He has represented a great man, who changed the face of the world, acting like a scoundrel, worthy of the gallows. He has no less absurdly travestied the character of Omar, which he has drawn like that of a cut-throat in a melodrama. (Las Cases 1823: 46)

In a sense, Napoleon missed the point. The fundamental question was not whether Voltaire had represented Muhammed accurately or not, but a deeper question concerning the purpose of theatre. In a late-1730s letter to Lanoue, Voltaire praised him for altering the historical character of the hero in his own play *Mahomet II* (1739), writing that 'an untruth producing a pleasing situation in theatre is preferable … to all the archives of the universe'. The untruth, he added, 'became true' (literally, 'devient vraie') by reproducing the right theatrical impression (1878 [1711–1778]: XXXV. 241). When *Le Fanatisme* was finally permitted onto the stage again in 1751, Voltaire acknowledged to his niece, Madame Denis, that Muslims were entitled to complain, since he had made Mahomet 'more evil than he was' (1878 [1711–1778]: XXXVII. 337). In fact, he confessed to the King of Prussia, it would not have been possible for Muhammed to commit the crime depicted in *Le Fanatisme*:

> I [have made] Mahomet … guilty of a crime which he was not, in fact, capable of committing. … [F]or a camel merchant to stir up sedition in his district

... to boast that he was entertained in heaven, and there received part of that unintelligible book which makes common sense shake on every page; that in order to procure respect for this book he should carry sword and fire into his country, murder fathers and ravish their daughters ... this is surely what no man will pretend to vindicate unless he was born a Turk and superstition had completely choked the light of nature out of him. (1753b [1741]: unpaginated)

For Voltaire, the virtue of *Le Fanatisme* lay not in its historical fidelity or consistency, but its capacity to condition people's emotional dispositions and hence their sense of morality. His task was not to represent facts, but, like Johann Engel in the second half of the eighteenth century, to '[delve] into the nature of the soul, into that of the passions and of their development, as well as the study of the changes they wrought in the human body' ('Translator's Preface' 1794: 12). Like a Renaissance prince, Voltaire sought to strengthen the 'weak souls' of his audiences against a 'foreign rage', by doing what theatre directors did best: stimulating the emotions and 'instructing the heart'.

I know that Mahomet did not devise precisely the type of treachery that is the subject of this tragedy. ... [B]ut whoever makes war upon his Country, and dares to make it in the name of God, is he not capable of everything? ... I will consider myself well rewarded if one or another of these weak souls, always ready to receive the impressions of a foreign fury not set in their heart, can strengthen itself against such fatal seductions by reading this work. (Voltaire 1753b [1741]: unpaginated)[20]

Edward Said famously argued that 'we need not look for correspondence between the language used to depict the Orient and the Orient itself, not so much because the language is inaccurate but because it is not even trying to be accurate'. 'What it is trying to do', he wrote, 'is at one and the same time to characterize the Orient as alien and to incorporate it schematically on a theatrical stage whose audience, manager, and actors are *for* Europe, and only for Europe' (Said 2003 [1978]: 71–2, emphasis original). As the foregoing passages show, Voltaire consciously deployed the Orient *for* Europe and was open about this fact. Indeed, Voltaire's self-reflections point to a striking conclusion: that Mahomet was in many ways an Islamized version of himself, a theatrical projection aligned with Voltaire's awareness of his own power as a stage director in control of people's emotions. Like Mahomet, Voltaire sought to 'enter the heart to establish his power' (1753b [1741]: 27). Like Mahomet's sidekick Omar, Lanoue could have boasted that 'More than one Judge seemed moved by my voice' (27).[21] Zopire at one point describes Mahomet's legacy as an 'incredible admixture of lies and audacity' (34). But Voltaire – by his own admission – had no particular concern for the truth either, using lies and audacity to achieve the strongest dramatic effect and thereby cement people's affections against a 'foreign fury not set in their heart'. Just as Mahomet chained Palmyre to the 'Fatherland' of the seraglio by conditioning her first sentiments ('The Fatherland is where the soul is enchained/Mahomet formed my first sentiments'; 9), Voltaire sought to consolidate his audience's attachment to France, 'audaciously' dissimulating this cultural work behind a veil of psychological projection.

Revolutionary terror and the fear of fear itself

When the Reign of Terror clamped down in the years following 1789, the purveyors of fear had a ready storehouse of knowledge concerning the manipulation of people's emotions through the politics of spectacle, not just from Voltaire and records of his terrifying performances, but from the heart of eighteenth-century political theory. 'When an impression of terror has no certain object', wrote Montesquieu in De l'Esprit des Lois (1748), 'it produces only clamour and abuse; it has, however, this good effect, that it puts all the springs of government into motion, and fixes the attention of every citizen' (1777a [1748]: 410). Similarly, Condorcet believed fear to be 'the origin of almost all human stupidities and above all of political stupidities' yet could not deny its political power. According to him, 'one is more sure of subjugating people's minds by frightening them, than by speaking to them of reason; for fear is an imperious passion' (Rothschild 2001: 13–14). The thrust of these ideas was anticipated by Father Senault, according to whom fear was a 'natural wisdom' which '[spread] herself over all the actions of our life' and was 'no less useful to religion than to the state'. For 'Though men talk of generosity in religion and wish to subordinate it to liberty, yet it must be confessed that fear has saved more guilty people than hope. Thus is she termed … the beginning of Wisdom, that is to say, the prop of Virtue' (1641: 413–14). By the eighteenth century, the chief model of a political system built on fear was, of course, Oriental despotism, though the latter could itself be presented as a reflex of the deeper and more pervasive system of religion. Nicolas Boulanger argued that religion bred the slavish mentality and bodily disposition required for despotism to take root, though ultimately both 'Idolatry and Despotism' stemmed from 'fears' and 'terrors' (1762 [1761]: 224). These ideas were later recapitulated by Bertrand Russell, according to whom religion is based 'primarily and mainly upon fear ... fear of the mysterious, fear of defeat, fear of death' (1957: 17).

Russell wrote out of an analytic tradition that valued reason above all else and equated emancipation from religion with emancipation from fear itself. Yet the situation was different in the eighteenth century. The Reign of Terror was preceded by several decades of theoretical and practical advances in the political manipulation of affect that tended to emphasize the utility of fear to projects of social improvement. Crucially, these took shape at least partially *within* the domain of the aesthetic. In Voltaire's case, a second order, 'othered' type of fear – the fear of fear itself, embodied in the figure of Mahomet – was explicitly aimed at reorienting people's affective dispositions away from religion and towards a secular habitus framed by the moral requirements of the emerging nation-state. If religion provided the *ur*-model of an ideology and set of practices in league with despotic power, *Le Fanatisme* and Lanoue's 'terrifying' performance exemplify a way of studying, reproducing and yoking religious bodies and affects to the aspirations and techniques of the secular, half a century before the national Cult of Reason absorbed such advances into itself.

Metaphor?

As noted in the Introduction, for many contemporary critics, to read *Le Fanatisme* as anything other than an attack on the Catholic Church or 'religious fanaticism' generally is to miss the referential irony underpinning the play, which transfigured Mahomet into the pope and Islam into Catholicism. A proper, metaphorical reading of the play defuses accusations of Islamophobia, since it was not about Islam anyway, but a simple medium for the critique of something wider (religious fanaticism) or something else (Catholicism).[22] In a letter to Mr. César de Missy, dated 1 September 1742, Voltaire explained he had 'tried to show the horrible excesses into which fanaticism, led by an impostor, can plunge weak minds' (1878 [1711–1778]: XXXVI. 157). Three years later (17 August 1745), he wrote to Pope Benedict XIV that *Le Fanatisme* was 'written in opposition to the founder of a false and barbarous sect' (1877 [1741]: III. 105). The first explanation allegorizes and universalizes, the second literalizes and particularizes. Which was true?

It would be easy to see the second as a smokescreen for the first. Voltaire's actual aim was to satirize fanaticism as whole – including Catholic fanaticism – but he dissimulated this behind a veil of anti-Islamism for his own safety, or to get *Le Fanatisme* back onto the stage after the papal ban of 1742. The universality of Voltaire's message was hidden behind the particularity of Islam, for reasons of expediency.

Without denying this component of the story, however, the reduction of *Le Fanatisme* to a mere vehicle for the representation of global principles risks obfuscating a crucial point: that Voltaire, like Montesquieu, criticized fanaticism through Islam *specifically*. By frictionlessly transfiguring Mahomet into the pope, commentators like Mullin or Rochaix do not explain why Muhammed and no one else could have stood for an excess of religious power or fanaticism in the eighteenth century, or why Muhammed and Islam became the examples *par excellence* of religious regressivity as the century progressed and attacks on religion intensified.

Allegory or metaphor may not be entirely misleading in the context of *Le Fanatisme*, if by this we mean something broader than a system of referential signs. According to theorists of language George Lakoff and Mark Johnsen, 'metaphors are not merely things to be seen beyond. ... [T]he ability to comprehend experience through metaphor [is like] a sense, like seeing or touching or hearing ... Metaphor is as much a part of our functioning as our sense of touch, and as precious' (2003 [1980]: 239). Similarly, Paul Ricoeur claims metaphors (unlike mere symbols) have the power to 'relate the semantic surface to the pre-semantic surface in the depths of human experience' (Ricœur 1976: 69). For most linguists, this capacity stems from its immediate relation to the affective and sensational; metaphor alone 'bypasses the objective and taps directly into the visceral' (Steuter and Wills 2008: xvi).

Yet whether *Le Fanatisme* was intended to be understood metaphorically or not, one point should be clear: to 'interpret' Mahomet as a simple medium or cypher for the critique of religious fanaticism or the pope is – by Voltaire's own account – to miss much of what made the play so powerful and so likely to cause members of the audience to cry 'as one bleeds from the nose'. Such a transfigurative manoeuvre radically underestimates both the power of 'mere' representation, as understood now and in the eighteenth century, and Voltaire's own articulated intentions behind the racialized construction of Mahomet. The Oriental despot did not translate or map onto the king and pope in a purely semiotic way, even in the eighteenth century. The 'overtones, allusions and associations' bound up with despotism and Islam were already well established by the late 1600s; audiences would already have considered the Prophet 'a lecherous villain in real life' (Gunny 2010: 96). As Magdy Gabriel Badir notes, 'the notion of an impostrous Mahomet was so anchored in people's minds, since the Middle Ages, that even the most enlightened philosophers of the eighteenth century like Bayle and Boulainvilliers firmly believed in the imposture of the Arab prophet. Liberals and apologists agreed on this point' (1974: 115). Given this consensus, the movement from plane (Oriental despot, Muslims) to plane (monarchs, pope, priests) could not have been – indeed, was not intended to be – purely formal or representative, and not clean. The aim of the play was not simply to contradict Christianity, but, in the words of Jean-François de La Harpe (1739–1803), to 'make Christianity odious' ('rendre le Christianisme odieux'; Badir 1974: 139).

The effect of this negative affect was arguably two-fold: it bolstered antipathy towards the pope or monarch, and it sustained a useful dichotomy between Occident and Orient even as empirical accounts of the degenerate East produced 'an image increasingly in keeping with historical truth' (Grosrichard 1998: 107; Pao 1998: 55). To understand how European discourse was able to resist the encroachments of more positive or empirically detailed accounts of the Orient and/or Islam from Bernier to Anquetil-Duperron, it is necessary to consider the utility of Orientalist representations to domestic projects of secular emancipation, almost a century before the onset of high colonialism. Against Wolff, *Le Fanatisme*'s portrayal of Muhammed as lecherous, treacherous, lascivious, power-obsessed and despotic, was designed on the back of exclusively home-grown concerns, with little or nothing to do with empire, but everything to do with religion.

Of course, the polemic force of secular, Orientalist works eventually transcended the boundaries of the Enlightenment. Mahomet's abjection was not simply transplanted onto the Western religious figure of authority or parsed out as an ideological embellishment, but became embedded in the structure of Western thought and feeling about the Orient.[23] According to Pao, the play '[participated] in a pre-colonial Orientalist discourse that would eventually be used to support the French invasion and colonization of the Middle East and North Africa' (1998: 59).[24] Voltairean representations of Islam and the Orient survived the transition to the 'pseudo-science' (Rubiés 2005: 110) of colonial Orientalism because their utility to imperial issues of legitimation overrode competing voices or concerns for nuance, but also, arguably, because the line between fiction and non-fiction was not always clear-cut, even to Voltaire. Many of Voltaire's negative aesthetic fabrications percolated seamlessly into non-fictional works like the *Essai sur les Moeurs* (1756) or the *Dictionnaire Philosophique* (1764), despite the presence of flatly contradictory, positive assessments of Islam and the Orient in the very same texts.[25] Somewhere between fiction and non-fiction, Enlightenment representations of Islam became the essence of late-eighteenth-century anti-religion and colonial-era Orientalism.

Conclusion: Universal religion, particular Islam – a Trojan story

'Power', wrote Voltaire, 'consists in making others act as I choose' (Arendt 1969: 36).[26] Making others act as one chose entailed manipulating the passions, since, in his words, 'One is sure to succeed [in theatre] when one speaks to people's passions more than their reason' (1877 [1732]: 539). This chapter has suggested that, in order to grasp the polemic force of *Le Fanatisme*, it is necessary to engage with Voltaire's racialization of Islam, in light of contemporaneous theories of the passions, received knowledge about their vulnerability to manipulation by images and the pressing issue of delegitimizing ecclesiastical power. I have argued that Voltaire's deployment of Islam was a key element in a carefully planned attack on Catholicism or 'external' religion that maximized the play's polemic effects through a strategic remoulding of aversion and desire. By Voltaire's own account, this affective work occurred in large part at the level of the representation itself (rather than the thing represented) and relied on emotionally valenced categorizations of race and nation. A framing of the play in terms of 'metaphor' is therefore appropriate only if it encompasses the full range of racist, emotional effects sought by Voltaire to secure a particular inhabitation of virtue; in other words, if it addresses Voltaire's definition of power.

Recall that Taylor characterizes the Cartesian understanding of the self as marked by a 'sharp division between mind and non-mental reality' that underpins 'a conception of thought and will as something self-contained, in principle quite clear and present to themselves, and capable of establishing their independence from the world of matter' (2007: 348). This understanding is taken by Taylor to instigate a gradual isolation of the self from the senses and surroundings, expressed during the eighteenth century in the 'cool, ironic' distance of Hume and Gibbon, and resulting in the buffered self of late modernity. Thus, according to Taylor, 'We sometimes find it hard to be frightened the way [our forerunners] were, and, indeed, we tend to invoke the uncanny things they feared with a pleasurable frisson, as if sitting through films about witches and sorcerers'. Unlike our modern selves trained in practices of aesthetic distancing, our forerunners 'would have found this incomprehensible' (Taylor 2011: 39).

It is not clear exactly where the dividing line between 'us' and 'our forerunners' lies. The last witch to be legally executed for witchcraft in Britain, Janet Horne, was burned in 1727 – well into the early modern era – and various forms of black magic, enchantment and possession continue to drive cultish terrors around the world, to say nothing of the political uncanny, such as the rogue state or suicide bomber.[27] But even if we accept that the twenty-first century self is in some way more aesthetically buffered than the pre-modern, this shift cannot be attributed to the French Enlightenment – mainstream or otherwise – which, as we have seen, evinced a deep commitment to the formative potential of the body and what 'passed before its eyes'. During his coaching for the role of Genghis Khan in *L'Orphelin de la Chine* (1753), the actor Henri Louis Cain or Lekain, recalled that, 'All the passions I expressed were graven in turn on [Voltaire's] features, which showed how he had been moved and touched' (Pao 1998: 54).[28] These comments illustrate the ideal relation between actor and audience, one of profound receptivity to the power of speech and images. They reveal a different kind of Enlightenment to Taylor's, one that foregrounds the body and its porousness to representation as non-negotiable aspects of individual and political subjectivity, and casts the Oriental stage as a key platform for the manipulation of the passions, in line with late-seventeenth- and early-eighteenth-century theories of the emotional body. For Voltaire, there could be no strict division between the aesthetic and the political, or the semiotic and the embodied on the theatrical stage. The empiricist backdrop of most of the Enlightenment ensured that 'thought and will' were absolutely undetachable from the world of matter and moving images. The theatre's sensual universe was politics in action, and, for Voltaire, Islam provided the raw material of terror.

Voltaire's logic of appealing to Islam for a critique of the developing category of 'religion' had repercussions beyond the immediate boundaries of the play. The Pope eventually revoked censorship of *Le Fanatisme* when he became satisfied the play was about Islam not Catholicism. But in aligning Islam and Catholicism along the single conceptual plane of 'religious fanaticism', Voltaire had already, at one level, conflated the two together in a manner analogous to Montesquieu's profanation of Catholicism through cultural and linguistic substitutions. One can see how the concept of religion would become an increasingly important polemic catch-all during the eighteenth century, holding these categories together. The cross-cultural qualifier 'religious' bound both religions to the same taxon, putting the Muslim despot to work as the affective 'Trojan horse' of Enlightenment anti-religion, though a peculiar one, perhaps, insofar as it both invaded and participated in the construction of its Troy. Inasmuch as

Europe 'shed some of its own superstitions by finding them shared by savages' (Kiernan 1990: 103), 'religion' constituted a powerful palimpsest on which cross-cultural differences could be laid out, compared, and in some cases collapsed. As the Catholic theologian Nicolas Sylvestre Bergier (1718–1790) suggested, Mahomet's wild dreams, when 'brought closer ... to a resemblance perceived in the Christian religion, and proposed upon the theatre', inevitably left a 'morbid impression' (Badir 1974: 139).

Conclusion

Since nature makes nothing that is not useful, and that, of the many things she produces, there is not one without its uses, hatred must find its use. And this passion which is born in us together with love, must find objects upon which it may innocently discharge its fury. But since nature loves her works, since this common mother bears affection to all her children, and nourishes them with such sweet intelligence that those who violate it pass for monsters, so must hatred respect them, and go out of the world to find a subject which may provoke its indignation. It must fight with the disorders of our soul, and attack such enemies as would destroy virtue.

Jean-François Senault, *De l'Usage des Passions* (1641: 286–7)

This book has examined the intimate relation between three aspects of seventeenth- and eighteenth-century philosophical culture: theories of the passions and habits, the growing issue of managing or suppressing religion, and representations of the Oriental despot in print and on stage. I have suggested that the epistemological and political implications of early works on the passions, like Descartes's *Les Passions de l'Âme* (1649), took root during the eighteenth century in a wide-ranging exploration of the body and emotion, and were elaborated into full-blown polemic strategies in the form and contents of some of the most radical anti-religious and Orientalist works of the French Enlightenment. Between the 1720s and 1790s, the figure of the Oriental despot evolved into a viscerally effective pedagogical tool for the inculcation of civic virtue, congruent with contemporaneous theories of emotional and habitual manipulation through the senses. There is thus a close connection between Enlightenment epistemology, the Enlightenment's challenge to the sharpening category of religion, and Enlightenment Orientalism – a connection which simultaneously challenges two key strands in recent theorizations of secular subjectivity: Charles Taylor and Charles Hirschkind's 'disengaged' theory of the secular body, and the specific issue of Eurocentrism in *A Secular Age* (2007).

As we have seen, the strategy of appealing to visceral images of civilizational otherness became more pronounced as the eighteenth century progressed. Representations of the despotic monster (and, through him, the Muslim other more generally) became cruder and more negative, until he came to stand exclusively for an excess of power, religious fanaticism and/or violence. This transformation, I have suggested, was inextricably linked to the emergence of 'religion' as a distinct problem of secular governmentality. If, as Larry Wolff argues, the despot could still be treated as a moral and political exemplar before the 1730s, this became increasingly difficult in the following decades, i.e. precisely the period during which explicitly anti-religious and pro-nationalist polemics took hold in mainstream French culture. At this point, the Oriental despot morphed into an exclusively negative figure of religious emotion and unreason, even as the passions retained their political value as tools for the cultivation of national sentiment.

This last point is important, for it suggests that negative representations of the Muslim despot not only turned people away from religion but served to mediate a contradiction between Enlightenment endorsements and devaluations of the passions for political purposes. As noted in Chapters 2 and 5, emotional Islam often acted as a foil not for the rational secular but rational Christianity. Yet the *philosophes* did not necessarily seek a middle way or mean between the twin extremes of Muslim fanaticism and Christian apathy. Although they warned against the dangers of Islamic fanaticism in terms of a generalized caution against excessive passionality, they themselves encouraged strong emotions in the domain of the secular and were as likely to accuse religion of suppressing the passions. This was a true contradiction, though one that easily slipped under the radar through the subterfuge of the affectively other. Religious passions could be imagined as wrong or dangerous, not because strong passions were wrong in principle, although occasionally portrayed as such, nor even because the aims to which they pointed were religious rather than secular, but because they were held by the wrong kind of people. This supra-semiotic work of othering arguably allowed Enlightenment philosophers to hold two positions simultaneously, to be both pro- and anti-emotional: the figure of the Oriental despot allowed the philosophes to take an anti-emotional stance when assuming the voice of secular reason and revert to a passionate, even fanatic patriotism when thinking more practically about how to bring about substantial change in pre-Revolutionary France. The emerging category of religion was capacious enough to represent both positions. Though Christianity had until then served as the *de facto* legitimator of Western exceptionality (e.g. in Hugo Grotius's Christocentric

Orientalism), the transition to secularity and repudiation of religion reproduced the schema of superior-West-versus-inferior-East in equally binary terms. The genius of the Enlightenment *philosophes* lay in their ability to combine the discursive power of this binary with a vigorous attack on the foundations of religion, so creating a powerfully affective 'secular assemblage'.

A number of questions remain to be answered for a fuller understanding of the history of the secular body. Anne Vincent-Buffault has suggested that, from the end of the eighteenth century, public displays of emotion were eventually suppressed and superseded by a colder, more restrained code of sociality based on the 'unsolvable separation of beings' (1991 [1986]: 96). If true, what conditions led to this shift? What role did Kant play in the eventual 'relegation of the passions' (Caygill 2006)? What is the wider context in which Kant's ideas spread and became established? How did inherited theories of the passions interact with biological and behavioural sciences during the nineteenth and early twentieth centuries? How did issues of legitimation surrounding European colonialism inflect discourse on religion and the body through this period? And what role did seminal representatives of secularism in the late nineteenth century, like Sigmund Freud and Karl Marx, play in the history of a perceived disengagement from the body and senses, now typically construed as a defining feature of the secular? These questions must await development in a longer, more comprehensive study.

Finally, a note on the remit of this work. *Secular Assemblages* combines traditional intellectual history with a critical perspective indebted to postcolonial theory and ideology critique, in order to trace an alternative genealogy of the secular that does not hedge on the possibility of a structure of affects distinctive to the secular. In staking out this ground, however, I do not wish to suggest that emotionalism or racist Orientalism are the only or even most important factors of the French Enlightenment. Different stories can be told, other narratives wound and unwound, that cast a different light on the history of the secular body. This will remain the case for as long as inconsistency and contradiction cut through the history of Western thought. Yet if it is impossible to edit the Enlightenment to a single story, one point is nevertheless clear: histories of the secular that purport to track the genealogy of Western secular experience without reference to other cultures or religions suffer from an intrinsic and deleterious blind spot, since core categories of the secular were formulated, articulated and propagated on the very basis of such references. A history of the secular body that would be 'other-wise' must take these into account.

Notes

Introduction

1   For an overview of different receptions of the play across different countries and time periods, see Spellberg (2004). When *Mahomet the Impostor* (as the play was known in James Miller's English adaptation) played the Theatre-Royal Smock Alley in Dublin in 1754, riots erupted at the second performance and the theatre was set on fire. According to Spellberg, this reaction 'had absolutely nothing to do with Islam or Catholicism or Protestantism, or pleas for religious tolerance or empire'. Instead, 'Once abstracted, the play became a facile, potentially universal allegory about tyranny, freedom and partisanship. The message in its Irish context transcended any definitions of authorial intent, either by Miller or Voltaire, and was readily recalibrated to the political rhetoric of Dublin party politics' (2004: 296–7).

2   Ironically, Voltaire shared more in common with Ramadan than Rochaix on the subject of self-censorship. He once reproached John Dryden for exposing too much in his translations of Racine, arguing that certain things should be 'veiled' on the stage, and that Frenchmen were distinguished precisely by their tactfulness: 'It is only through a hundred clouds that one should glimpse such ideas as make us blush when presented too closely. It is this veil that gives honest people their charm ... The French have known this rule for longer than other people' (1877 [1732]: 552–3).

3   On the eighteenth century as a turning point for the release of printing from monarchic/state control, see Lise Andries (1997). According to Andries, censorship at this time became virtually impossible, since 'Too many obstacles run against it: the constant increase in the number of books, the improving trade of clandestine books, founded on substantial networks of contraband, and finally, the severity of regulations which paradoxically encourage infractions' (193, translation mine).

4   See also Mahmood: 'the emergence of the modern category of the secular (to be distinguished from the pre-modern use of the Latin term *saeculum*) is constitutively related to the rise of the modern concept of religion wherein it is impossible to track the history of one without simultaneously tracking the history of the other' (2008b: unpaginated); and Beaman: 'the secular is always entangled with the religious, and the question that is most interesting is *how* rather than *whether* they are entangled'. See also Sheehan (2003: 1072) and Hurd (2011: 172).

5   References to Kant are ubiquitous in secular studies. For example, Craig Calhoun traces the 'European Enlightenment tradition of imagining religion to be properly

outside the frame of the public sphere' (2011: 80) explicitly to Kant, while Mahmood sees the 'secular concept of religion' as underpinned by 'the Kantian model of autonomous reason' (2006: 345; see also 342, fn. 48). See also Owen and Owen (2010: 10). Cf. Connolly's essay 'Europe: A Minor Tradition' (2006), in which Asad is questioned for his own emphasis on Kant: 'Much of what Asad says seems right to me, although – and I imagine Asad may agree – the contemporary focus on Kant as *the* key figure of the Enlightenment speaks as much to the assumptions and demands of contemporary academic politics as it does to the plurality of perspectives in play during the seventeenth and eighteenth centuries' (2006: 80). Against this Kantian paradigm, and in some ways against his own earlier work in *Why I Am Not*, Connolly outlines a number of alternative Enlightenment strands of thought bracketed under the notion of a 'minor tradition', originating in Epicurus and Lucretius, building through Spinoza and ending in Deleuze. On the problem of a retroactive construction of a 'rational' Enlightenment mainstream and a post- or anti-rational periphery, see below.

6   Cf. Hurd, who warns: 'A fixed understanding of religion in relation to the secular supports an understanding of the secular as that which is associated with normal, rational politics. Religion becomes a repository for a range of nonrational and nonuniversal dimensions of politics that fall outside the range of "normal" politics, including belief, culture, tradition, mood, and emotion' (2011: 170).

7   See also Asad (2003: 159–80).

8   Mahmood: 'Both [notions of blasphemy and freedom of speech] presuppose a semiotic ideology in which signifiers are arbitrarily linked to concepts, their meaning open to people's reading in accord with a particular code they share between them. What might appear to be a symbol of mirth and merrymaking to some may well be interpreted as blasphemous by others … [T]his rather impoverished understanding of images, icons, and signs not only naturalizes a certain concept of a *religious* subject but also fails to attend to the affective and embodied practices through which a subject comes to relate to a particular sign' (2009: 841–2). On the 'semiotic ideology' that allows 'responses to the desecration of sacred objects and texts, or to the legal regulation of such things as headscarves and crucifixes' to seem 'to be irrational and archaic restrictions on the freedom that people should claim for themselves', see Keane (2015: 62). On the control of this semiotics by state powers, with special reference to legislation on the veil, see Asad (2004: 3). Particularly interesting in this regard is a pernicious double-standard concerning the semiotics of Islamic iconography and the semiotics of Islamic female dress, where the former is considered flexible, arbitrary and unstable (and therefore inadequate cause for 'religious' offence), and the latter strictly fixed (and therefore grounds for 'secular' offence). Consider e.g. French philosopher and political commentator Elisabeth Badinter's comments on the unambiguously

'unpatriotic' semiotics of the veil and the violence enacted by the veil on the wearers' 'oppressed sisters': 'In a modern democracy, where we are trying to establish transparency and gender equality, you signify to us brutally that none of this is your business, that relations with other people do not concern you, and that our battles are not yours. So I ask myself: why not return to Saudi or Afghan lands, where no one will ask you to show your face, where your daughters will be veiled, where your husband can indulge his polygamy and reject you when he pleases …? In truth, you use democratic liberties to turn them against democracy. [But] the scandal is less the offence caused by your rejection than the blow you address to your oppressed sisters who risk death to enjoy the very liberties you disdain' (2010: unpaginated, translation mine).

9   On the relative youth and instability of these categories, see Fernando (2014: 10). On the constructive force of 'misidentification' and the permanently frustrated desire that leads national subjects to identify as 'national', see Mazzarella (2009: 299, 302).

10 For an example of the political nature of secular discrimination against non-majority religions and cultures in a legal context, see Mahmood's essay 'Religious Reason and Secular Affect' (2009), in which the arguments of two lawsuits (*Otto-Preminger Institut vs Austria*, 1994, and *Wingrove vs United Kingdom*, 1997) are compared to the rhetoric surrounding the *Jyllands Posten* debacle in 2005. According to Mahmood, the lawsuits demonstrated a bias towards Western forms of offence, since in the end both lawsuits concluded with a ban on 'the display and circulation of films for offending devout Christians'. They also highlighted close links between secularism and the pragmatics of statecraft, since 'These decisions notably did not ground their judgment in European blasphemy laws but in article 10 of the convention that ensures the right to freedom of expression. Notably, while article 10(1) of the ECHR holds "freedom of expression" to be an absolute right, article 10(2) allows for this right to be limited if the restrictions are prescribed by law and *are understood to be necessary to the functioning of a democratic society*' (854–5, emphasis mine).

11 In the 2007 electoral programme of the PVV (Partij Voor de Vrijheid [Dutch Party for Freedom]), Geerts Wilders combined Christian and Enlightenment history in one breath by declaring the 'superiority of Judeo-Christian, secular culture'. Similarly, Martin Bosma has written that 'Dutch citizens should cherish above all the Christian background of this country. Almost all our crucial accomplishments are connected to Christianity. Democracy, separation of Church and State, tolerance' (2010: 68). I am grateful to Ernst van den Hemel for sharing and translating these quotations.

12 Augustine himself drew on an older tradition of negative, instrumentalizing thought surrounding the passions. Plato's *Timaeus* described the physical relations

leading to the ethical life in terms of a straightforward dominance of the passions: 'First, sensation, the same for all, arising from violent impressions; second, desire blended with pleasure and pain, and besides these fear and anger and all the feelings that accompany these and all that are of a contrary nature: and if they would master these passions they would live in righteousness; if they were mastered by them, in unrighteousness' (Caygill 2006: 218).

13 Thus, according to Locke, 'that church can have no right to be tolerated by the magistrate, which is constituted upon such a bottom, that all those who enter into it, do thereby, *ipso facto*, deliver themselves up to the protection and service of another prince. For by this means the magistrate would give way to the settling of a foreign jurisdiction in his own country, and suffer his own people to be lifted, as it were, for soldiers against his own government' (1796 [1689]: 55–6). Rousseau agrees: 'by giving men two systems of legislation, two rulers and two countries, [Roman Catholicism] subjects them to contradictory duties, and prevents them from being devoted at once to god and to country'. This type of religion is 'so obviously bad that it is a waste of time to go to the trouble of proving it' since 'Anything which breaks the unity of society is worthless' (1986 [1762–1772]: 148). For an anti-Christian (rather than anti-Catholic) attack on supra-national, religious allegiances, see Holbach: 'wherever Christianity is admitted, two opposed legislations are established, at war with one another' (1972 [1761]: 125).

14 See Victoria Kahn and Neil Saccamano on 'benevolence', 'sympathy' and 'pity' as necessary passions for the regulation of the modern state: 'Eighteenth-century moral and political philosophers were concerned to manage the conflictive potential of the passions without necessarily advocating the absolutism of state power. The managing of the passion of self-preservation was sought not through the repression of passion by the authority of reason or by the sovereignty of public regulation but through the "discovery" of other, socially beneficent and constitutive feelings such as benevolence, sympathy, and pity' (2006: 4).

15 E.g. 'The [English] Restoration sees a reaction against fanaticism and "enthusiasm"' (Taylor 2007: 224; see also 226, 263, 287; and Taylor 2011: 33, 35, 224). At one point Taylor does distinguish fanaticism from enthusiasm, writing that '"Fanaticism" designated the kind of religious certainty that seemed to the agent concerned to licence going well beyond, and even committing gross violations against the order of mutual benefit. While "enthusiasm" meant the certainty that one heard the voice of God, and could act on it, without having to rely on external authority, ecclesiastical or civil' (2007: 239). As should be clear, this distinction, while usefully separating two modes of autonomous religious action and belief, has no evaluative bearing on the latter's emotional or embodied quality. Like fanaticism, enthusiasm is later equated with its modern 'hot' or 'emotional' meaning and contrasted with Edward Gibbon and David Hume's 'cool distance', 'ironic wit' and 'unflappable stance' (2007: 241).

16 On positive valuations of *fanatisme* in the *Encyclopédie*, see Hirschman (1977: 27). According to Hirschman, 'the idea of engineering social progress by cleverly setting up one passion [especially the patriotic sentiment] to fight another [the religious sentiment] became a fairly common pastime in the course of the eighteenth century' (26). As Amy Schmitter writes, '"passion" didn't even begin to get its contemporary flavor of violent, often sexually charged emotions until the middle of the eighteenth century (at the earliest)' (2006: unpaginated).

17 For an argument that enchantment persists through the aestheticization and sublimation of 'religious feelings', see Philip Fisher (1998: 1–2). According to Fisher, the writings of T. E. Hulme indicate that 'the emotions inspired in us by God, eternity, and the universe as a whole and held within the jar of religion – feelings of the infinite, adoration, fear, the sublime – spill out in the process of secularization onto such parts of experience as our relation to landscape, the nearly religious importance of romantic love, and our worshipful interest in our own subjectivity. … The sublime secularized feelings of the infinite and of the relative insignificance of human powers in an attractive way, allowing the modern intellectual to hold onto covert religious feelings under an aesthetic disguise' (1–2).

18 Or again, 'I am less [a] critic [of the disenchantment story] than its trash collector. … I dust off and shine up what it discards, that is, the experiences of wonder and surprise that endure alongside a cynical world of business as usual, nature as manmade, and affect as the effect of commercial strategy. The experiences that I recycle … are not invaders of the major tale but underground or background residents of it' (Bennett 2001: 8).

19 'I am not merely suggesting that the rationalizing, disenchanting institutions of modernity need to be understood as vulnerable because there always remains a vital "outside" or "other" that exceeds their normalizing grasp. It has for example by now become quite routine to argue (not least with reference to colonial and postcolonial settings) that the panoptic, capillary ambition of modern governmentality in fact leaves large swathes of local lifeworlds relatively untouched and therefore external to its sway. Unabsorbed, these dense thickets of vernacular sociality then perennially return as the uncanny repressed of the political order, unsettling and denaturing claims to rule by singular sovereign reason' (Mazzarella 2009: 298).

20 For a concise summary of this argument, see Wendy Brown's immediate response to *ASA* at *The Immanent Frame*: '[A]bsent from Taylor's account is every stripe of outsider to Latin Christendom, from Jews and Muslims in Europe to colonized natives and other outsiders, as well as dissident voices, reversals and disruptions to what he calls his "story." The missing elements make it more provincially European, monolithic, colonial, than it needs to be. Above all, they make the emergence of Euro-Atlantic secularism a product of tensions within Christendom rather than, in part, a feature of Christendom's encounter with others and especially with its

constitutive outside. More than a problem of historiography or comprehensiveness, this omission has consequential politics; today, Western secularism is so relentlessly defined through its imagined opposite in Islamic theocracy that to render secularism as generated exclusively through Western Christian European history is to literally eschew the production of ourselves as secular through and against our imagined opposite. It is to be locked into Thomas Friedman's conceit about "our" secular modernity and "their" need for it' (2007: unpaginated).

21   A similar point is made by Peter Danchin in the context of contemporary religious appeals to the secular narrative of religious freedom. Reflecting on Winnifred Sullivan's study of American Catholic bishopry, Danchin writes, 'the Catholic bishops paradoxically accept the priority of the religion clauses of the First Amendment ("our first liberty") just as they challenge the dreaded spectre of "secular humanism." And they do so explicitly in terms of a dominant Enlightenment narrative that holds that this liberty is both exceptionally "ours" (America as the "particular guardian of freedom") as well as "universal" (valid "for all nations and people who yearn to be free")' (2015: 175).

22   According to Rousseau and Porter, 'the [Enlightenment's] highly popular imaginative enterprise of "conjectural history" (philosophizing what would have happened in history had been rational) dovetailed with an actual geography. The peoples and stages of civilization of the European past were readily mapped on to the tribes contemporaries encountered in Africa or America; thereby the "here and then" was mapped upon the "there and now"' (1990: 9).

23   For Masuzawa (2005), the abstract category of 'world religions' is dependent on a relativization of Christianity and simultaneous projection of Christian concepts and values that could only have happened through a history of imperial encounters. Fitzgerald argues that 'the secular' *qua* distinct realm of life separate from 'religion' was *demanded* by colonialism, as a means of securing the superiority of Western civilization *vis-à-vis* the religious other: 'The construction of "religion" and "religions" as global, crosscultural objects of study has been part of a wider historical process of western imperialism, colonialism, and neocolonialism. Part of this process has been to establish an ideologically loaded distinction between the realm of religion and the realm of non-religion or the secular' (2000: 8). See also Mahmood (2010): 'Not only did the discovery of and subsequent knowledge produced on other religious traditions serve as the mirror against which European Christianity fashioned itself, but the very concept of "religion" – its conceptual contours, its classificatory system and attendant calculus of inferior and superior civilizations – was crafted in the crucible of this encounter' (286). And Asad (2003): 'modernity is neither a totally coherent object nor a clearly bounded one … many of its elements originate in relations with the histories of peoples outside of Europe' (13). On links between the writings of Hobbes, Locke, Montesquieu and Rousseau and selective readings of non-European peoples, see Nisbet (1980: 149).

24 Casanova agrees with Taylor that 'contemporary genealogies of secularism fail to recognize the extent to which the formation of the secular is itself inextricably linked with the internal transformation of European Christianity, from the so-called Papal Revolution to the Protestant Reformation, and from the ascetic and pietistic sects of the seventeenth and eighteenth centuries to the emergence of evangelical denominational Protestantism in nineteenth-century America'. Unlike Taylor, however, he insists on the importance of taking *all* religions into account: 'A proper rethinking of secularization will require a critical examination of the diverse patterns of differentiation and fusion of the religious and the secular and their mutual constitution across all the religions of the world, and especially across the so-called "world religions"' (2008: 104).

25 According to Hurd, 'The secular/religious binary operates such that *not* to be secular is to be emotional, irrational, unpredictable, and behind the march of progress. Quietly at work here is the notion that only the West, with its narrative of secularization, has found a way out of the woods, while other civilizations continue to cast about in a desperate search to answer the questions that the West resolved centuries ago' (2011: 169).

26 In Jessica Riskin's words, 'Enlightenment thinkers' ... extreme sensitivity to the possibility of rationalist excess led them to write their own epitaph' (2002: 280). Note the difference between this approach, and one that unearths 'Counter-Enlightenment' resistances contemporaneous with, but not part of, the Enlightenment, as exemplified by Darrin McMahon. According to McMahon 'a good number of the more violent claims against the Enlightenment [both left and right] have been with us since the movement itself' (2001: 13). McMahon challenges Isaiah Berlin's claim that the Enlightenment and Counter-Enlightenment can be parsed on the basis of their geographical location, with the Enlightenment occurring in France, and the Counter-Enlightenment in Germany. According to him, 'At the most basic level, it is clear, opposition to the Enlightenment was neither exclusively German nor predominantly philosophical. First and foremost French, and first and foremost religious, it extended outward from there into other countries and realms of inquiry. ... It stands to reason that the reaction to the Enlightenment should also have occurred first in the place of its birth and been spearheaded by the very institution – the Catholic Church – charged with maintaining the faith and morals of the realm' (9). As should be clear, this book does not seek out forces antithetical to and contemporaneous with the Enlightenment – religious or otherwise – but 'Counter-Enlightenment' elements within the Enlightenment itself. For more on the Counter-Enlightenment, see Chapter 2.

27 'Literature is an assemblage. It has nothing to do with ideology. There is no ideology and never has been' (1987 [1980]: 4).

28 Cf. Foucault: 'The frontiers of a book are never clear-cut: beyond the title, the first lines, and the last full stop, beyond its internal configuration and its autonomous

form, it is caught up in a system of references to other books, other texts, other sentences: it is a node within a network. ... The book is not simply the object that one holds in one's hands; and it cannot remain within the little parallelepiped that contains it: its unity is variable and relative. As soon as one questions that unity, it loses self-evidence; it indicates itself, constructs itself, only on the basis of a complex field of discourse' (1972: 23).

29 As Sheehan has argued, a 'media reading' of the Enlightenment suggests the intention of the Enlightenment philosophes may be secondary to the form in which their arguments emerged: such a reading would not ask '*what* Bayle meant' but '*how* Bayle's text functioned'. The articles of Bayle's *Dictionnaire* 'did not need to cohere, nor were positions set in stone.' Rather, 'its form opened up horizons of interpretive behavior unknown in the previous age' (2003: 1077).

Chapter 1

1 '[D]efining is a historical act and when the definition is deployed, it does different things at different times and in different circumstances, and responds to different questions, needs, and pressures. The concept "religion" is not merely a word: it belongs to vocabularies that bring persons and things, desires and practices together in particular traditions in distinctive ways. [...] [L]iberal democracy [...] requires that *belief* be taken as the essence of religiosity' (2011: 39–40). Although Asad recognizes that 'the idea of belief in Taylor's story does not always have the sense of a proposition,' he nevertheless worries that 'the notion of "construal" by the buffered self in [Taylor's] story seems to presuppose something that is capable of being articulated – if not propositionally, then in the form of a narrative' (48).

2 Taylor elsewhere provides a shorthand definition of 'disengaged reason' as 'a reasoning which in no way draws insight from the significance things have for us as embodied, social beings, who mark moral or aesthetic distinctions in things and actions' (2012: 18).

3 See also Taylor 1989: 162, 2012: 18.

4 Cf. Habermas (1989 [1962]: 30–1).

5 See also: '[the public sphere] is supposed to be listened to by power, but it is not itself an exercise of power' (Taylor 2007: 190).

6 The only available translation of *De l'Usage* is Henry Carey's *The Use of Passions* (1650). Since this translation is reliable but stylistically older than Stoothoff's translation of the *Passions* (below), I have updated Carey's text for consistency, with occasional reference to the French for clarification of key terms.

7 Citations are from the standard modern translation by Robert Stoothoff in *Philosophical Writings of Descartes, Vol. I* (1985: 325–404), with occasional

reference to the French, and to the first, anonymous translation of 1650 where relevant. Although Stoothoff's translation is the standard reference for contemporary Descartes Studies, cross-referencing with the French and the older 1650 translation reveals occasional divergences in meaning, along with a subtly rationalistic bias in the modern rendition. I have therefore modified Stoothoff's translation where appropriate, and signalled changes by including the original term in square brackets within the quotation, accompanied by Stoothoff's translation in a footnote. E.g.: 'the soul cannot suddenly [*promptement*] change or stop [*arrester*] its passions' (1985a: 345) substitutes 'suddenly' and 'stop' for Stoothoff's 'readily' and 'suspend'.

8   '[W]hen a husband mourns his dead wife, it sometimes happens that he would be sorry to see her brought to life again. It may be that his heart is torn by the sadness aroused in him by the funeral display and by the absence of a person to whose company he was accustomed. And it may be that some remnants of love or pity occur in his imagination and draw genuine tears from his eyes. Nevertheless he feels at the same time a secret joy in his innermost soul, and the emotion of this joy has such power that the concomitant sadness and tears can do nothing to diminish its force' (1985a: 381). For a literal interpretation of this passage, see Kahn (2006).

9   For an overview of these common assumptions, see Cottingham (2008: 243).

10   'I am convinced of this by the observation that all the other parts of our brain are double, as also are all the organs of our external senses – eyes, hands, ears and so on. But in so far as we have only one simple thought about a given object at any one time, there must necessarily be some place where the two images coming through the two eyes, or the two impressions coming from a single object through the double organs of any other sense, can come together in a single image or impression before reaching the soul, so that they do not to present to it two objects instead of one' (1985a: 340).

11   For an example of early distortions on this score, see Jonathan Israel's observation in *Radical Enlightenment* (2001), that, as part of a general anti-Cartesian revolt, Louis XIV prescribed 'seven fundamental doctrines of metaphysics directly contrary to those of Descartes', including the doctrine that 'the soul is really present in, and united with, the whole human body' (2001: 40).

12   Cf. Taylor's claim in *SotS* that 'For Descartes, there could have been minds without bodies' (1989: 188). In what sense such a mind would 'be' following the dissolution of the assemblage of its organs is not clear, since the mind has no extension; lacking the required material support for earthly life, it could only conceivably exist in the afterlife.

13   Cf. Senault: 'For though [God's] infinite spirit does not depend upon the world he has created … yet is he dispersed into all its parts; there is no space he does not fill up. … So is the soul dispersed in the body, and penetrates all its parts. *It is as noble*

in the hand as in the heart, and though it accommodates itself to the disposition of the organs, speaks by the mouth, sees by the eyes, and hears by the ears, yet is it but one spirit in its essence. And in its differing functions, its unity is not divided, nor its power weakened. ... [T]he soul, whose power is limited, cannot operate independently of the organs' (1641: 12–13, emphasis mine).

14   Not only is this concept missing from Taylor's reading of Descartes, but *SotS* explicitly describes 'habit' as a twentieth-century term traceable to Locke and the 'uneasiness of desire'. According to Taylor, Locke represents the roots of 'the remote origins of modern reductive psychology and the theory of reinforcement': 'Where twentieth-century psychologists speak of "habits," Locke speaks of the association that each of us makes between our inner unease and certain goods as our "relish"' (1989: 170).

15   I have adjusted Stoothoff's translation of this passage, since he unjustifiably cuts out the last half of Descartes's sentence ('do they tend ... syllables'), erasing the essential dualism Descartes sets up between the sense experience of hearing or seeing language, and the extra-sensual act of interpretation – an erasure that makes the passage redundant and almost meaningless. Stoothoff renders the passage: 'Words produce in the gland movements which are ordained by nature to represent to the soul only the sounds of their syllables when they are spoken or the shape of their letters when they are written, because we have acquired the habit of thinking of this meaning when we hear them spoken or see them written' (348). The original passage is: '[les] paroles, qui excitent des mouvements en la glande, lesquels selon l'institution de la nature ne representent à l'âme que leur son, lors qu'elles sont proferées de la voix, ou la figure de leurs lettres lors qu'elles sont escrites, and qui neantmoins par l'habitude qu'on a acquise en pensant à ce qu'elles signifient, lors qu'on a ouy leur son, ou bien qu'on a vû leurs lettres, ont coustume de faire concevoir cette signification, plustot que la figure de leurs lettres, ou bien le son de leurs syllabes' (1649: 76). The 1671 translation by Henry Carey is more faithful on this point. According to the latter, words 'excite the motions of the kernell' by 'represent[ing] only to the soul their sound ... or by the figure of their letters when they are written', yet 'by a habit acquired by thinking what they signifie, as soon as ever their sound is heard, or their letters seen, use to make us conceive the signification rather than the form of our letters or the sound of their sillables' (1671 [1649]: 43).

16   Cf. Spinoza: 'If the human Body has once been affected by two or more bodies at the same time, then when the Mind subsequently imagines one of them, it will immediately recollect the others also' (1985 [1677]: 465).

17   See also Descartes's recorded impression on persons with 'squints': 'When I was a child, I loved a girl of my own age who had a slight squint. The impression made by sight in my brain when I looked at her cross-eyes became so closely connected

to the simultaneous impression which aroused in me the passion of love that for a long time afterwards when I saw persons with a squint I felt a special inclination to love them simply because they had that defect; yet I had no idea myself that this was why it was' (cited in Kirkebøen 2001: 183).

18 Subst. 'readily' and 'suspend'; 1649: 65.

19 Subst. 'suppressed'; 1649: 64.

20 Whereas in *SotS* Taylor *contrasts* Cartesian with Aristotelian ethics (1989: 148–9), suggesting that Descartes reversed the latter through a rejection of embodied practice, Cottingham sees Descartes as standing precisely in the Aristotelian tradition (2008: 245). The difference between coercion and self-fashioning may be conceptualized, as it was by Senault, in terms of a critical difference between patriarchy and absolute sovereignty. Although Senault insists on the sovereignty of reason, and occasionally articulates this sovereignty through a martial language of conflict and coercion ('we [must] reduce these rebels [the passions] under obedience, and ... make such soldiers march under the banners of virtue', 1641: 21), he also admits that certain passions 'must be treated gently to make them obedient to reason' (117). In this case, the proper relation of reason to the passions is less that of a sovereign than a father who affectionately guides and rears his children into the proper avenues: 'Although they are subjects, they are not slaves, and the spirit which governs them is rather their father than their sovereign. Others would be cozened, and though virtue is so generous, it must accommodate itself to the weakness of the passions, and employ cunning when force will not prevail. Love is of this nature. Unable to banish it from out of our hearts, we must divert it. We must lay before it legitimate objects, and make it virtuous by an innocent cozenage' (117).

21 In *SotS* Taylor defines the passions as 'functional devices that the Creator has designed for us to help preserve the body-soul substantial union' (1989: 150).

22 Subst. 'simply'; Fr.: 'l'utilité de toutes les passions ne consiste qu'en ce qu'elles fortifient et font durer en l'âme des pensées' (Descartes 1649: 100).

23 See also Article 161: 'It should also be noted that ... thoughts may be produced by the soul alone; but it often happens that some movement of the spirits strengthens them, and in this case they are both actions of virtue and at the same time passions of the soul' (1985a: 387–8). And Article 160: 'I see no reason why the same movement of the spirits which serves to strengthen a thought which has bad foundations might not also strengthen one that is well-founded' (1985a: 386).

24 On the role of the passions in Cartesian aesthetics, Cottingham cites Descartes's language of admiration at the end of the *Third Meditation*, where he 'gazes at, wonders at, and adores the beauty of this immense light'. According to Cottingham, this language 'involves a remarkable fusing of cognitive intuition with an outpouring of passion' (2008: 112). Philip Fisher's *Wonder, the Rainbow, and the Aesthetics of Rare Experiences* (1998) argues that Descartes's 'first and central

passion', wonder, is a pure and involuntary 'experience of the senses' that precedes wilful action: whereas 'memory' and 'expectation … presume the part of the will within experience … Wonder in its first moment stands outside the will' (2008: 16–18). See also Shapiro (2003: 233).

25   On our passivity *vis-à-vis* the passions in general, see Cottingham: 'The etymology of the term "passion" (derived from the Latin verb for "to suffer") suggests something contrasted with an action – something that *happens* to a person, as opposed to that which he initiates' (2008: 242).

26   On the idea that, for Descartes, 'virtue is defined as, at least in part, a matter of *virtù*, a surplus of power or a strategic manipulation of the passions by means of the passions themselves', see Kahn (2006: 108).

27   On the equivalence of God and nature in Descartes, see the *Sixth Meditation*: 'if nature is considered in its general aspect, then I understand by the term nothing other than God himself, or the ordered system of created things established by God. And by my own nature in particular I understand nothing other than the totality of things bestowed on me by God' (1984 [1641]: 56). Cf. Spinoza (1985 [1677]: 544). Contrast Cottingham's reading with Taylor's claim in *SotS* that 'the spiritual attitude' which focuses upon the mysteriousness and strangeness of our conscious emergence from an unconscious universe 'is in flat contradiction to the Cartesian'. According to Taylor, for Descartes, 'the dominant idea is of the purity of the thinking being, of its *utter heterogeneity from blind physical nature*, and of its transcendently higher status' (1989: 347, emphasis mine). On the secondariness of the will to the dictates of nature, see also Article 44, where Descartes explains the uncontrolled contraction of the pupil following the volition to look at a distant object ('if we think only of enlarging the pupils, we may indeed have such a volition, but we do not thereby enlarge them', 1985a: 344), as a result of 'natural' annexation: 'For the movement of the gland, whereby the spirits are driven to the optic nerve in the way required for enlarging or contracting the pupils, has been joined by nature with the volition to look at distant or nearby objects, rather than with the volition to enlarge or contract the pupils' (1985a: 344). For an argument that Descartes's explanation of the body-mind is fundamentally 'teleological', in the sense that 'the associations between body and mind are as they are in virtue of their promotion of the *human good*', see Shapiro (2003: 211–48, emphasis original).

28   This reading of Descartes is prevalent within classical psychology. See e.g. Corson and Corson's essay 'From Descartes to Pavlov to Anokhin' (1985). According to the authors, 'René Descartes developed a mechanistic notion of reflex action in an attempt to describe automatic acts of "soulless" machine-like "unfeeling" animals, in contrast to rational voluntary behaviour of humans directed by a "soul" via the pineal gland' (1985: 679). Cf. Pavlov on Descartes, below.

29   See also Article 38: 'the body may be moved to take flight by the mere disposition of the organs, without any contribution from the soul' (1985a: 343).

30 '[W]e cannot have too ardent a desire for virtue. ... [T]he mistake we usually
    make in this regard is never that we desire too much; it is rather that we desire too
    little' (1985a: 378). See also Descartes's *Letter to Elisabeth* of June 1645: 'I know
    indeed that it is almost impossible not to give in to the disturbances which new
    misfortunes initially arouse in us. I know too that ordinarily the best minds are
    those in which the passions are most violent and act most strongly on their bodies'
    (1991a: 253). Also Cottingham (2008: 250, fn. 57).

31 Interestingly, a similar discrepancy underlies Senault's *De l'Usage*. On one hand,
    Senault claims that 'reason is sovereign of the passions' (1641: 119), and that even
    'our most insolent passions may be subject to reason' (7); on the other, he assigns
    this power to love: '[I]f there are diverse passions, love is their sovereign ... it is so
    absolute in its kingdom, that its subjects undertake nothing except its orders. It is
    the prime mover [*premier mobile*] which supports them, setting them in motion
    and bringing them to rest. Its gaze [*regard*] irritates and appeases them, and its
    examples have such power over all the affections of our soul, that its goodness or
    malice renders them good or evil' (31).

32 Cf. Corson and Corson: '*In contradistinction to Cartesian dualism*, Pavlov
    introduced the monistic concept of an integrated organism (theory of nerves) and
    of conditional reflexes enabling all animals to modify their behaviour in response
    to changing environmental situations' (1985: 679, emphasis mine).

33 Subst. 'worth noting' and 'effort'; 1649: 78. This last, crucial term is translated
    from the French *industrie*, which in the seventeenth century would have had
    connotations of *invention* and *savoir-faire*, as well as, or instead of, the modern
    sense of economically productive activity or effort (e.g. Voltaire uses it in the sense
    of *capacité technique*; Harsin 1930: 236). For an analysis of the term in seventeenth-
    and eighteenth-century France, and its transition to the modern sense, see Paul
    Harsin (1930).

34 Subst. 'guiding'; 1649: 78. Cf. Senault, according to whom the passions are 'born
    with us' and 'borrow their strength from our constitution', 'yet they draw their
    nourishment from exterior things; and if they are not entertained by objects,
    they die or pine away' (1641: 132). Among 'exterior things', the arts in particular
    '[seduced] men by the means of passions' (179), and thus it was reason's duty to
    'always keep watch over subjects that may excite our passions' and guard our senses
    against their 'surprizes' (116–17). On the power of rhetoric, Senault wrote: 'Orators
    who wish to seize the soul by means of the senses, join handsome language to good
    reasons, flatter the ear to touch the heart, and employ all the tropes to move the
    affections. They attack the two parts whereof man is composed, using the weakest
    to subdue the stronger. And as the devil undid man by means of woman, they gain
    reason by means of passion' (186–7).

35 Subst. 'are presented'; 1649: 202–3.

Chapter 2

1   As Connor writes, 'the national bond is subconscious and emotional rather
than conscious and rational its inspiration. It can be analysed but not explained
rationally' (1994: 204). Anderson argues that the 'profound emotional legitimacy'
commanded by the nation is explicable by reference to the 'cultural roots' of
nationalism – cultural roots which share much in common with religion: 'Part
of the difficulty is that one tends unconsciously to hypostasize the existence of
Nationalism-with-a-big-N (rather as one might Age-with-a-capital-A) and then
to classify "it" as an ideology ... It would, I think, make things easier if one treated
it as if it belonged with "kinship" and "religion," rather than with liberalism or
"fascism"' (2006: 4–7). Drawing on Étienne Balibar, Smith-Rosenberg writes
that 'For a nation to live, its heterogeneous, often contentious inhabitants must
experience themselves as parts of a collective "We, the people." Rhetoric, images,
and words lie at the heart of the daily practices that create collective national
identity ... National identities are scripts that take form and feel natural as a result
of repetitive, ritualized enactments' (2010: 18).

2   According to Anderson, 'The century of the Enlightenment, of rationalist
secularism brought with it its own modern darkness. With the ebbing of religious
belief, the suffering which belief in part composed did not disappear. Disintegration
of paradise: nothing makes fatality more arbitrary. Absurdity of salvation: nothing
makes another style of continuity more necessary. What then was required was a
secular transformation of fatality into continuity, contingency into meaning ... few
things were (are) better suited to this end than an idea of nation' (2006: 11).

3   Cf. Horkheimer and Adorno: 'the cause of enlightenment's relapse into mythology
is to be sought not so much in the nationalist, pagan, or other modern mythologies
concocted specifically to cause such a relapse as in the fear of truth which petrifies
enlightenment itself' (2002 [1944]: xvi).

4   In his *Dictionnaire des Synonymes* (1701–1800), Étienne Bonnot de Condillac
defined 'culture' as 'the care one gives to a piece of land to render it fertile', as was
'said figuratively of customs, the mind, the sciences, etc.'. Jessica Riskin glosses this
definition in terms of a return to the body: to cultivate the 'mind, the memory,
the arts, the sciences' during the Enlightenment was 'a matter of developing one's
responsiveness to this organic process – one's sensibilities and intuitions – more
than one's rational faculty' (2002: 231–2).

5   See Taylor on the generation of a social imaginary: 'it very often happens that what
start off as theories held by a few people may come to infiltrate the social imaginary,
first of élites perhaps, then of the whole society' (2007: 172).

6   Rothschild also challenges the widespread view that enlightened ideas were
essentially Stoic. According to her, 'stoical apathy and indifference' were odious to

Enlightenment thinkers like Adam Smith, and especially so when they impinged on the 'private and domestic affections': 'Smith's ethics is founded on his description of moral sentiments; on the emotions which we feel for our friends and "nearest connections," but which are in turn the sentiments by which entire societies are united. ... This is the opposite, in Smith's description, of Stoic positions. The sentiments which the Stoics seek to repress become for Smith the foundations of ethics (and even of politics)' (2001: 132, 133, 137).

7   Pinker recognizes that Enlightenment thinkers rejected 'the implausible claim that humans are perfectly rational agents', but also claims that Enlightenment philosophers from Hume to Kant called out 'our irrational passions and foibles' in order to 'overcome them' (2018: 9). This directly contradicts Hume's famous declaration that 'reason is, and ought only to be the slave of the passions' (1739: 415).

8   Since 9/11 especially, the Enlightenment has become an ideological flashpoint for the convergence of secularism and right-wing populism. As Ian Buruma explains in *Murder in Amsterdam* (2006): 'Until recently not much attention was paid outside the universities to the currents and crosscurrents of the Enlightenment and the Counter-Enlightenment. It was the attack on the World Trade Center on September 11, 2001 ... that brought the Enlightenment back to the center of political debate' (2006: 28). On Buruma's account, the Enlightenment has been newly politicized because 'Islamist extremism' has come to stand for its opposite: the parochial, atomizing and regressive politics of a contemporary Muslim 'Counter-Enlightenment'. Under these conditions, Muslim immigration threatens not only Europe, but the 'fortress of Enlightenment' itself (28–9). On the post-9/11 emergence of 'patriotic atheism', see Bullivant (2010).

9   Historian of atheism Michael J. Buckley agrees with a traditional assessment of the *Système* as 'the most important demonstration of materialism and atheism' until the middle of the twentieth century (1987: 32). Michel Onfray complains in his *Atheist Manifesto* (2005) that 'the work of Baron d'Holbach cannot be found in the university: no scholarly or scientific edition by any philosophical publisher worthy of the name; no works, theses, or ongoing research; no paperback edition, of course (whereas editions of Rousseau, Voltaire, Kant, or Montesquieu abound); no classes or seminars devoted to analytic examination and propagation of his thinking; not one biography ... Painful!' (2005: 30).

10   See also McMahon 2001: 8.

11   I include Roger Hausheer's Introduction to *Against the Current* in this summary, since it neatly summarizes the principal ideas of the book and is formally endorsed by Berlin as a 'sympathetic and luminous account' of the views discussed in his essays (1979: front matter, unpaginated).

12   See also 2007: 139: 'the disengaged, disciplined stance first restricts intimacy, and then makes us take a distance from our powerful emotions and our bodily

functions'. And 2007: 142: 'the disciplined, disengaged agent completes another facet of what I've been calling the buffered self. Not only is there a firm inner/outer boundary in a world which has been disenchanted, but further barriers are raised against strong physical desires and the fascination with the body. The barriers are raised by and in the name of the central identity as agent of disengaged discipline, keeping its distance from this zone of abandon. But since this is also a zone in which feelings flow between people, and a kind of intimacy of mutual arousal can easily arise, this distance also drastically narrows the range of permitted intimacy. Outside the narrow circles of intimacy which remain, we are trained to relate to each other as dignified subjects of rational control, whose defining relations are no longer intimate ones, and indeed, which prepare each other eventually to transcend defining relations altogether'.

13 Curtis's work is especially interesting for the way it focuses discussions of religious freedom on the meta-framework, the excess of conditions, which shape the way 'religious freedom' is constructed and deployed across different contexts and for different political purposes. In the course of his argument, Curtis sets up three key antitheses between Bushnell's theological liberalism and the Enlightenment, based upon the importance for the former of, and blindness of the second to sentiments of the heart, habits and virtues (2016: 51).

14 See also Jonathan Israel, who posits two enlightenments, 'mainstream' and 'radical', the first associated with Locke and the doctrine of religious toleration, and the second with the wholesale destruction of the old order. According to Israel, the second succeeded the first and made unprecedented appeals to emotion. This was part of a growing politicization of atheism, as the philosophes came to realize the nature of the power they wielded (2001: 5–11). While it is true that the 'radical' Enlightenment appealed to emotion, it was just as – if not more – wedded to Locke's ideas than the 'tolerant' mainstream. The 'radical Enlightenment' simply built on Lockean epistemology rather than Lockean political doctrine. The tension between a Lockean epistemology that traces all knowledge to the senses, and a Lockean political doctrine that refuses sensual (i.e. external) religion presents a fascinating problem for the genealogy of the secular, though one which, unfortunately, lies outside the scope of this work.

15 'Modern enlightened culture is very theory-oriented. We tend to live in our heads, trusting our disengaged understandings: of experience, of beauty … even the ethical: we think that the only valid form of ethical self-direction is through rational maxims or understanding. We can't accept that part of being good is opening ourselves to certain feelings; either the horror at infanticide, or agape as a gut feeling' (2007: 555).

16 In the fourth century, Augustine declared that 'I see in myself a body and a soul, one external, the other internal', and that 'What is inward is superior' (1992

[397–400]: 184). Reflecting on 'the pleasure of the bodily senses', Augustine thought this 'not even worth considering', for the true seeker '[climbs] beyond all corporeal objects and the heaven itself, where sun, moon and stars shed light on the earth' (171).

17 Contrast Diderot's pre-revolutionary enthusiasm for fanatical nationalism, with Condorcet's post-revolutionary reversion to the emancipatory power of pure reason: 'hypocrisy covers Europe with executions at the stake, and assassinations. The monster, fanaticism, maddened by the wounds it has received, appears to redouble its fury, and hastens to burn its victims in heaps, fearful that reason might be approaching to deliver them from his hands' (1796 [1795]: 166–7). Diderot elsewhere belittles the *économistes* for naïvely ignoring 'the deceits, the passions, all the ruses of avidity, all the ruses of fear' constitutive of modern economics. For Diderot, such economics are not 'tranquil' but rather present 'a tumultuous conflict of fear, of avidity, of greed' (Rothschild 2001: 20). On Diderot's Nietzschean deferral to instinct and the will to power over reason, see also his *Philosophical Thoughts*: 'None of the vain speculations of metaphysics have the cogency of an argument *ad hominem*. In order to convince, it is sometimes only necessary to rouse the physical or moral instinct. The Pyrrhonist was convinced by a stick that he was wrong in doubting his own existence. Cartouche, pistol in hand, might have taught Hobbes a similar lesson: 'Your money or your life; we are alone, I am the stronger, and between us there is no question of justice' (1916 [1746–1751]: 34).

18 See also 1795 [1791]: 305.

19 In this respect, Christians were comparable to sensorily incapacitated persons, such as the blind. As Riskin notes, Diderot's *Lettre sur les Aveugles* (1749) argued that 'blind people thought like mathematicians and mathematicians like blind people: both were unusually impervious to sensory experience, therefore lacking in sensibility. This insensibility stunted the moral as well as intellectual faculties, Diderot suggested, and so he "suspected blind people" and, by implication, mathematicians of "inhumanity"' (Riskin 2002: 11).

20 Spinoza's example is particularly interesting, for the light he sheds on the distinctness of the *philosophes*. According to Hirschman, Spinoza does not see the counteraction of passions with passions as an end in itself, but merely a stage on the path to pure reason. He recognizes the power of the passions only to emphasize the great difficulty of reaching that destination – that destination being 'the triumph of reason and love of God over the passions'; the idea of the countervailing passion is a mere 'station' to this final goal (1977: 23–4). Unlike Bacon and against the later *philosophes*, Spinoza had 'no intention whatever of translating this idea into the realm of practical moral or political engineering, even though he had a lively appreciation of such possibilities' (24). So long as Spinozist rationalism restricted itself to theology, philosophy or metaphysics, it had no need for emotion

or the body as substantial components of the good. This was not the case for many eighteenth-century *philosophes*, for whom emotions were intrinsic to the means *and* end of social reform.

21   See also: 'Nature does not make man either good or wicked; she combines machines more or less active, mobile and energetic; she furnishes him with organs, with temperament, of which his passions, more or less impetuous, are the necessary consequence; these passions have always his happiness for their object; therefore they are legitimate and natural, and they can only be called bad or good, relatively to the influence they have on the beings of his species' (1889 [1770]: 345).

22   See also: 'When [man's] passions have been moderate, and have tended to the public good, they are legitimate, and we approve those actions which are their effects' (1857 [1768]: 251–2). Or again, 'it is [the Freethinker's] duty to moderate his passions … Thus, relatively to his morality, the Freethinker has principles more sure than those of superstition and fanaticism' (1857 [1768]: 276).

23   *Micromégas* tells the story of two giants from space, who visit Earth and strike up a conversation with a group of philosophers. After mocking the supporters of Aristotle, Descartes, Malebranche and Leibniz, the giants are thrilled to hear about Locke: 'A tiny Lockean stood nearby, and when he was finally addressed, said: " … I have only ever thought on the basis of my senses … " The animal from Sirius smiled: he found this one the wisest of the lot, and the dwarf from Saturn would have embraced the supporter of Locke if there had not been such an extreme disproportion [in their sizes]' (Voltaire 1877 [1752]: XXI. 122).

24   Condorcet's conception of right was similarly based, at least partly, on the fact that man feels: 'After ages of error, after wandering in all the mazes of vague and defective theories, writers upon politics and the law of nations at length arrived at the knowledge of the true rights of man, which they deduced from this simple principle: that *he is a being endowed with sensation, capable of reasoning upon and understanding his interests, and of acquiring moral ideas*' (1796 [1795]: 185, emphasis original).

25   Like Holbach, Diderot could sometimes revert to a straightforward rationalism, even in matters of morality. So twenty pages earlier in the same book, he writes, 'There are many things which we think we learn through [the senses'] medium and of which we have not a full assurance. When, therefore, the evidence of the senses is inconsistent with, or does not outweigh, the authority of reason, we have no choice; logically, we must decide for reason' (1916 [1746–1751]: 62).

26   When Voltaire mourned Blaise Pascal's loss of reason in later life, he put this down to 'melancholy' – an emotional condition no more mysterious than a physical illness: 'It is not surprising, after all, that a man of delicate temperament, of melancholy imagination … should, because of his bad diet [*mauvais régime*], manage to disturb his brain's organs. This sickness is neither more surprising,

nor more humiliating than a fever or migraine' (1753a [1741]: 108–9). See also Voltaire's, entry for *fanatisme* in his *Dictionnaire Philosophique* (1764), which literally portrays fanaticism as a disease to be cured by the 'philosophical spirit': 'Once fanaticism has gangrened a brain, the sickness is practically incurable. I have seen epileptics [*convulsionnaires*] who, describing the miracles of saint Paris, gradually grew hotter in spite of themselves: their eyes flamed, their limbs trembled, fury disfigured their faces, and they would have killed whomever contradicted them. There is no cure to this epidemic than the philosophical spirit which, spread from acquaintance to acquaintance, softens the customs of men and prevents the accessions of evil; as soon as this evil makes any progress, one must run away and wait for the air to clear' (1878 [1764]: XIX. 81).

27 Cf. Montesquieu's *Lettres Persanes* (1721): 'The air is charged, like plants, by particles indigenous to the soil of each country. It has such an effect on us, that our temperament is fixed by it. When transported into another country, we become ill. Liquids being accustomed to a certain consistency, solids to a certain disposition, and both to a certain degree of movement, they cannot suffer change, and resist new permutations' (1973 [1721]: 271).

28 '[T]he opinions, whether good or bad, injurious or beneficial, true or false, which form themselves in his mind, are never more than the effect of those physical impulsions which the brain receives by the medium of the senses' (1889 [1770]: 75).

29 Contrast this understanding of the imagination as shaped by external factors, to Riskin's suggestion that Enlightenment sensationism '[set] the imagination up as the antithesis of sensibility. While sensibility focused the mind outward through the senses, imagination drew the mind inward, away from its sensory interface with the outside world' (2002: 192, fn. 121). Cf. fn. 27 below.

30 'Q. Do objects that act upon our senses leave any impression or trace? A. Yes, the traces left by objects are called ideas or images; thought reveals them in ourselves. The memory of images is called imagination. Q. What is thought? A. It is the action that takes place within man every time he receives or retraces the impression that external objects or his own organs have made upon him' (1790: 25).

31 'Thus, it may be observed, that a man of a sanguine constitution is commonly lively, ingenious, full of imagination, passionate, voluptuous, enterprising; whilst the phlegmatic man is dull, of a heavy understanding, slow of conception, inactive, difficult to be moved, pusillanimous, without imagination, or possessing it in a less lively degree, incapable of taking any strong measures, or of willing resolutely' (1889 [1770]: 61).

32 On the importance of imagination to Rousseau's politics of social sentiments, see Patrick Coleman, according to whom 'Rousseau presents the civil religion as something to be taken on faith. Sentiments of sociability can only emerge

through a consciousness that is active but unreflective, in other words through the imagination' (2006: 159–160).

33   As Rothschild notes, for Condorcet, the object of political economy was to seek 'a general law in "this apparent chaos," this "external shock of opposing interests," "this astonishing variety of works and products, of needs and resources; in this frightening complexity of interests, which links to the general system of societies, the subsistence, the well-being of an isolated individual; which makes him dependent on *all the accidents of nature*, on *all events of politics*; which extends, in some respects, to the entire globe his capacity to experience either enjoyments or deprivations"' (2001: 237, emphasis mine).

34   Cf. Voltaire: 'To what do we owe revolutions! A slightly harder blow from a stone ... would give another destiny to the world' (1878 [1764]: XVII. 106).

35   See also: 'in examining the primitive sources of this strange revolution, what were the concealed causes that had an influence over this man, that excited his peculiar passions, that modified his temperament? What was the matter from the combination of which resulted a crafty, ambitious, enthusiastic and eloquent man; in short, a personage competent to impose on his fellow creatures, and capable of making them concur in his views? They were the insensible particles of his blood, the imperceptible texture of his fibres, the salts, more or less acrid, that stimulated his nerves, the proportion of igneous fluid that circulated in his system. From whence came these elements? It was from the womb of his mother, from the aliments which nourished him, from the climate in which he had his birth, from the ideas he received, from the air which he respired, without reckoning a thousand inappreciable and transitory causes, that, in the instance given, had modified, had determined the passions of this important being, who had thereby acquired the capacity to change the face of this mundane sphere' (1889 [1770]: 115).

36   '[Man] takes those for innate ideas, of which he has forgotten the origin; he no longer recalls to himself either the precise epoch or the successive circumstances when these ideas were first consigned to his brain: arrived at a certain age, he believes he has always had the same notions; his memory, crowded with experience and a multitude of facts, is no longer able to distinguish the particular circumstances which have contributed to give his brain its present modifications, its instantaneous mode of thinking, its actual opinions' (1889 [1770]: 80).

37   Asad critiques Judith Perkins's argument that Stoicism, as a ruling ideology, sustained and encouraged an unequal status quo. According to him, 'Stoicism was an ethic intended for the elite rather than the masses. As such, it encouraged withdrawal from corrupt public life and inattention to social and material conditions'. Asad therefore questions whether Stoicism was 'an ideology well suited to active involvement in imperial rule' (2003: 86), implicitly setting it up – like Taylor – as an important facet of secular self-perception and self-rule.

Chapter 3

1 As critically minded scholars of the secular have pointed out, 'external' (and therefore particular) religion has often been presented as something 'other' cultures have, in contrast to European science or internalized forms of Protestant faith. Fitzgerald (2000) and Cavanaugh (2009), for example, argue that the universal applicability of Enlightenment has served as the justification for liberating societies still trapped in the bondage of historically contingent tradition, religion or culture.

2 By 'statecraft' I have in mind Asad's idea of a form of governance that uses '*neither* compulsion (force) *nor* negotiation (consent) *but* ... "self-discipline" and "participation," "law" and "economy" as elements of political strategy' (2003: 3, emphasis original).

3 See e.g. Condorcet: 'Now it unfortunately happens, that ... travellers are almost always inaccurate observers; they see objects with too much rapidity, through the medium of the prejudices of their own country, and not unfrequently by the eyes of the men of the country they run through: their conferences are held with such men as accident has connected them with; and the answer is, in almost every case, dictated by interest, party spirit, national pride or ill-humour' (1796 [1795]: 247).

4 A similar argument was recently made by Pim Fortuyn against Calvinism, and through it, Islam: 'Calvinists are always lying. Why? Because their moral principles are raised so high that it's not humanly possible to live up to them. You see the same thing in Muslim culture' (Buruma 2006: 57).

5 A similar retrenchment of particularistic sentiments and values against rational universalism is notoriously at work in Rousseau's limited sociality. According to *Émile*, 'Every patriot hates foreigners; they are only men, and nothing to him. This defect is inevitable, but of little importance. The great thing is to be kind to our neighbours. ... Distrust those cosmopolitans who search out remote duties in their books and neglect those that lie nearest. Such philosophers will love the Tartars to avoid loving their neighbour' (1921 [1762]: 7).

6 By contrast, Condorcet took resemblances between the moral systems of various religions as evidence of the *independence* of morality from religion, and therefore religion's redundancy. For him, 'This resemblance between the moral precepts of all systems of religion, and all sects of philosophy, would be sufficient to prove that they have a foundation independent of the dogmas of those religions, or the principles of those sects; that it is in the moral constitution of man we must seek the basis of his duties, the origin of his ideas of justice and virtue' (1796 [1795]: 95).

7 See also: 'Man's innate ideas ... have all come to him through the medium of some of his senses ... these pretended inherent ideas of his soul, are the effect of education, of example, above all, of habit, which, by reiterated motion, has taught his brain to associate his ideas, either in a confused or perspicuous manner; to

familiarize itself with systems, either rational or absurd' (1889 [1770]: 80). Or again: 'Our moral ideas are the fruits of experience alone. The sentiments of paternal and filial affection are the result of reflection and habit' (345).

8   Cf. Voltaire: 'Nature being everywhere the same, men were necessarily forced to adopt the same truths and the same errors with regard to the objects [*choses*] that come under the senses and strike the imagination most intensely' (1878 [1756]: 16). But contrast with Voltaire's self-reflexive thoughts on the distinctiveness of Islam: describing the Arabic practice of displaying poems at the temple of Mecca, and the great Meccan poet Abid's conversion to Islam upon seeing Mahomet's second chapter, Voltaire reflects that 'Here are mores, customs [*usages*], facts so different from anything that happens among us that they must demonstrate how varied the canvas of the universe is, and *how much we should guard ourselves against our habit of judging everything by our own customs*' (1878 [1756]: 208, emphasis mine).

9   Cf. Condillac's *Essay on the Origin of Human Knowledge*: 'By [the] history of the progress of language, everybody can see that languages, well-understood, would portray the character and genius of each people. They would see how imagination has combined ideas according to prejudices and passions; they would see forming in each nation a different mind, in proportion to the less interaction there is between nations' (cited in Vyverberg 1989: 77).

10 See e.g. Asad's argument that (implicitly secular) notions of legal responsibility rely upon a conception of the self invulnerable to the 'external' force of the passions: 'the responsibility of individuals refers to an action in opposition to passion. That is the reasoning behind the legal doctrine that "crimes of passion" are less culpable than calculated crimes since in them the agent's capacity for reason … is diminished by the intrusion of an "external force." Like the act of an insane person, a crime of passion is not considered to be the consequence of an agent's *own* intention. Now that emotions are generally thought of as part of the internal economy of the self, the notion is reinforced that agency means the self-ownership of the individual to whom external power always signifies a potential threat' (2003: 75, emphasis original).

11 Cf. Holbach's definition of education in *Éléments de la Morale Universelle*: 'Q. So what is education? A. It is the art of causing man to contract during his youth the habits that can contribute to his happiness' (1790: 34–5).

12 Cf. Spinoza: 'From this we clearly understand what Memory is. For it is nothing other than a certain connection of ideas involving the nature of things which are outside the human Body – a connection that is in the Mind according to the order and connection of the affections of the human Body' (1985 [1677]: 465). As Robin Douglass observes, regarding the relation between Rousseau's politics and his theories of education, the legislator's role in 'forming the will of citizens [was] analogous to the role of the governor in *Émile*' (2015: 169–70). While seeming to

flatten the distribution of power (by e.g. fusing self and social interests) Rousseau really opened the door for the arrogation of civil power to an elite body of decision-makers who would bear responsibility for 'being there first', in the same way that parents preceded their children.

13 Cf. Augustine: 'Woe to you, torrent of human custom!' (1992 [397–400]: 18).

14 See also Condorcet: 'Is not the impetuosity of our passions the continual result, either of habits to which we addict ourselves from a false calculation, or of ignorance of the means by which to resist their first impulse, to divert, govern, and direct their action?' (1796 [1795]: 277–8). Condorcet linked the habits especially to despotism, which he defines as 'the oppression of a people by a single man, who governs it by opinion, by habit and, above all, by a military force' (1796 [1795]: 48). See also Condorcet 1847 [1791–1792]: 184.

15 The unaccountability of individuals to an all-perceiving God was a central concern among both defenders *and* attackers of religious belief in the eighteenth century. On 'undetected crime' as a concern lodged against Helvétius's atheistic tract *De l'Esprit*, see D. W. Smith 1965: 86.

16 Rothschild parses the Enlightenment into a 'disposition' and a 'sect'. According to her, the first sense conjures something quite diffuse and gradual: Enlightenment as a slow alteration of people's 'way of thinking and seeing', as it 'seeped into men's thoughts like a "perfume," or like an "infection"' (2001: 15).

17 There is a striking resemblance between this example and Augustine's account of his mother's fall into alcoholism. According to Augustine, '[A] weakness for wine gradually got a grip upon [my mother]. By custom her parents used to send her, a sober girl, to fetch wine from the cask. She would plunge the cup through the aperture at the top. Before she poured the wine into a jug, she used to take a tiny sip with the tip of her lips. … Accordingly, to that sip of wine she added more sips every day … until she had fallen into the habit of gulping down almost full cups of wine' (1992 [397–400]: 167).

18 Augustine: 'step by step I ascended from bodies to the soul which perceives through the body, and from there to its inward force, to which bodily senses report external sensations, this being as high as the beasts go. From there again I ascended to the power of reasoning to which is attributed the power of judging the deliverances of the bodily senses. This power, which in myself I found to be mutable, raised itself to the level of its own intelligence, and led my thinking out of the ruts of habit. It withdrew itself from the contradictory swarms of imaginative fantasies, so as to discover the light by which it was flooded' (1992 [397–400]: 127).

19 See also Rousseau: 'Before bodily habits become fixed you may teach what habits you will without any risk, but once habits are established any change is fraught with peril. A child will bear changes which a man cannot bear, the muscles of the one are soft and flexible, they take whatever direction you give them without any effort; the

muscles of the grown man are harder and they only change their accustomed mode of action when subjected to violence' (1921 [1762]: 15). And Holbach: 'Q. When is man most susceptible to contracting habits? A. It is in childhood, because then his organs are more tender, more supple, and offer no resistance to movements one wishes to imprint there' (1790: 34).

20 See also Condorcet: '[The priests] possessed themselves of the soft and flexible mind of the child, of the boy, and directed at their pleasure the first unfinished thoughts of man. … To the secular power they left the superintendence of those studies which had for their object jurisprudence, medicine, scientific analysis, literature and the humanities, the schools of which were less numerous, and received no pupils who were not already broken to the sacerdotal yoke' (1796 [1795]: 173).

21 See Rousseau on the close relation of ideas, affect, desire and habit in the early child: 'The child's first mental experiences are purely affective, he is only aware of pleasure and pain; it takes him a long time to acquire the definite sensations which show him things outside himself, but before these things present and withdraw themselves, so to speak, from his sight, taking size and shape for him, the recurrence of emotional experiences is beginning to subject the child to the rule of habit. You see his eyes constantly follow the light, and if the light comes from the side the eyes turn towards it, so that one must be careful to turn his head towards the light lest he should squint. He must also be accustomed from the first to the dark, or he will cry if he misses the light. Food and sleep, too, exactly measured, become necessary at regular intervals, and soon desire is no longer the effect of need, but of habit, or rather habit adds a fresh need to those of nature. You must be on your guard against this' (1921 [1762]: 29–30).

22 In *The Enchantment of Modern Life* (2001) Jane Bennett notes an etymological connection between the word *enchant* and the French verb *to sing* (*chanter*). To 'en-chant' means 'to surround with song or incantation; hence, to cast a spell with sounds, to make fall under the sway of a magical refrain, to carry away on a sonorous stream'. Drawing on Deleuze and Guattari, Bennett describes the refrain in terms of a 'catalytic function', whereby 'the repetition of word sounds not only exaggerates the tempo of an ordinary phrase and not only eventually renders a meaningful phrase nonsense' but 'can also provoke new ideas, perspectives and identities'. According to Bennett, the sonorous dimension of language, more than anything else, makes possible 'plays on words, the spell-binding effect of stories told aloud, the enchantment power of chants' (2001: 6).

23 'It is impossible that these innumerable judgements should not happen in one's head, without one's knowledge [*à votre insu*]' (de Tracy 1817 [1804]: 278). See also: 'It must be admitted that a prodigious number of movements continually takes place within us, and that, at every instant, an incredible quantity of intellectual operations is executed simultaneously, of which we are not even conscious' (277).

24 This phrase is drawn from D. W. Smith on Holbach's friend, Helvétius: 'Since all human actions were motivated by self-interest, Helvétius concluded that all a state had to do to secure the greatest happiness of the greatest number was to make it worth men's while to work for the public benefit. An artificial system of punishments and rewards, a system of sticks and carrots for the human donkey, would force men to do only those things which contributed to public happiness. … Men in their right minds could not help but be good citizens: "Si les citoyens ne pouvaient faire leur bonheur particulier sans faire le bien public, il n'y aurait alors de vicieux que les fous; tous les hommes seraient nécessités à la vertu; et la félicité des nations serait un bienfait de la morale"' (1965: 116).

25 On the notion that seventeenth- to eighteenth-century approaches to sociability (particularly for Samuel Richardson, Laurence Sterne and David Hume) centred upon 'the communication of passions and sentiments', see Mullan (1988), Pinch (1996) and Riskin (2002: 8, fn. 22).

Chapter 4

1 For an argument that the three stages in Turner's analysis of rite can be mapped onto the values of the French Revolution (liberty, equality, fraternity) see Arpad Szakolcai's *Comedy and the Public Sphere* (2013: 23–4). According to Szakolcai, the rupture of community through initiation entails a new liberty from social conventions, followed by an equality of status among initiants (equivalent to Turner's concept of 'communitas') and by the invigorated fraternity of social reintegration. Because these values are unachievable in a permanent way, they must necessarily be seen as liminal: they engender nightmares when enforced as absolute and timeless.

2 See Joan-Pau Rubiés: 'The historical influence of the concept [of Oriental despotism] which Montesquieu crystallized in the *Esprit des Lois* needs little argument, since (as Franco Venturi showed) it was widely discussed within the Enlightenment, and, for example, cast its shadow upon the early justification and criticism of the British conquest' (2005: 109).

3 Malmesbury: 'I imagine that [the Persian Sultan's] empire has continued for so long and still increases because the people are unwarlike, and being deficient in active blood, know not how to cast off slavery when once admitted … But the western nations, bold and fierce, disdain long-continued subjugation to any people whatever, often delivering themselves of servitude and imposing it on others' (Rubiés 2005: 116).

4 Cf. Çirakman (2001: 49).

5 Distilling these advertisements to their empirical essence, Honoré de Balzac explained that they worked 'by deploying fantastical characters, bizarre collages,

vignettes, and, later, lithographs which made of the poster *a poem for the eyes*' (Todd 1989: 547, translation and emphasis mine).

6   Voltaire suggests something of this atmosphere when reproaching his contemporaries for romanticizing Muslims as a people still formed by 'the simplicity of heroic times': 'They had, it is said, the simplicity of heroic ages; but what were the heroic ages? They were times when one slaughtered one another for a water well, or for a cistern, as we do nowadays for a province' (1878 [1764]: XVII. 105). See also Voltaire's comment that 'Contemporary Arabs wrote about Muhammed's life in the greatest detail. Everything exudes the barbarous simplicity of the times we call heroic' (1878 [1756]: XI. 208).

7   The idea that Arabs are particularly prone to thievery and that this tendency grew in proportion to their Muslimness was a commonplace of Enlightenment literature. In Voltaire's play *Le Fanatisme* (1741) (the subject of the following chapter), Mahomet boasts to Zopire that 'My law makes heroes', to which Zopire answers 'Say rather brigands' (1753b [1741]: 37). Later in the century, Condorcet wrote that 'At the extremities of Asia, and upon the confines of Africa, there existed a people, who ... derived their subsistence from agriculture, while others observed a pastoral life; all pursued commerce, and some addicted themselves to robbery' (1796 [1795]: 126).

8   Çırakman's developmental theory of tyranny and despotism should not be overstated, since, even in the late sixteenth century, Giovanni Botero (1544–1617) had observed that the need for violence and coercion tended to vanish among second-generation slaves, who were likely to 'become Turks without realizing it, never knowing a father other than the Great Lord at whose expense they live, nor a fatherland other than the one upon which they [depended]' (Çırakman 2001: 53).

9   Wolff has touched on the relation between theories of emotion in the 'long eighteenth century' and the changing face of the Oriental despot on European stages from Paris to Vienna: 'In the history of emotions, the long eighteenth century, from the 1680s to the 1820s, witnessed on the one hand an emphasis on emotional discipline, as suggested by Norbert Elias's account of mannerly restraint in the "civilizing process," but on the other hand the cultural articulation of emotions in a variety of styles from baroque passions, to Rousseauist sensibility, to *Sturm und Drang*, right up to the age of Romanticism. The dynamics of emotional expression and emotional control were therefore implicit in operatic representations, comic or tragic, and the singing Turk became a prominent protagonist in this enlightened exploration of emotional development and the civilizing process' (2017: 9).

10   This shift may be seen as reflective of an older distinction between self-government of the passions by a 'sovereign' and government by a 'father' in Senault's *De l'Usage des Passions* (1641; see Chapter One, fn. 23). According to Senault, a failure to take

control of the objects of experience would lead people into despotic subjugation by the passions, as they would eventually come to 'love their servitude', 'kiss their irons' and 'fear the end of their imprisonment' (1641: 95–6).

11 Montesquieu's use of surprise, destabilization incorporation and integration in the *Lettres*, maps very accurately onto the two stages of wonder and judgement in Descartes's account of our engagement with foreign objects. The first part of this account is thoroughly embodied, standing strictly outside the 'neo-Stoic' theory of the hegemony of the will. *Étonnement*, for Descartes, is what one experiences in a state of raw alertness, before reason or the will hold sway. Since wonder involves no activation of sense-making memory, but is instead 'an experience of the senses', 'wonder in its first moment stands outside the will' (Fisher 1998: 18). As the object of attention becomes familiar, however, wonder or surprise are replaced by a judgement of attraction or repulsion, depending on the object's usefulness. According to Lisa Shapiro, 'As we come to be better acquainted with [the object of attention] we should cease to feel the wonder we first felt and come to feel differently, in accordance with how that thing might be important to us' (2003: 233). Just as 'It is easy to imagine that upon our first encounter with a boa constrictor we find ourselves impressed with its immense size', as we get used the snake, 'we realize that this same size poses a real threat to us': 'Here, what was new becomes more commonplace, and we move on to feel the fear that is in keeping with that snake's power to crush us' (233). The Persians' 'surprise' *vis-à-vis* European religious culture echoes the suspension of the will outlined by Descartes as the first stage in the apprehension of a foreign object. Their lack of a narrative frame or set of memories for making sense of the new world triggers, first, surprise or a suspension of the normal sense-making faculties; and second, a reconfiguration of the chains of association surrounding heretofore familiar objects, so that the new can be combined with the old, creating new assemblages of aversion and desire.

12 Usbek on Louis XIV: 'he has often been heard saying that, of all the governments in the world, that of the Turks, or our august Sultan, would please him best; thus does he plead the case of Oriental politics!' (Montesquieu 1973 [1721]:114).

13 On 'Eroticism and Politics in the *Lettres Persanes*', see Vartanian 1969.

14 On the sexualization of the religious other in the Chinese, Dutch and French Revolutionary contexts, see van der Veer: 'Clerics are portrayed in [the press of the late Qing period] as visiting houses of pleasure. The main theme here is, in fact, that monastic celibacy and techniques of self-improvement are a *disguise* for a lawless, unbridled sexuality. This theme of sexual scandal is certainly crucial in the emergence of the popular press in the nineteenth century everywhere, but the Chinese focus on clerics recalls especially the pornography that was printed in the Netherlands but distributed in revolutionary circles in France in the decades

before the French Revolution. Here we see a genealogy of *laïcité* in the underbelly of the Enlightenment that connects religion with sexuality in ways that are never made explicit but that are, in my view, also behind the social energy in anti-Islamic gestures today in France' (2011: 273).

15 According to Rica, poets are 'not rare' among Orientals, where the hotter sun seems to 'heat imaginations themselves' (Montesquieu 1973 [1721]: 304). Cf. Henri de Boulainvillier's *Vie de Mahomet* (1730), which reverses this dynamic in a politically motivated apologia for Islamic violence. Following Boulainvilliers, the latter was always driven by pure motives (noble and religious), whereas Christian violence was driven by cruelty and thirst for material gain: 'Indeed, to what degree have ambition, love, jealousy and politics carried the men of our northern regions to barbarity? Even among us, cruelty is joined to the exercise of justice. Arabs, instead accustomed to considering objects in cold blood and organizing their lives only rarely, sacrifice others' [lives] without scruple or anxiety, in accordance with intentions they believe to be God's own' (Badir 1974: 61, translation mine).

16 On the polemic device of the inferior civilizational gaze brought to bear on Western society in William Hogarth's paintings, see Rousseau and Porter: 'when Hogarth painted blacks ... such figures encoded complex and perhaps contradictory meanings for the white society upon whom they stood in silent judgement. They were victims – slaves, domestics – yet they were also muscularly threatening – warning symbols of physical power and animal eroticism, unlike the sickly and decaying flesh of their masters. Above all, *they* too (as captured by Hogarth) were anthropologists, watching the bizarre, exotic rituals daily enacted at Church, at *levées*, at the Old Bailey, St. James's, the developing West End, or Tyburn. As with so much *philosophe* satire, the tables were turned, the watchers were watched, and the anthropological eye trained back, through a mirror, upon itself' (1990: 12–13, emphasis original). Voltaire understood this principle well, when he wrote that 'One must above all agree that Canadians and Kaffirs, whom we have taken pleasure in calling savages, are infinitely superior to our [people]. The Huron, the Algonquin, the Illinois, the Kaffir, the Hottentot, possess the art to make for themselves everything they need, and this art is lacking among our yokels. The people of America and Africa are free, yet our savages do not even have a conception of freedom' (1878 [1756]: XI. 19).

17 As Starobinski concludes, 'No matter how severe the criticism explicitly or implicitly formulated by the foreign visitors, no matter how evident the recourse to appearances and hypocritical behaviours, it nevertheless remains that Christian France, compared to Persia, is a country where one lives with an uncovered face, where women dare to appear in public, where joy can reign among chosen friends. And no matter how laughable the concern for honour ... it carries public and private consequences that are less threatening than the *fear* which prevails in Persia,

Muscovy, or China, in brief, any place dominated by despotism. This remains unalterable at the end of the day' (1973: 18, emphasis original).

18　For some context on the theory of climatic variation, and Montesquieu's precedents in French intellectual history, see Vyverberg (1989: 66 and *passim*), Rubiés (2005) and Curtis (2009). Six centuries earlier, William of Malmesbury had argued that 'Asians are more reflective but lack courage, whilst northerners are courageous but lack prudence. Only the "Francs" living in a temperate zone, combine the two' (Rubiés 2005: 116). Jean Chardin later claimed that '"the cause or the origin of the customs and the habits of the Orientals" lay in the nature of their climate' (Curtis 2009: 45).

19　This point is later picked up by Rousseau, who argued that 'monarchy is suitable only to large states' (1986 [1762–1772]: 78).

20　For an argument that 'the issue of "orientalism," defined as a self-interested (even if perhaps unconscious) misrepresentation, was recognized as a problem within the Enlightenment', see Rubiés (2005: 114). Cf. Usbek's critique of Christian hypocrisy in *Lettres*: 'Christian princes long ago enfranchized all slaves within their states, because, so they claimed, Christianity renders all men equal. This act of religion was indeed very useful to them. They thereby lowered lords from the power invested in them by the people. They then made conquests in countries where they saw it would be advantageous to hold slaves, and allowed the purchase and sale [of slaves], forgetting this religious principle that so concerned them' (1973 [1721]: 190).

21　As Lauriol explains, 'The church reproached Montesquieu for reasoning as if there had been no revelation, not distinguishing among religions the only true one' (2013: unpaginated). See also Vyverberg on Guillaume-François Berthier (1704–1782), long-time editor of the influential Jesuit *Journal of Trévoux*. Berthier was strongly against climatic, relativistic theory. 'Montesquieu, he wrote had ignored the religious and ethical absolutism of true religious principle and had floundered in cultural relativism. He had revelled in speculation about the physical factors of climate and soil, following human and not divine reason, and had scorned universal truth and justice. Among moral causes of cultural differentiation, Montesquieu had emphasized the arbitrary customs of various peoples and nations and had thrust aside the eternal edicts of God' (1989: 72).

22　Cf. Descartes on the passions: 'even a false joy is often more valuable than a sadness whose cause is true' (1985a [1649]: 378). And Spinoza: 'Nothing positive which a false idea has is removed by the presence of the true insofar as it is true' (1985 [1677]: 547). In *Le Fanatisme*, Voltaire attributes a similar idea to Mahomet ('Whether true or false, my cult is necessary', 1753b [1741]: 37), and in *Lettres Persanes*, Usbek advocates 'observing religions with zeal' because they all contain 'precepts useful to society' (1973 [1721]: 207–8). Cf. Mandeville 'It is certain, that

Christianity being once stript of the Severity of its Discipline, and its most essential Precepts, the Design of it may be so skilfully perverted from its original Scope, as to be made subservient to any worldly End or Purpose, a Politician can have Occasion for' (1732: 236).

23   E.g. D. W. Smith (1965: 121).

Chapter 5

1   Saba Mahmood: 'Arguments about the racialization of Muslims provoke the fear among Europeans that if this premise is conceded or accorded legal recognition then European Muslims will resort to European hate-speech laws to unduly regulate forms of speech that they regard as injurious to their religious sensibilities. Many Europeans who champion freedom of speech reject the claim that the Danish cartoons have anything to do with racism or Islamophobia, arguing instead that Muslim extremists are using this language for their own nefarious purposes. ... Such voices caution soft-hearted liberals and multiculturalists not to fall for such an opportunistic misuse of antidiscrimination and human rights discourse because, they warn ominously, "Islam [will] force its values upon Europe" to the ultimate destruction of the "Europe of the Enlightenment"' (2009: 851–2). Quotation from András Sajó (2007: 299).

2   On the difficulty of recovering European visions of Islam through the ages, with particular reference to medieval Europe, see Sénac (1983: 10).

3   On the relation between eighteenth-century theories of climatic or environmental variation and the birth of modern, scientific racism, see Rousseau and Porter: 'It was during the eighteenth century that the project of classifying the different races of mankind by use of secular scientific terms ... first deserves the name "anthropology." Growing awareness of the roles played by climate and environment in creating difference, and by custom fixing it, further contributed to a sense of the exotic as indelibly distinct, itself encouraging a rising, if aberrant, current of polygenism' (1990: 10). See also Burke (1972) and Duchet (1971).

4   In James Miller and John Hoadly's 1744 English adaptation, Mahomet is 'an arrogant imposter'; 'a tyrant' (1773 [1744]: 5, 10); a 'conqu'ror, prince and pontiff' (6); a 'usurper' whose 'savage hand' killed Alcanor's wife and children (6); a 'subtile robber' who holds a licentious Haram (9); a man 'inspir'd/By that tremendous pow'r whose sword he bears' (9); a 'fierce Arab' (9); a 'robber' and 'scap'd felon', 'scoffer at all faiths' (10); a tyrant who wrongs Palmyre's youth with 'vile illusions, and fanatic terrors' (10); 'A pil'fring Camel driver, one so vile his own vile crew renounc'd him' (12); 'spoiler of the earth' (21); and a 'bad man! who com'st with serpent-guile to sow dissension in the realms of peace' (21).

5   See also Voltaire's entry for 'Arabia' in *Essai sur les Mœurs* (1878 [1756]): '[Mecca exists] in a land so dusty and wretched that it does not seem likely it was founded before river-side cities. … More than half of Arabia is a vast desert, of sand or rocks' (44).

6   I have translated single words and lines of *Le Fanatisme* in-text, and extended references in footnotes, in order to preserve the rhyme structure and integrity of the original. Literal translation (henceforth 'LT'): 'The sword and Qur'an in my bloody hands/Would impose silence on the rest of humanity./My voice would affect them like thunder/And I would see their foreheads attached to the earth'.

7   'Invincibles soutiens de mon Pouvoir Suprême,/Noble et sublime Ali, Morad, Hercide, Ammon,/Retournez vers ce Peuple, instruisez-le en mon nom./Promettez, menacez, que la Vérité règne;/Qu'on adore mon Dieu, mais surtout qu'on le craigne' (1753b [1741]: 28, 31). LT: 'Invincible supports of my supreme power,/Noble and sublime Ali, Morad, Hercide, Ammon,/Return to this people, instruct it in my name./Promise, threaten, so that Truth reigns;/May my God be adored, but above all feared'.

8   On the seventeenth- and eighteenth-century representation of the seraglio as the archetypal form of despotic government, see Rousseau and Porter (1990: 13).

9   LT: 'Without parents, without fatherland, slaves from childhood,/In our equality we cherish our irons'. Already in *Zaïre*, Voltaire had relativized religion by assigning it to one's country of birth, on the basis that everything is acquired. Thus, Zaïre explains, 'La coutume, la loi plia mes premiers ans/… J'eusse été près du Gange esclave des faux dieux,/Chrétienne dans Paris, musulmane en ces lieux./L'instruction fait tout; et la main de nos pères/Grave en nos faibles cœurs ces premiers caractères' (1877 [1732]: 560). LT: 'Customs and the law formed my first years./I would have been a slave to false gods, had I been born near the Ganges,/Christian in Paris, Muslim in these places./Instruction makes everything, and the hand of our fathers/Engraves in our weak hearts these first characters'. Like the 'willing slave' of Montesquieu's 'letter within a letter' (see previous chapter), Zaïre's 'free' choices result from her infant conditioning. 'Far from her parents and abandoned to the irons' she finds in a barbarian a 'generous protector', and 'unites' with him willingly (586). Nérestan (Zaïre's brother) provides the explanation for this in his earlier discussion with the character Chatillon: 'Votre prison, la sienne, et Césarée en cendre/Sont les premiers objets, sont les premiers revers/Qui frappèrent mes yeux à peine encore ouverts' (571). LT: 'Your prison, hers, and Caesarea in ashes/Are the first objects, the first appearances/That struck my barely-opened eyes'.

10 LT: 'Could your heart feel, without fear,/A feeling I did not dictate?/…/Slave to your laws, submitted at your feet,/My heart, of a faint respect, does not shed the habit'.

11 LT: 'Nature in my eyes is nothing but habit,/That of obeying me was her only study'.

12 Orosmane in many ways epitomizes the psychology of the Enlightenment, challenging his father's despotism and putting the people's happiness before his

own. Yet, as Pao points out, if Orosmane is able to speak and act like an enlightened European, it is not because he miraculously swims against the grain of eighteenth-century conventions surrounding the degenerate Orient, but because he is not truly Oriental. Unlike Mahomet, he is not Arab. Indeed, he is not even 'Asian': 'Je ne suis point formé du sang asiatique:/Né parmi les rochers, au sein de la Taurique,/Des Scythes mes aïeux je garde la fierté,/Leurs mœurs, leurs passions, leur générosité' (1877 [1732]: 583). LT: 'I am not made of Asiatic blood:/Born among rocks, in the heart of Tauric,/Of my forefathers the Scythians I retain the pride,/Their mores, their passions, their generosity'. Scythians were generally regarded as an exception in the Middle East of the eighteenth century; they were more easily recognized as European because they originated from Taurique, modern-day Crimea, i.e. 'that part of the Ottoman Empire that extended into the European continent' (Pao 1998: 42). By singling out Orosmane as an historical abnormality, Voltaire attempted a daringly subtle calibration of Orosmane's national character, one which preserved the Orientalist schema but also left Voltaire open to charges of misrepresentation for not making Orosmane *Oriental enough*. Indeed, the ambiguity of Orosmane's character caused some consternation for one reviewer, writing for the *Courrier de l'Europe* in 1810: 'It may be that Orosmane does not afford an entirely accurate portrayal of the Oriental character, but it may also be that he would be less appealing if he were truly Turkish; besides, he is so fine in his love, in his jealous transports, that too much would be lost if Voltaire had not softened the Muslim severity in depicting him' (Pao 1998: 49). As this critic suggests, it is arguable that Voltaire did not spare Orosmane because he actually thought Scythians were less degenerate than 'true Turks', but because the dynamics of tragedy required a sympathetic protagonist. The strategism of Voltaire's character creation is demonstrated – as in *Lettres Persanes* – by occasional reversions to negative Oriental stereotypes, both inside and outside the play. When Orosmane is threatened by Zaïre and Nérestan, he reverts to the standard model, threatening to close the seraglio forever and rule by terror, in accordance with the 'ancient customs of Oriental kings' (1877 [1732]: 593). Later, in his *Essai sur les Moeurs* (1756), Voltaire criticized the 'affectations' of 'malign' historians who 'eulogized the Scythians, whom they did not know' (1878 [1756]: 42). Hypocritically, he claimed that if Horace praised these 'barbarians', it was because he spoke as a 'satirical poet, for whom it is easy to elevate strangers at the expense of one's country'. In fact, Voltaire wrote, 'Scythians are these same barbarians we now call Tartars; the same who, long before Alexander, had already ravaged Asia several times, and degraded a large part of the continent. … Here are these disinterested and righteous men whose equanimity today's historians are so keen to praise' (43).

13   On the success of the play during initial performances in Lille, in which the audience hollered for extra showings, see Badir (1974: 90).

14 Prior to the play's performance, Voltaire worried that it would not be effective enough to solicit the wished-for tears. 'The play's force', Voltaire wrote to d'Argental, 'will strike the soul rather than the heart', and 'few tears' could therefore be expected (1878 [1711–1778]: XXXVI. 11).

15 According to Brooks, late-eighteenth- and early-nineteenth-century directors considered gesture 'the first and ultimately the most passionate form of communication, that which comes to the fore when the code of verbal language lapses into inadequacy ... Only the body can speak for the soul at such moments' (1994: 19–20).

16 'Spectators attribute ideas to the gestural signification of pantomime that the gestures have merely awakened in their own memory. ... Amongst all the subjects [of Greek poetry] it sufficed ... for the pantomime to awaken in spectators' spirits the principal idea indicated by each situation, for their memory to develop the series of all those linked to it' ('Translator's Preface' 1794: 21–2).

17 Such indexes were found throughout the French Enlightenment, from the explicit racism of Voltaire's *Essai sur les Moeurs* to the categorizations of the *Encyclopédie*, reinforcing the idea that strict divisions existed between different peoples, and that the latter felt and acted in accordance with their race or nationality. See e.g. Voltaire's introduction to *Essai sur les Mœurs*: 'Only a blind man can doubt that Whites, Negros, Albinos, Hottentots, Samis, Chinese and Americans, are entirely different races. ... The round eyes of [Negros], their wide nose, their inevitably broad lips, their differently figured ears, the wool on their head, even the measure of their intelligence, put prodigious distances between them and the other species of man. ... Samoyeds, Samis, the inhabitants of Northern Siberia, those of Kamchatka, are even less advanced than the peoples of America. The majority of Negros, all Kaffirs, are buried in the same stupidity and will stagnate there for a long time' (1878 [1756]: 5–9).

18 LT: 'The master of this place, the powerful Orosmane,/Knows, my lord, how to acquire and cherish virtue./This generous Frenchman who is unknown to you,/By glory brought back from the coasts of France'. Outside his plays, Voltaire constantly eulogized the French for their cultural sophistication, concision and their mastery at representing the passions (1877 [1732]: 545, 554 and below). On the question of Voltaire's relation to nationalism and the passions, it is interesting to note that Miller and Hoadly's English adaptation, which is more rationalistic and anti-passional than Voltaire's original, extends the category of fanaticism to include nationalism, unlike the French. When Zaphna falls to his father's feet in shame, he cites 'Love of my duty, *nation* and religion' as inspirations for an 'act more black more horrid, than e'er the sun cast eye on' (1773 [1744]: 49, emphasis mine).

19 Engel's translator encouraged modern theatre directors to treat their art as 'a national matter' ('Translator's Preface' 1794: 3).

20 This comment was advanced in explicit defiance of the 'cold chimeras' of rationalistic
    pedants like 'boring' Leibniz, who, with their obsessive attention to truth and the
    minutiae of reality, never understood the pleasure (or utility) of a well-delivered
    lie. In a letter to M. de Formont, written shortly before *Le Fanatisme* hit the stage,
    Voltaire accused Leibniz's 'methodical and common spirit' of an essential mediocrity
    and insensitivity to the value of artifice: 'puisqu'il nous faut des erreurs,/Que nos
    mensonges sachent plaire./L'esprit méthodique et commun/Qui calcule un par un
    donne un,/S'il fait ce métier importun,/C'est qu'il n'est pas né pour mieux faire' (1878
    [1711–1778]: XXXVI. 24). LT: 'since we need errors,/Let our untruths please./The
    methodical and common spirit/Which calculates one-by-one produces one,/If it
    carries out this unwelcome task,/It is because it is not born for anything better'.

21 On the extraordinary eloquence attributed to Muhammed, see Badir on
    Boulainvilliers's *Vie de Mahomet* (1730). According to Boulainvilliers, it was
    principally through eloquence and 'the gift of persuasion' that Mahomet succeeded
    in his mission to proselytize Islam throughout the world (Badir 1974: 64). The
    passivity of Omar's audience and its vulnerability to emotional manipulation is
    vividly brought out in Miller and Hoadly's adaptation, where the equivalent passage
    is rendered as: 'the silent and desponding crowd broke out in murmurs, plaints, and
    last in shouts, and each mechanic grew a Mussulman' (1773 [1744]: 52). Cf. Victoria
    Kahn on theatrical power in Descartes's *Passions of the Soul*. According to Kahn,
    Descartes described the King's automata in terms of a new theatrical display of
    power, and a new understanding of the subject that accompanies it: 'the only human
    agent who appears is entirely deprived of thought: "sans y penser"' (2006: 100).

22 For examples of this argument in relation to Enlightenment Orientalism generally,
    see Rousseau and Porter (1990: 12) and Netton (1990: 23–45).

23 For a basic argument that '[Voltaire's] one-sided presentation of Islam cannot be
    dismissed as a mere allegory that did not affect the perception of the literal Other in
    eighteenth-century consciousness', see Stephanie Hilger (2009: 100).

24 On the relation between Enlightenment Orientalism, nationalism, colonial
    legitimation and domestic issues of governance in the American context, see Hurd
    (2003: 31).

25 Voltaire's non-fictional statements about Islam are notoriously contradictory. In
    his 1764 *Dictionnaire Philosophique*, he conceded Islam's sophistication *against*
    the 'infinity of stupidities' written by Christian monks polemically engaged in
    caricaturing the Turkish enemy, following the fall of Constantinople (1878 [1764]:
    46). This work overturned a series of already common assumptions about the
    degeneracy of Islam, spotlighting their utility for domestic issues of legitimacy. For
    example, Voltaire criticized the tendency, common among his contemporaries, to
    politicize the female body: 'Our authors … did not have much trouble co-opting our
    women to their cause: they persuaded them that Mahomet did not regard them as
    intelligent animals, that they were all slaves, according to the laws of the Qur'an, that

they possessed nothing in this world, and that, in the other, they would have no part in paradise. All this is obviously false, and all this has been firmly believed. Although one only had to read the second and fourth sura or chapter of the Qur'an to be set straight' (46). This Voltaire would have had little patience for facile caricatures of Islam as a religion of violence. On the contrary, he claimed, Islam was 'a simple and wise religion', spread as much 'through the word as the sword' (48). Yet Voltaire was extraordinarily inconsistent, slipping into the crudest caricatures when it suited him. Indeed, he reversed his position just eighty lines later, stating that 'The first Muslims were animated, through Muhammed, by the rage of enthusiasm. Nothing is more terrifying than a people who, having nothing to lose, fights at once with a spirit of rapaciousness and religion' (48; see also 1878 [1756]: 206). In his *Essai sur les Mœurs*, Voltaire claimed that 'It was not through weapons that Islam was established in more than half our hemisphere, but by enthusiasm, by persuasion, and especially by the example of victors' (1878 [1756]: 220–1). But this claim is directly contradicted on the very same page, in a spurious contrast between Islam and Christianity: 'the legislator of Muslims, a powerful and terrifying man, established his dogmas through his courage and his weapons' (221). For an argument that Voltaire's more positive assessments of Islam in the *Essai* derive from his opposition to the Judaeo-centrism of Bossuet's *Discours sur l'Histoire Universelle* (1681), see Badir (1974: 151–82).

26 I have not been able to trace Hannah Arendt's source for this quotation.

27 The suicide bomber is in some ways the epitome of the modern, anti-buffered self, insofar as she or he transgresses notions of personhood by mixing bodies with weapons, flesh with flesh, and blood with blood: 'The suicide bomber, whether in Israel, Sri Lanka, New York, Iraq, or London, is the darkest possible version of the liberal value placed on the individual, the number "one." The suicide bomber today is the ideal type of the terrorist, since in this figure several nightmares are condensed. He or she … completely closes the boundary between the body and the weapon of terror. Whether by strapping bombs to his or her body or by otherwise disguising explosives in his or her body, the suicide bomber is an explosive body that promises to distribute its own bloody fragments and mix them in with the bloody parts of the civilian populations it is intended to decimate. Thus, not only does the suicide bomber elude detection, he or she also produces a horrible mixture of blood and body between enemies, thus violating not only the soil of the nation but the very bodies of the victims, infecting them with the blood of the martyr' (Appadurai 2006: 77–8).

28 Cf. Diderot: 'What affects us in the spectacle of a man animated by great passions? Is it words [*discours*]? Sometimes. But what always moves people are laughs, unarticulated words, broken voices, a few monosyllables let out in bursts, some sort of throat whisper between the teeth. … [I]t is not the expression *I love you* that triumphs over the severities of a prude, over the schemes of a seductress, over the virtues of a sensitive woman: it is the tremor of the voice in which it is pronounced; the tears which accompany it' (1821 [1757]: 142).

Bibliography

Ahmed, Sara (2014), *The Cultural Politics of Emotion*, Edinburgh: Edinburgh University Press.

Althusser, Louis (1972), *Politics and History: Montesquieu, Rousseau, Hegel and Marx*, trans. B. Brewster, London: New Left Books.

Anderson, Benedict (2006), *Imagined Communities: Reflections on the Origin and Spread of Nationalism*, London: Verso Books.

Andries, Lise (1997), 'Le Colportage des Livres au XVIIIe Siècle, Entre Orthodoxie et Clandestinité', in Olivier Bloch and Antony McKenna (eds.), *La Lettre Clandestine (n°5–1996): Tendances Actuelles dans la Recherche sur les Clandestins à l'Âge Classique*, 193–200, Paris: Presses de l'Université de Paris-Sorbonne.

Anidjar, Gil (2006), 'Secularism', *Critical Inquiry* 33 (1): 52–77.

App, Urs (2010), *The Birth of Orientalism*, Philadelphia: Pennsylvania University Press.

Appadurai, Arjun (2006), *Fear of Small Numbers: An Essay on the Geography of Anger*, Durham, NC; London: Duke University Press.

Arendt, Hannah (1969), *On Violence*, New York: Harcourt Brace Jovanovich.

Aristotle (1921), *The Works of Aristotle Vol. X: Politica*, trans. Benjamin Jowett, Oxford: Oxford Clarendon Press.

Armanios, Rachid (2005), 'Voltaire Échappe à la Censure', *Le Courrier*, 9 December, available online: https://forums.lecourrier.ch/index.php?name=Newsandfile=articlea ndsid=40589 (accessed 4 March 2016).

Asad, T., W. Brown, J. Butler and S. Mahmood (2013), *Is Critique Secular? Blasphemy, Injury, and Free Speech*, New York: Oxford University Press.

Asad, Talal (1993), *Genealogies of Religion: Discipline and Reasons of Power in Christianity and Islam*, Baltimore: Johns Hopkins University Press.

Asad, Talal (2003), *Formations of the Secular: Christianity, Islam, Modernity*, Stanford, CA: Stanford University Press.

Asad, Talal (2004), 'Reflections on *Laïcité* and the Public Sphere', Keynote Address at the *Beirut Conference on Public Spheres, October 22–24 (Excerpts)*, available online: https://www.scribd.com/document/36116973/Talal-Asad-Reflections-on-Secularism-and-the-Public-Sphere (accessed 24 June 2016).

Asad, Talal (2011), 'Thinking about Religion, Belief, and Politics', in Robert A. Orsi (ed.), *The Cambridge Companion to Religious Studies*, 36–57, Cambridge: Cambridge University Press.

Augustine (1992 [397–400]), *Confessions*, trans. Henry Chadwick, Oxford: Oxford University Press.

Badinter, Elisabeth (2010), 'Message d'Elisabeth Badinter à Celles qui Portent Volontairement la Burqa et Audition à l'Assemblée Nationale', *Le Huffington Post*, 1 February, available online: http://archives-lepost.huffingtonpost.fr/article/2010/02/01/1917208_message-d-elisabeth-badinter-a-celles-qui-portent-volontairement-la-burqa.html (accessed 5 September 2015).

Badir, Magdy Gabriel (1974), *Voltaire et l'Islam*, Banbury: Voltaire Foundation.

Baudier, Michel (1631), *Histoire Générale du Sérail et de la Cour du Grand Seigneur*, Paris: Claude Cramoisy.

Beaman, Lori (2015), 'Beyond Establishment', in Winnifred Fallers Sullivan, Elizabeth Shakman Hurd, Saba Mahmood and Peter G. Danchin (eds.), *Politics of Religious Freedom*, 207–19, Chicago: The University of Chicago Press.

Bennett, Jane (2001), *The Enchantment of Modern Life: Attachments, Crossings, and Ethics*, Oxford; Princeton, NJ: Princeton University Press.

Berlin, Isaiah (1979), *Against the Current: Essays in the History of Ideas*, ed. Henry Hardy, London: Hogarth Press.

Berlinerblau, Jacques (2012), *How to Be Secular: A Call to Arms for Religious Freedom*, New York: Houghton Mifflin Harcourt.

Berlinerblau, Jacques (2014), 'The Crisis in Secular Studies', *The Chronicle of Higher Education*, 8 September, available online: http://www.chronicle.com/article/The-Crisis-in-Secular-Studies/148599 (accessed 17 January 2015).

Bernays, Edward (1928), *Propaganda*, New York: Horace Liveright.

Bloch, O. and A. McKenna (eds.) (1997), *La Lettre Clandestine (n°5–1996): Tendances Actuelles dans la Recherche sur les Clandestins à l'Âge Classique*, Paris: Presses de l'Université de Paris-Sorbonne.

Bosma, Martin (2010), *De Schijn-Élite van de Valse Munters*, Amsterdam: Bert Bakker.

Boulanger, Nicolas (1762 [1761]), *Recherches sur l'Origine du Despotisme Oriental*, London: Seyffert.

Bourdieu, Pierre (1990 [1980]), *The Logic of Practice*, Cambridge: Polity Press.

Bristow, William (2017), 'Enlightenment', in Edward N. Zalta (ed.), *The Stanford Encyclopedia of Philosophy*, Fall Edition, available online: https://plato.stanford.edu/archives/fall2017/entries/enlightenment/ (accessed 26 January 2018).

Brooks, Peter (1994), 'Melodrama, Body, Revolution', in Jacky Bratton, Jim Cook and Christine Gledhill (eds.), *Melodrama: Stage, Picture, Screen*, 11–24, London: British Film Institute.

Brown, Wendy (2007), 'Idealism, Materialism, Secularism?', *The Immanent Frame*, available online: http://blogs.ssrc.org/tif/2007/10/22/idealism-materialism-secularism/ (accessed 15 March 2016).

Bruce, Harold L. (1918), 'Voltaire on the English Stage', *University of California Publications in Modern Philology* 8 (1): 1–152.

Buckley, Michael J. (1987), *At the Origins of Modern Atheism*, New Haven, CT; London: Yale University Press.

Bullivant, Steven (2010), 'The New Atheism and Sociology: Why Here? Why Now? What Next?', in Amarasingam Amarnath (ed.), *Religion and the New Atheism: A Critical Appraisal*, 109–24, Leiden; Boston, MA: Brill.

Burke, J. G. (1972), 'The Wild Man's Pedigree: Scientific Method and Racial Anthropology', in E. Dudley and M. E. Novak (eds.), *The Wild Man Within: An Image in Western Thought from the Renaissance to Romanticism*, 259–80, Pittsburgh: Pittsburgh University Press.

Buruma, Ian (2006), *Murder in Amsterdam: The Death of Theo van Gogh and the Limits of Tolerance*, London: Atlantic Books.

Calhoun, Craig J. (2010), 'Rethinking Secularism', *The Hedgehog Review* 12 (3): 35–48.

Calhoun, Craig J. (2011), 'Secularism, Citizenship and the Public Sphere', in Craig J. Calhoun, Mark Juergensmeyer and Jonathan VanAntwerpen (eds.), *Rethinking Secularism*, 75–91, Oxford: Oxford University Press.

Calhoun, C. J., M. Juergensmeyer and J. VanAntwerpen (eds.) (2011), *Rethinking Secularism*, Oxford: Oxford University Press.

Casanova, José (2006), 'Public Religions Revisited' in Hent de Vries (ed.), *Religion: Beyond a Concept*, 101–119, New York: Fordham University Press.

Casanova, José (2010), 'A Secular Age: Dawn or Twilight', in Michael Warner, Jonathan VanAntwerpen and Craig J. Calhoun (eds.), *Varieties of Secularism in a Secular Age*, 265–281, Cambridge, MA; London: Harvard University Press.

Cavanaugh, William T. (2009), *The Myth of Religious Violence: Secular Ideology and the Roots of Modern Conflict*, New York; Oxford: Oxford University Press.

Cavanaugh, William T. (2012), 'The Invention of Fanaticism', in Sarah Coakley (ed.), *Faith, Rationality, and the Passions*, 29–40, Oxford: Wiley-Blackwell.

Caygill, Howard (2006), 'Kant and the Relegation of the Passions', in Victoria Kahn, Neil Saccamano and Daniela Coli (eds.), *Politics and the Passions, 1500-1850*, 217–30, Princeton, NJ: Princeton University Press.

Channel 4 News (2018), 'Cambridge Analytica Uncovered: Secret Filming Reveals Election Tricks', *Channel 4 News YouTube Channel*, 19 March, available online: https://www.youtube.com/watch?v=mpbeOCKZFfQ&frags=pl%2Cwn (accessed 30 December 2018).

Çırakman, Aslı (2001), 'From Tyranny to Despotism: The Enlightenment's Unenlightened Image of the Turks', *International Journal of Middle East Studies* 33 (1): 49–68.

Coakley, Sarah (ed.) (2012), *Faith, Rationality, and the Passions*, Oxford: Wiley-Blackwell.

Coleman, Patrick (2006), 'Rousseau's Quarrel with Gratitude', in Victoria Kahn, Neil Saccamano and Daniela Coli (eds.), *Politics and the Passions, 1500-1850*, 151–74, Princeton, NJ: Princeton University Press.

Condorcet, Marquis de (1796 [1795]), *Outlines of an Historical View of the Progress of the Human Mind*, trans. anonymous, New York: Lang and Ustick.

Condorcet, Marquis de (1847 [1791–1792]), 'Sur l'Instruction Publique', in Arthur O'Connor and François Arago (eds.), *Oeuvres de Condorcet Vol. XVII*, 167–437, Paris: Firmin Didot.

Connolly, William E. (1999), *Why I Am Not a Secularist*, Minneapolis; London: University of Minnesota Press.

Connolly, William E. (2006), 'Europe: A Minor Tradition', in David Scott and Charles Hirschkind (eds.), *Powers of the Secular Modern: Talal Asad and His Interlocutors*, 75–92, Stanford, CA: Stanford University Press.

Connor, Walker (1994), *Ethnonationalism: The Quest for Understanding*, Princeton, NJ: Princeton University Press.

Cooke, Rachel (2017), 'Spare Us the Moral Hysteria That Threatens a New Age of Censorship', *Guardian*, 17 December, available online: https://www.theguardian.com/commentisfree/2017/dec/17/censorship-sexual-harassment-theatre-art (accessed 17 December 2017).

Corson, S. and E. Corson (1985), 'From Descartes to Pavlov to Anokhin: The Evolution of General Systems Concepts in Biomedical Sciences in Eastern Europe', in P. Pichot, P. Berner, R. Wolf and K. Thau (eds.), *Psychiatry: The State of the Art: Biological Psychiatry, Higher Nervous Activity*, 679–83, New York: Plenum Press.

Cottingham, John (2008), *Cartesian Reflections: Essays on Descartes's Philosophy*, Oxford: Oxford University Press.

Cottingham, John (2012), 'Sceptical Detachment or Loving Submission to the Good? Reason Faith, and the Passions in Descartes', in Sarah Coakley (ed.), *Faith, Rationality, and the Passions*, 107–16, Oxford: Wiley-Blackwell.

Cox, Christoph (1999), *Nietzsche: Naturalism and Interpretation*, London: University of California Press.

Curtis, Finbarr (2016), *The Production of American Religious Freedom*, New York: New York University Press.

Curtis, Michael (2009), *Orientalism and Islam: European Thinkers on Oriental Despotism in the Middle East and India*, Cambridge; New York: Cambridge University Press.

Damasio, Antonio R. (1994), *Descartes' Error: Emotion, Reason, and the Human Brain*, New York: G.P. Putnam.

Danchin, Peter G. (2015), 'Religious Freedom in the Panopticon of Enlightenment Rationality', in Winnifred Fallers Sullivan, Elizabeth Shakman Hurd, Saba Mahmood and Peter G. Danchin (eds.), *Politics of Religious Freedom*, 240–52, Chicago: University of Chicago Press.

Daniel, Norman (1993), *Islam and the West: The Making of an Image*, Oxford: OneWorld.

Darnton, Robert (1991), *Édition et Sédition: L'Univers de la Littérature Clandestine au XVIIIe Siècle*, Paris: Gallimard.

De Sousa, Ronald (1987), *The Rationality of Emotion*, Cambridge, MA; London: MIT Press.

Deleuze, G. and F. Guattari (1987 [1980]), *A Thousand Plateaus: Capitalism and Schizophrenia*, trans. and foreword by Brian Massumi, Minneapolis; London: University of Minnesota Press.

Derrida, Jacques (2001 [1967]), *Writing and Difference*, Abingdon; New York: Routledge.

Descartes, René (1649), *Les Passions de l'Âme*, Paris: Henry le Gras.

Descartes, René (1671 [1649]), *The Passions of the Soule in Three Books: The First, Treating of the Passions in Generall, and Occasionally of the Whole Nature of Man. The Second, of the Number, and Order of the Passions, and the Explication of the Six Primitive Ones. The Third, of Particular Passions*, trans. anonymous, London: J. Martin and J. Ridley.

Descartes, René (1973), *Oeuvres de Descartes*, ed. Charles Adam and Paul Tannery, Paris: Vrin.

Descartes, René (1985 [1641]), 'Meditations on First Philosophy', trans. John Cottingham, in John Cottingham, Robert Stoothoff and Dugald Murdoch (eds.), *The Philosophical Writings of Descartes Vol. I*, 1–62, Cambridge: Cambridge University Press.

Descartes, René (1985a [1649]), 'The Passions of the Soul', trans. Robert Stoothoff, in John Cottingham, Robert Stoothoff and Dugald Murdoch (eds.), *The Philosophical Writings of Descartes Vol. I*, 325–404, Cambridge: Cambridge University Press.

Descartes, René (1985b [1649]), *The Philosophical Writings of Descartes Vol. I*, trans. and ed. John Cottingham, Robert Stoothoff and Dugald Murdoch, Cambridge: Cambridge University Press.

Descartes, René (1991a [1619–1650]), 'Letters', trans. Robert Stoothoff, in John Cottingham, Robert Stoothoff, Dugald Murdoch and Anthony Kenny (eds.), *The Philosophical Writings of Descartes Vol. III*, 1–384, Cambridge: Cambridge University Press.

Descartes, René (1991b [1619–1650]), *The Philosophical Writings of Descartes Vol. III*, trans. and ed. John Cottingham, Robert Stoothoff and Dugald Murdoch, Cambridge: Cambridge University Press.

Diderot, Denis (1821 [1757]), 'Entretiens sur le Fils Naturel', in J. Brière (ed.), *Oeuvres Complètes de Denis Diderot Vol. IV*, 113–235, Paris: J. L. J. Brière.

Diderot, Denis (1821 [1757–1758]), *Oeuvres Complètes de Denis Diderot Vol. IV*, ed. J. Brière, Paris: J. L. J. Brière.

Diderot, Denis (1916 [1746–1751]), *Diderot's Early Philosophical Works*, trans. and ed. Margaret Jourdain, Chicago; London: Open Court Publishing Ltd.

Diderot, D. and J. d'Alembert (eds.) (2016 [1751–1782]), *Encyclopédie, ou Dictionnaire Raisonné des Sciences, des Arts et des Métiers, Etc.*, ed. Robert Morrissey and Glenn Roe, Chicago: University of Chicago, ARTFL Encyclopédie Project, available online: http://encyclopedie.uchicago.edu/ (accessed 23 March 2016–12 July 2018).

Donne, John (1633), *Poems, by J. D. with Elegies on the Authors Death*, London: M. F. for John Marriott.

Douglass, Robin (2015), *Rousseau and Hobbes: Nature, Free Will, and the Passions*, Oxford: Oxford University Press.

Dube, Saurabh (2009), *Enchantments of Modernity: Empire, Nation, Globalization*, New Delhi: Routledge.

Duchet, M. (1971), *Anthropologie et Histoire au Siècle des Lumières: Buffon, Voltaire, Rousseau, Helvétius, Diderot*, Paris: François Maspero.

Elias, Norbert (1994 [1939]), *The Civilizing Process: The History of Manners and State Formation and Civilization*, Oxford: Blackwell.

Engel, Johann Jakob (1794 [1788]), *Idées sur le Geste et l'Action Théâtrale Vol. I*, trans. anonymous, Paris: H. J. Jansen and Co.

Fassin, Didier (2006), 'Nommer, Interpréter: Le Sens Commun de la Question Raciale', in Didier Fassin and Eric Fassin (eds.), *De la Question Sociale à la Question Raciale? Representer la Société Française*, 19–36, Paris: La Découverte.

Fernando, Mayanthi L. (2014), *The Republic Unsettled: Muslim French and the Contradictions of Secularism*, Durham, NC: Duke University Press.

Fisher, Philip (1998), *Wonder, the Rainbow, and the Aesthetics of Rare Experiences*, Cambridge, MA: Harvard University Press.

Fitzgerald, Timothy (2000), *The Ideology of Religious Studies*, New York; Oxford: Oxford University Press.

Foucault, Michel (1972), *The Archaeology of Knowledge*, New York: Tavistock Ltd.

Foucault, Michel (1978 [1976]), *The History of Sexuality Vol. I*, trans. Robert Hurley, New York: Pantheon Books.

Foucault, Michel (2003 [1975]), *Abnormal: Lectures at the Collège de France 1974–1975*, London; New York: Verso.

Fourest, Caroline (2007), *Brother Tariq: The Doublespeak of Tariq Ramadan*, trans. Ioana Wieder and John Atherton, New York; London: Encounter Books.

Freeden, Michael (2007), *The Meaning of Ideology: Cross-Disciplinary Perspectives*, London: Routledge.

Geertz, Clifford (1973), *The Interpretation of Cultures: Selected Essays*, New York: Basic Books.

Grosrichard, Alain (1979), *Structure du Sérail: La Fiction du Despotisme Asiatique dans l'Occident Classique*, Paris: Éditions du Seuil.

Grosrichard, Alain (1998), *The Sultan's Court: European Fantasies of the East*, New York: Verso.

Gunny, Ahmad (2010), *Prophet Muhammad in French and English Literature: 1650 to the Present*, Markfield: Kube Publishing Ltd.

Habermas, Jürgen (1984 [1981]), *The Theory of Communicative Action Vol. I*, trans. Thomas McCarthy, Cambridge: Polity Press.

Habermas, Jürgen (1989 [1962]), *The Structural Transformation of the Public Sphere: An Inquiry into a Category of Bourgeois Society*, trans. Thomas Burger and Frederick Lawrence, Cambridge: Polity Press.

Hammerbeck, David (2003), 'Voltaire's *Mahomet*, the Persistence of Cultural Memory and Pre-Modern Orientalism', *Agora* 2 (2): 1–20.

Harsin, Paul (1930), 'De Quand Date le Mot "Industrie"?', *Annales d'Histoire Économique et Sociale* 6: 235–42.

Hausheer, Roger (1979), 'Introduction', in Isaiah Berlin and Henry Hardy (eds.), *Against the Current: Essays in the History of Ideas*, xxxi–lxxxiii, London: Hogarth Press.

Helvétius, Claude Adrien (1759 [1758]), *De l'Esprit*, Paris: Durand.

Helvétius, Claude Adrien (2009 [1737–1772]), 'Letters', in A. Dainard, J. Orsoni, D. Smith and P. Allan (eds.), *Electronic Enlightenment Correspondence*, available online: http://www.e-enlightenment.com/item/helvclUT0020118a1c (accessed 3 May 2016).

Herder, Johann G. (1803 [1784]), *Outlines of a Philosophy of the History of Man Vol. II*, trans. T. Churchill, London: Hanfard.

Higgins, Andrew (2006), 'Blame It on Voltaire', *The Wall Street Journal*, 6 March, available online: https://www.wsj.com/articles/SB114161327867090087 (accessed 19 September 2016).

Hilger, Stephanie M. (2009), *Women Write Back*, Amsterdam; New York: Rodopi.

Hirschkind, Charles (2011), 'Is There a Secular Body?', *Cultural Anthropology* 26: 633–47.

Hirschman, Albert O. (2013 [1977]), *The Passions and the Interests: Political Arguments for Capitalism before Its Triumph*, Princeton, NJ: Princeton University Press.

Holbach, Paul-Henri Thiry d' (1768), *La Contagion Sacrée, ou Histoire Naturelle de la Superstition Vol. I*, London: publisher unknown.

Holbach, Paul-Henri Thiry d' (1770), *Histoire Critique de Jésus-Christ, ou Analyse Raisonnée des Evangiles*, publisher unknown.

Holbach, Paul-Henri Thiry d' (1776 [1766]), *Le Christianisme Devoilé, ou Examen des Principes et des Effets de la Religion Chrétienne*, London: publisher unknown.

Holbach, Paul-Henri Thiry d' (1790), *Éléments de la Morale Universelle, ou Catéchisme de la Nature*, Paris: G. de Bure.

Holbach, Paul-Henri Thiry d' (1857 [1768]), *Letters to Eugenia, or, A Preservative against Religious Prejudices*, trans. Anthony C. Middleton, Boston, MA: J. P. Mendum.

Holbach, Paul-Henri Thiry d' (1889 [1770]), *The System of Nature, or, Laws of the Physical and Moral World Vols I and II*, trans. H. D. Robinson, Boston, MA: J. P. Mendum.

Holbach, Paul-Henri Thiry d' (1972 [1761]), *Premières Oeuvres: Le Christianisme Devoilé, La Contagion Sacrée, Histoire Critique de Jésus-Christ*, preface and notes Paulette Charbonnel, Paris: Les Éditions Sociales.

Horkheimer, M. and T. Adorno (2002 [1944]), *Dialectic of Enlightenment: Philosophical Fragments*, ed. Gunzelin Schmid Noerr, trans. Edmund Jephcott, Stanford, CA: Stanford University Press.

Hume, David (1739), *A Treatise on Human Nature: Being an Attempt to Introduce the Experimental Method of Reasoning into Moral Subjects Vol I: Of the Understanding*, London: John Noon.

Hume, David (1987 [1742]), *Essays, Moral, Political, and Literary*, ed. Eugene F. Miller, Indianapolis: Liberty Fund.

Hurd, Elizabeth S. (2003), 'Appropriating Islam: The Islamic Other in the Consolidation of Western Modernity', *Critical Middle Eastern Studies* 12 (1): 25–41.

Hurd, Elizabeth S. (2011), 'A Suspension of (Dis)Belief: The Secular-Religious Binary and the Study of International Relations', in Craig J. Calhoun, Mark Juergensmeyer and Jonathan VanAntwerpen (eds.), *Rethinking Secularism*, 166–84, Oxford: Oxford University Press.

Israel, Jonathan I. (2001), *Radical Enlightenment: Philosophy and the Making of Modernity, 1650–1750*, Oxford: Oxford University Press.

Jakobsen, Janet (2005), 'Sex + Freedom = Regulation: WHY?', *Social Text* 23 (3–4): 285–308.

Jakobsen, J. and A. Pellegrini (2008), *Secularisms*, Durham, NC: Duke University Press.

Juergensmeyer, Mark (2011), 'Rethinking the Secular and Religious Aspects of Violence', in Craig J. Calhoun, Mark Juergensmeyer and Jonathan VanAntwerpen (eds.), *Rethinking Secularism*, 185–203, Oxford: Oxford University Press.

Kahn, Victoria (2006), 'Happy Tears: Baroque Politics in Descartes' *Passions de l'Âme*', in Victoria Kahn, Neil Saccamano and Daniela Coli (eds.), *Politics and the Passions, 1500–1850*, 93–110, Princeton, NJ: Princeton University Press.

Kahn, V., N. Saccamano and D. Coli (eds.) (2006), *Politics and the Passions, 1500–1850*, Princeton, NJ: Princeton University Press.

Kant, Immanuel (2006 [1785]), *Anthropology from a Pragmatic Point of View*, trans. Robert L. Louden, Cambridge: Cambridge University Press.

Keane, Webb (2015), 'What Is Religious Freedom Supposed to Free?', in Winnifred Fallers Sullivan, Elizabeth Shakman Hurd, Saba Mahmood and Peter G. Danchin (eds.), *Politics of Religious Freedom*, 57–65, Chicago: University of Chicago Press.

Kiernan, V. G. (1990), 'Noble and Ignoble Savages', in G. S. Rousseau and Roy Porter (eds.), *Exoticism in the Enlightenment*, 86–116, Manchester: Manchester University Press.

Kirkebøen, Geir (2001), 'Descartes's Embodied Psychology: Descartes's or Damasio's Error?', *Journal of the History of the Neurosciences* 10: 173–91.

Koch, Erec R. (2008), *The Aesthetic Body: Passion, Sensibility, and Corporeality in Seventeenth-Century France*, Newark: University of Delaware Press.

Lakoff, G. and M. Johnsen (2003 [1980]), *The Metaphors We Live By*, London: University of Chicago Press.

Landes, Joan B. (2001), *Visualizing the Nation: Gender, Representation, and Revolution in Eighteenth-Century France*, Ithaca, NY; London: Cornell University Press.

Landy, J. and M. T. Saler (2009), *The Re-Enchantment of the World: Secular Magic in a Rational Age*, Stanford, CA: Stanford University Press.

Las Cases, Emmanuel (1823), *Mémorial de Saint Hélène: Journal of the Private Life and Conversations of the Emperor Napoleon at Saint Helena Vol. II*, trans. anonymous, Boston, MA: Wells and Lilly.

Lauriol, Claude (2013), 'Quarrel over *L'Esprit des Lois*', trans. Philip Stewart, in Catherine Volpilhac-Auger (ed.), *A Montesquieu Dictionary*, ENS Lyon, available online: http://dictionnaire-montesquieu.ens-lyon.fr/en/article/1377637845/en (accessed 13 March 2016).

LeDoux, Joseph E. (1996), *The Emotional Brain: The Mysterious Underpinnings of Emotional Life*, New York: Simon and Schuster.

LeDrew, Stephen (2016), *The Evolution of Atheism: The Politics of a Modern Movement*, New York: Oxford University Press.

Locke, John (1796 [1689]), *A Letter Concerning Toleration*, Huddersfield: J. Brook.

Loichemol, Hervé (2006), 'Une Fatwa Contre Voltaire?', *Le Monde*, 14 February, available online: http://www.lemonde.fr/idees/article/2006/02/14/une-fatwa-contre-voltaire-par-herve-loichemol_741217_3232.html (accessed 28 October 2017).

Machiavelli (1988 [1532]), *The Prince*, ed. Quentin Skinner and Russell Price, Cambridge: Cambridge University Press.

Mahmood, Saba (2006), 'Secularism, Hermeneutics, and Empire: The Politics of Islamic Reformation', *Public Culture* 18 (2): 323–47.

Mahmood, Saba (2008a), 'Is Critique Secular?', *The Immanent Frame*, available online: http://blogs.ssrc.org/tif/2008/03/30/is-critique-secular-2/ (accessed 4 February 2015).

Mahmood, Saba (2008b), 'Secular Imperatives?', *The Immanent Frame*, available online: http://blogs.ssrc.org/tif/2008/05/07/secular-imperatives/ (accessed 4 February 2015).

Mahmood, Saba (2009), 'Religious Reason and Secular Affect: An Incommensurable Divide?', *Critical Inquiry* 35: 836–62.

Mahmood, Saba (2010), 'Can Secularism Be Other-Wise?', in Michael Warner, Jonathan VanAntwerpen and Craig J. Calhoun (eds.), *Varieties of Secularism in a Secular Age*, 282–299, Cambridge, MA; London: Harvard University Press.

Mali, J. and R. Wokler (eds.) (2003), 'Isaiah Berlin's Counter-Enlightenment', *Transactions of the American Philosophical Society* 93 (5): i–196.

Mandeville, Bernard de (1732), *An Enquiry into the Origin of Honour, and the Usefulness of Christianity in War*, London: John Brotherton.

Massumi, Brian (2002), *Parables for the Virtual: Movement, Affect, Sensation*, Durham, NC; London: Duke University Press.

Masuzawa, Tomoko (2005), *The Invention of World Religions, or, How European Universalism Was Preserved in the Language of Pluralism*, Chicago; London: University of Chicago Press.

Mauss, Marcel (1973 [1934]), 'Techniques of the Body', *Economy and Society* 2 (1): 70–88.

Mazzarella, William (2009), 'Affect: What Is It Good For?', in Saurabh Dube (ed.), *Enchantments of Modernity: Empire, Nation, Globalization*, 291–309, New Delhi: Routledge.

McMahon, Darrin M. (2001), *Enemies of the Enlightenment: The French Counter-Enlightenment and the Making of Modernity*, Oxford; New York: Oxford University Press.

Melville, Herman (1967 [1851]), *Moby-Dick: An Authoritative Text, Reviews and Letters by Melville, Analogues and Sources, Criticism*, ed. Harrison Hayford and Hershel Parker, New York; London: Norton.

Milbank, J., C. Pickstock and G. Ward (1999), 'Introduction', in John Milbank, Catherine Pickstock and Graham Ward (eds.), *Radical Orthodoxy: A New Theology*, 1–20, London: Routledge.

Mill, James (1817), *The History of British India Vol. I*, London: Baldwin, Cradock and Joy.

Minuti, Rolando (2012), 'Oriental Despotism', *European History Online*, available online: http://ieg-ego.eu/en/threads/backgrounds/european-encounters/rolando-minuti-oriental-despotism (accessed 19 November 2017).

Modern, John Lardas (2011), *Secularism in Antebellum America: With Reference to Ghosts, Protestant Subcultures, Machines, and Their Metaphors; Featuring Discussions of Mass Media, Moby-Dick, Spirituality, Phrenology, Anthropology, Sing Sing State Penitentiary, and Sex with the New Motive Power*, Chicago: University of Chicago Press.

Modood, Tariq (2007), *Multiculturalism: A Civic Idea*, Cambridge: Polity Press.

Montaigne, Michel de (1940), *Essais (Extraits) Vol. I: L'Homme*, Paris: Larousse.

Montesquieu, Charles de Secondat, Baron de (1777a [1748]), *The Complete Works of M. de Montesquieu, Vol. I: The Spirit of the Laws*, London: T. Evans and W. Davis.

Montesquieu, Charles de Secondat, Baron de (1777b [1748]), *The Complete Works of M. de Montesquieu, Vol. II: The Spirit of the Laws*, London: T. Evans and W. Davis.

Montesquieu, Charles de Secondat, Baron de (1973 [1721]), *Lettres Persanes*, ed. Jean Starobinsky, Paris: Gallimard.

Mullan, John (1988), *Sentiment and Sociability: The Language of Feeling in the Eighteenth Century*, New York: Oxford University Press.

Mullin, Ross (1994), 'Voltaire Censored – Again', *Truth Seeker* 121 (4), available online: http://web.archive.org/web/20060323115950/www.banned-books.com/truth-seeker/1994archive/121_4/ts214d.html (accessed 13 September 2017).

Netton, Ian Richard (1990), 'The Mysteries of Islam', in G. S. Rousseau and Roy Porter (eds.), *Exoticism in the Enlightenment*, 23–45, Manchester: Manchester University Press.

Nisbet, Robert A. (1980), *History of the Idea of Progress*, London: Heinemann.

Nussbaum, Martha C. (2013), *Political Emotions: Why Love Matters for Justice*, Cambridge, MA; London: Belknap Press of Harvard University Press.

Onfray, Michel (2005), *Atheist Manifesto: The Case against Christianity, Judaism, and Islam*, New York: Arcade Publishing.

Ong, Walter (2005 [1958]), *Ramus, Method and the Decay of Dialogue: From the Art of Discourse to the Art of Reason*, Chicago: University of Chicago Press.

Owen, J. M. and J. J. Owen (2010), *Religion, the Enlightenment, and the New Global Order*, New York; Chichester: Columbia University Press.

Pao, Angela C. (1998), *The Orient of the Boulevards: Exoticism, Empire, and Nineteenth-Century French Theater*, Philadelphia: University of Pennsylvania Press.

Pavlov, I. P. and G. V. Anrep (1960), *Conditioned Reflexes: An Investigation of the Physiological Activity of the Cerebral Cortex*, New York: Dover.

Pellegrini, Ann (2015), 'Everson's Children', in Winnifred Fallers Sullivan, Elizabeth Shakman Hurd, Saba Mahmood and Peter G. Danchin (eds.), *Politics of Religious Freedom*, 253–64, Chicago: University of Chicago Press.

Pellegrini, A. and J. Jakobsen (eds.) (2008), *Secularisms*, Durham, N.C.: Duke University Press.

Pinch, A. (1996), *Strange Fits of Passion: Epistemologies of Emotion, Hume to Austen*, Stanford, CA: Stanford University Press.

Pinker, S. (2018), *Enlightenment Now: The Case for Reason, Science, Humanism, and Progress*, London: Penguin Books.

Pocock, J. G. A. (2000), *Barbarism and Religion Vol. I: The Enlightenments of Edward Gibbon, 1737–1764*, Cambridge: Cambridge University Press.

Pullman, Philip (2017), 'My Daemon Is a Raven, a Bird That Steals Things', *The Observer*, 22 October, available online: https://www.theguardian.com/books/2017/oct/22/philip-pullman-my-daemon-is-a-raven-la-belle-sauvage-interview-questions (accessed 23 October 2017).

Ramadan, Tariq (1993), 'Lettre Ouverte à M. Hervé Loichemol', *Tribune de Genève*, 7 October, available online: https://tariqramadan.com/arabic/2006/02/23/se-prendre-pour-voltaire/ (accessed 17 September 2017).

Ramadan, Tariq (2006), 'Une Lettre de Tariq Ramadan', *Le Monde*, 23 February, available online: http://www.lemonde.fr/disparitions/article/2006/02/23/une-lettre-de-tariq-ramadan-le-monde-date-vendredi-24-fevrier_744336_3382.html (accessed 2 October 2017).

Rasmussen, Dennis C. (2014), *The Pragmatic Enlightenment: Recovering the Liberalism of Hume, Smith, Montesquieu, and Voltaire*, New York: Cambridge University Press.

Ricoeur, Paul (1976), *Interpretation Theory: Discourse and the Surplus of Meaning*, Texas: Texas Christian University Press.

Riskin, Jessica (2002), *Science in the Age of Sensibility: The Sentimental Empiricists of the French Enlightenment*, Chicago; London: University of Chicago Press.

Rothschild, Emma (2001), *Economic Sentiments: Adam Smith, Condorcet and the Enlightenment*, Cambridge, MA: Harvard University Press.

Rousseau, G. S. and R. Porter (1990), *Exoticism in the Enlightenment*, Manchester: Manchester University Press.

Rousseau, Jean-Jacques (1921 [1762]), *Emile, or Education*, trans. Barbara Foxley, London; Toronto: J. M. Dent and Sons.

Rousseau, Jean-Jacques (1986 [1762–1772]), *Political Writings: Containing the Social Contract, Considerations on the Government of Poland, and Part I of The*

Constitutional Project for Corsica, trans. Frederick Mundell Watkins, Wisconsin: University of Wisconsin Press.

Rubiés, Joan-Pau (2005), 'Oriental Despotism and European Orientalism: Botero to Montesquieu', *Journal of Early Modern History* 9 (1–2): 109–80.

Ruse, Michael (2015), *Atheism: What Everyone Needs to Know*, New York: Oxford University Press.

Russell, Bertrand (1957), *Why I Am Not a Christian*, London: George Allen and Unwin Ltd.

Said, Edward W. (2003 [1978]), *Orientalism*, London: Penguin Books.

Sajó, András (2007), 'Countervailing Duties as Applied to Danish Cheese and Danish Cartoons', in András Sajó (ed.), *Censorial Sensitivities: Free Speech and Religion in a Fundamentalist World (Issues in Constitutional Law)*, Utrecht: Eleven International Publishing, 273–308.

Sawer, Marian (1977), *Marxism and the Question of the Asiatic Mode of Production*, The Hague: Nijhoff.

Schmitter, Amy (2006), '17th and 18th Century Theories of Emotion', in *Stanford Encyclopedia of Philosophy*, available online: https://plato.stanford.edu/entries/ emotions-17th18th/ (accessed 6 March 2016).

Scott, D. and C. Hirschkind (eds.) (2006), *Powers of the Secular Modern: Talal Asad and His Interlocutors*, Stanford, CA: Stanford University Press.

Sénac, Paul (1983), *L'Image de l'Autre: L'Occident Médiéval Face à l'Islam*, Paris: Flammarion.

Senault, Jean-François (1641), *De l'Usage des Passions*, Paris: Jean Camusat.

Senault, Jean-François (1671 [1641]), *The Use of Passions*, trans. Henry, Earl of Monmouth, London: W. G.

Shapiro, Lisa (2003), 'Descartes' *Passions of the Soul* and the Union of Mind and Body', *Archiv für Geschichte der Philosophie* 85 (3): 211–48.

Sheehan, Jonathan (2003), 'Enlightenment, Religion, and the Enigma of Secularization: A Review Essay', *The American Historical Review* 108 (4): 1061–1080.

Smith, David W. (1965), *Helvétius: A Study in Persecution*, Oxford: Clarendon Press.

Smith, Jonathan Z. (1982), *Imagining Religion: From Babylon to Jonestown*, Chicago: University of Chicago Press.

Smith, Jonathan Z. (1998), 'Religion, Religions, Religious', in Mark C. Taylor (ed.), *Critical Terms for Religious Studies*, 269–84, London; Chicago: University of Chicago Press.

Smith, Wilfred C. (1964), *The Meaning and End of Religion: A New Approach to the Religious Traditions of Mankind*, New York: New American Library.

Smith-Rosenberg, C. (2010), *This Violent Empire: The Birth of an American National Identity*, Chapel Hill: University of North Carolina Press.

Spellberg, Denise A. (2004), 'Islam on the Eighteenth-Century Stage: Voltaire's *Mahomet* Crosses the Atlantic', in Neguin Yavari, Lawrence G. Potter and Jean-Marc

R. Oppenheim (eds.), *Views from the Edge: Essays in Honor of Richard W. Bulliet*, 291–302, New York: Columbia University Press.

Spinoza, Baruch (1985 [1677]), 'Ethics', in Edwin Curley (trans. and ed.), *The Collected Works of Spinoza Vol. I*, 408–617, Princeton, NJ: Princeton University Press.

Starobinsky, Jean (1973), 'Preface', in *Lettres Persanes* by Charles de Secondat, Baron de Montesquieu, 7–40, Paris: Gallimard.

Steuter, E. and D. Wills (2008), *At War with Metaphor: Media, Propaganda, and Racism in the War on Terror*, Lanham, MD: Lexington Books.

Sullivan, W. F., E. S. Hurd, S. Mahmood and P. G. Danchin (eds.) (2015), *Politics of Religious Freedom*, Chicago: University of Chicago Press.

Szakolcai, Arpad (2013), *Comedy and the Public Sphere: The Rebirth of Theatre as Comedy and the Genealogy of the Modern Public Arena*, New York; Abingdon: Routledge.

Talleyrand, Charles Maurice de (1791), *Rapport sur l'Instruction Publique, Fait au Nom du Comité de Constitution à l'Assemblée Nationale, les 10, 11 et 19 Septembre 1791*, Paris: L'Imprimerie Nationale.

Taylor, Charles (1989), *Sources of the Self: The Making of the Modern Identity*, Cambridge: Cambridge University Press.

Taylor, Charles (2007), *A Secular Age*, Cambridge, MA; London: Belknap Press of Harvard University Press.

Taylor, Charles (2010), 'Afterword: Apologia Pro Libro Suo', in Michael Warner, Jonathan VanAntwerpen and Craig J. Calhoun (eds.), *Varieties of Secularism in a Secular Age*, 300–324, Cambridge, MA; London: Harvard University Press.

Taylor, Charles (2011), 'Western Secularism', in Craig J. Calhoun, Mark Juergensmeyer and Jonathan VanAntwerpen (eds.), *Rethinking Secularism*, 31–53, Oxford: Oxford University Press.

Taylor, Charles (2012), 'Reason, Faith, and Meaning', in Sarah Coakley (ed.), *Faith, Rationality, and the Passions*, 13–28, Oxford: Wiley-Blackwell.

Todd, Christopher (1989), 'French Advertising in the Eighteenth Century', in *Studies on Voltaire and the Eighteenth Century Vol. CCLXVI*, 513–48, Oxford: Alden Press.

Tracy, Destutt de (1817 [1804]), *Élémens d'Idéologie Vol. I: Idéologie Proprement Dite*, Paris: Courcier.

Translator's Preface to Johann Jakob Engels, *Idées sur le Geste et l'Action Théatrale* (1794), 1–31, Paris: Jansen and Co.

Trouillot, Michel-Rolph (2003), *Global Transformations*, New York: Palgrave Macmillan.

Turner, Victor (1964), 'Betwixt and Between: The Liminal Period in "Rites de Passage"', in June Helm (ed.), *Symposium on New Approaches to the Study of Religion: Proceedings of the 1964 Annual Spring Meeting of the American Ethnological Society*, 4–20, Seattle: American Ethnological Society.

Valensi, L. and A. Denner (1993), *The Birth of the Despot: Venice and the Sublime Porte*, Ithaca, NY; London: Cornell University Press.

Van der Veer, Peter (2001), *Imperial Encounters: Religion and Modernity in India and Britain*, Princeton, NY; Oxford: Princeton University Press.

Van der Veer, Peter (2011), 'Smash Temples, Burn Books: Comparing Secularist Projects in India and China', in Craig J. Calhoun, Mark Juergensmeyer and Jonathan VanAntwerpen (eds.), *Rethinking Secularism*, 270–81, Oxford: Oxford University Press.

Vartanian, Aram (1969), 'Eroticism and Politics in the *Lettres Persanes*', *Romanic Review* 60 (1): 23–33.

Vincent-Buffault, Anne (1991 [1986]), *The History of Tears: Sensibility and Sentimentality in France*, trans. Teresa Bridgeman, London: Macmillan.

Volney, Constantin François de Chasseboeuf, Comte de (1795 [1791]), *The Ruins, or, A Survey of the Revolutions of Empire*, trans. anonymous, London: J. Johnson.

Voltaire (1753a [1741]), 'Lettre de l'Auteur à Mr. De S****', in *Le Fanatisme ou Mahomet le Prophète*, 106–112, Amsterdam: Ledet and Compagnie.

Voltaire (1753b [1741]), *Le Fanatisme ou Mahomet le Prophète*, Amsterdam: Ledet and Compagnie.

Voltaire (1773 [1744]), *Mahomet the Impostor: A Tragedy*, trans. James Miller and John Hoadly, Edinburgh: Peter Williamson.

Voltaire (1877 [1732]), 'Zaïre', in Louis Moland (ed.), *Œuvres Complètes de Voltaire Vol. II*, 556–618, Paris: Garnier.

Voltaire (1877 [1741]), 'Lettre au Pape Benoît XIV', in Louis Moland (ed.), *Œuvres Complètes de Voltaire Vol. III*, 105, Paris: Garnier.

Voltaire (1877 [1752]), 'Micromégas', in Louis Moland (ed.), *Œuvres Complètes de Voltaire Vol. XXI*, 122, Paris: Garnier.

Voltaire (1878 [1711–1778]), 'Correspondance', in Louis Moland (ed.), *Œuvres Complètes de Voltaire Vols XXXIII–L*, Paris: Garnier.

Voltaire (1878 [1756]), 'Essai sur les Mœurs et l'Esprit des Nations', in Louis Moland (ed.), *Œuvres Complètes de Voltaire Vols XI–XIII*, Paris: Garnier.

Voltaire (1878 [1764]), 'Dictionnaire Philosophique', in Louis Moland (ed.), *Œuvres Complètes de Voltaire Vols XVII–XIX*, Paris: Garnier.

Vyverberg, Henry (1989), *Human Nature, Cultural Diversity, and the French Enlightenment*, New York: Oxford University Press.

Ward, Graham (2010), 'History, Belief and Imagination in Charles Taylor's *A Secular Age*', *Modern Theology* 26 (3): 337–48.

Warner, Michael (1990), *The Letters of the Republic: Publication and the Public Sphere in Eighteenth-Century America*, Cambridge, MA; London: Harvard University Press.

Warner, M., J. VanAntwerpen and C. J. Calhoun (eds.) (2010), *Varieties of Secularism in a Secular Age*, Cambridge, MA; London: Harvard University Press.

William (of Malmesbury) (1854 [12th century]), 'History of the Kings of England', trans. by John Sharpe Williams, in Joseph Stevenson (ed.), *Church Historians of England Vol II*, 1–380, London: Seeleys.

Wolff, Larry (2017), *The Singing Turk: Ottoman Power and Operatic Emotions on the European Stage from the Siege of Vienna to the Age of Napoleon*, Stanford, CA: Stanford University Press.

Yavari, N., L. G. Potter and J. M. Oppenheim (eds.) (2004), *Views from the Edge: Essays in Honor of Richard W. Bulliet*, New York: Columbia University Press.

Index

www.ingramcontent.com/pod-product-compliance
Lightning Source LLC
Chambersburg PA
CBHW050419280326
41932CB00013BA/1915